Praise for Jodee Blanco an
Bestseller *Please Stop L*

"From cover to cover, Blanco reasons through what happened to her, laying the groundwork for what may become an anti-bullying Bible."

—*Illinois Association of School Boards*

". . . the author's courageous and honest memoir of the years she spent as the victim of her contemporaries points smartly to the inability of adults to deal with issues of serious bullying."

—*Publishers Weekly*

"Many will take comfort both in the universality of the experiences and in Blanco's transformation from an unhappy, embittered ugly duckling to a poised, accomplished swan. Others, if they are honest, just might recognize bullying tendencies in themselves and become sufficiently chagrined to reexamine their views and actions toward nonconformists of all stripes."

—*School Library Journal*

"Blanco's story is often painful to read, but her eventual success and triumph over the past are inspiring."

—*Booklist*

"*Please Stop Laughing at Me* . . . is honest and upfront. I highly recommend this work for parents and educators. . . ."

—*Hispanic Magazine*

"It's important that all kids read *Please Stop Laughing at Me . . .* to realize the severe physical and emotional damage students receive at school. It's an important read for parents and teachers. . . . Readers will not be left laughing at the pranks and jokes played on Jodee, but wondering how human beings could treat each other this way. It leaves a long-lasting impression that will change the way you look at the loners and popular kids in your school or community."

—*St. Petersburg Times*

"A must-read for youth . . . most definitely there is hope for victims of peer abuse."

—*Philadelphia Tribune*

"*Please Stop Laughing at Me . . .* should be required reading for every child in school. Jodee Blanco's relentless audacity for doing the right thing should be taught to all of our children."

—WomensSelfEsteem.com

"Judging by the standing ovation Jodee Blanco received at Valparaiso High School, her message about bullying got through to students."

—*Valparaiso Post Tribune*

"Later that day, when Blanco was leaving the school, a teacher stopped her and said, 'Thanks for giving that student a hug.' The teacher told Blanco that particular student was the most popular student in school but was also the biggest bully, adding that she would never bully anyone again after Blanco's speech."

—*Dodge City Daily Globe*

Please Stop
Laughing at Us ...

One Survivor's Extraordinary Quest to
Prevent School Bullying

Jodee Blanco

BENBELLA

BENBELLA BOOKS, INC.
Dallas, Texas

BenBella Books, Inc.
6440 N. Central Expressway, Suite 503
Dallas, TX 75206
Send feedback to feedback@benbellabooks.com
www.benbellabooks.com

Printed in the United States of America
10 9 8 7 6 5 4 3 2 1

Library of Congress Cataloging-in-Publication Data

Blanco, Jodee, 1964-
   Please stop laughing at us-- : one survivor's extraordinary quest to prevent school bullying / Jodee Blanco.
       p. cm.
   Sequel to: Please stop laughing at me.
   Includes bibliographical references and index.
   ISBN 1-933771-29-1 (alk. paper)
   1. Bullying in schools--United States--Prevention. I. Blanco, Jodee, 1964-
Please stop laughing at me. II. Title.

   LB3013.32.B53 2007
   371.7'82--dc22

                              2007041586

Cover design by Melody Cadungog
Cover photo by Ross Hamilton
Text design and composition by Laura Watkins
Proofreading by Stacia Seaman
Printed by Bang Printing

Distributed by Independent Publishers Group
To order call (800) 888-4741
www.ipgbook.com

For special sales, contact Robyn White at Robyn@benbellabooks.com

Author's Note

When I wrote *Please Stop Laughing at Me . . .*, I knew I had a story worth telling, I just never imagined it would become so successful that there would be a demand for a sequel. In both books, some of the characters are composites, assembled from more than one actual person, but the story is true. I've also changed certain names, dates, and places in the interest of protecting people's privacy.

Contents

Dedication

To my mom for loving me through it all.

To my husband for loving me despite it all.

To Chester, Sasha, and Kelly, for being love itself.

. . . and to Aunt Ann, Paul Day, Judy, and Hail, without whom I couldn't have written this book.

And in loving memory of my father.

I cherish all of you *so* much.

Acknowledgments

If it weren't for the following people, this book wouldn't exist. They were my strength and my inspiration, and I will forever be in their debt:

Kent Carroll, my editor, mentor, and most cherished friend, who gave his heart and soul to this project. Thank you for believing in me, even on those days when I didn't believe in myself. You are the reason I had the courage to write this book.

Eileen, "the Little General" Hunsicker, who put her life on hold and sacrificed everything to join my crusade against school bullying. Your love and support were my oxygen. And I would also like to thank Jeffrey, her husband, whose unselfishness knows no bounds, and her daughter Jillian and son Jeff. You are what every family should be.

Dee Salinas, my comfort and sunlight, and the person I rely on most to protect me from myself. I'm convinced that you were the inspiration for Wonder Woman. And Nicky and Joey, thank you for sharing your mom with me.

My cousin Jeanine Woolet, who never allowed me to feel alone, especially during those long weeks spent writing day and night, worried that I wouldn't finish this book. I cannot thank you enough.

Kathy Gibbons and Kyle Weber, thank you for taking care of my pets so that I could stay locked away in my writing studio. You'll never know the peace of mind you gave my husband and me.

Don "Deet" Taylor, who provided a much-needed port in

a storm and who also helped me to understand post-traumatic stress disorder. I owe you a brick at the Farmer's Daughter.

My amazing stepdaughters, Amber and Valerie Pantaleo, you are my greatest teachers. And my thanks to Amber's friends Kylie Hayes, Ellie Markham, Jenna Opferman, and Samantha Ollry, for our wonderful conversation at the lake. I became a better writer because of it.

Kim Malloy, Debbie Mendoza, and everyone at DAT International/Exel Transportation, I will never be able to repay you for your patience during the writing of this book.

Terri Carr, the person who became a surrogate cyber-mom to thousands of kids in crisis and their families. You are an angel.

Ross Hamilton, a talented photographer and wonderful human being. Thank you for sharing your talents and insights with me. They enriched this book.

Dr. Damptz, who helped me hold on to my self-worth when the world was ripping it out of my hands. You are more than my family doctor. You *are* family.

Becky Heim and her children Bailey, Tayler, and Matthew "Cookie Foot," who blessed me with their love and light, and who inspired much of the wisdom in this book.

Dean "Mr. Wonderful" Stump, who taught me that some friendships are worth waiting for no matter how long it takes. The love and respect we have for each other is not only an important part of this book, it's also one of the reasons I'm able to give so many kids hope.

Karyn Ivancich, whose friendship has helped me to grow in ways I couldn't have predicted. Thank you for making me take a long, hard look at myself.

Carol Anderson, my copyeditor, who pirouetted through hoops to accommodate the deadline on this book. You're a miracle worker.

My publisher, Glenn Yeffeth, and the caring, dedicated team at BenBella Books. You are a comfort and a blessing, and I thank God every day that I'm being published by you.

Mark Suchomel and the gang at IPG, you motivate me to want to make you proud.

The thousands of students, parents, educators, and adult survivors who left their indelible imprint on my soul and whose stories are commemorated in these pages. This book is in honor of your grace, courage, and unrelenting ability to love.

Thank you all.

Introduction

So much has happened in the past few years. I wrote my memoir, *Please Stop Laughing at Me . . .* because, in the wake of all the school violence erupting across America, I decided it was time to go public with my story. I felt that too many people in this country didn't understand that kids shooting other kids wasn't about gun control, anger management, or any of the other politically correct catchphrases popping up in newspaper editorials and on afternoon talk shows. It was loneliness. I'm not talking about one lonely weekend spent pouting because the phone doesn't ring. The kind of loneliness I'm referring to is a much darker version, one that, sadly, has been afflicting kids long before any school shooting ever made the headlines. It's the desperate sadness of the outcast child, the kid who, no matter how hard he tries, just can't seem to fit in with his peers. The one who's simply "different." I know, because I *was* that kid. From fifth grade through the end of high school, I suffered from chronic loneliness, a state of heart that, believe me, can twist your head into a pretzel and your spirit into a dead, tangled mess.

I wrote my memoir because I wanted kids everywhere who were being bullied by their peers, who dreaded going to school, who cried themselves to sleep night after night, who felt misunderstood by grown-ups and hated by classmates, to have a voice. I knew I was someone whom they could identify with, because I had been through it myself and survived. I also knew that I'd have credibility with their parents and teachers, because I was an adult with a successful career much like them. Secretly, I hoped that writing the book would be a catharsis, and help me overcome the residual insecurity and anger from those painful school years.

Writing *Please Stop Laughing at Me* . . . was the hardest challenge I ever undertook. On a professional level, confessing my past to the world and how that would affect my business was scary enough. I was a high-profile publicist whose job was to keep her famous clients in the limelight, not do anything that would put *her* in the public eye. Personally, the idea of stepping forward was even tougher. It was horrible reliving all those experiences: the name-calling, being spit on and kicked, the mean giggling behind my back, the physical threats, the fear; and even worse, the feeling of being invisible. I ended up having to see a therapist during the writing of the book, because I was having night sweats and bad dreams.

But something kept me going. It was as if there were hands on my back pushing me forward. Every time I felt like I couldn't finish a chapter, the courage to continue seemed to come from a place inside me that I never knew was there. So I persevered.

Five days after I delivered the manuscript to my publisher, it was my twentieth high school reunion. I was terrified to attend, since all those memories were so fresh in my mind. If anyone ever tells you that one night can't change your life, you tell them that you have a friend named Jodee Blanco who says they're wrong. One night not only changed my life, but affected the lives of thousands of others.

Speaking of that night, I originally had a different last chapter. When I got back to my mom's house early the following morning I knew what I had to do or my heart would burst. At my high school reunion, I felt all the darkness inside me lift, and for the first time I could see my future and my purpose. It was as if I had been living in a tiny cave and had been there so long that I'd convinced myself that being cold, hungry, and alone was normal. Then, suddenly, someone with a giant flashlight illuminated the way out. In that moment, I learned that I didn't have to be in the blackness anymore, that I could come out now and help guide others to the same bright place of self-acceptance I had found. This miracle of freedom occurred on the one night that I thought would surely destroy me. I immediately sat down at the computer, deleted the original last chapter, and wrote the new one. My publisher had to pull my book out of production in order to accommodate the switch. That weekend transformed my memoir from a story of survival to a celebration of forgiveness.

The day *Please Stop Laughing at Me . . .* was published, President Bush declared war on Iraq. My publisher and my agent groaned, because they knew that books launched during a major international event fail. Indeed, every media appearance my publicist had scheduled for me was canceled. I was sick inside. How would my hopeful message reach the kids who needed it? Yes, I ached because we were at war, but what about all the wars being fought in the school hallways and locker rooms that only made the news if blood was spilled? What about the kids who face another kind of battlefield every day, just navigating the safest way to get from homeroom to study hall without being wounded?

I *had* to write this book, and now it appeared as if my efforts were doomed. My mom had always told me that it's always darkest before the dawn. I used to get irritated every time she said that to me, but in this instance she was prophetic. Despite Iraq dominating every newscast and talk show, within forty-eight hours of my book's launch it appeared on the *New York Times* bestseller list. I began receiving hundreds of e-mails and letters from kids and parents across the country, all thanking me for sharing my story and showing them that they, too, can survive. But the real kicker? Almost every person who wrote me mentioned the last chapter, and how it was the forgiveness that gave them hope. How ironic is *that*? Because the night that inspired that last chapter almost left me in my car in a parking lot, too terrified to face my classmates.

The night of my twentieth reunion was only the beginning. In the last few years, everything in my life has changed. Professionally, I gave up my PR firm working with Hollywood stars to embrace the new stars in my life: kids in crisis. I travel across the country, speaking at schools, helping students, teachers, families, and entire communities with bullying survival and prevention. I've been fortunate to be assisted by an extraordinary team of people whose passion and commitment to this issue encourage me every day. You'll be shocked, inspired, incensed, and amazed when you hear some of the stories from these schools.

I see the American school system from a perspective few

others do. I see the pain and frustration in teachers' eyes as they witness peer abuse, wanting to stop it but unsure of what to do. I meet principals who are dedicated, committed people who sacrifice so much to help students. I also come across administrators who are more concerned about a manicure appointment than they are about a student caught brandishing a razor. I see the best of our schools and the worst. I celebrate the hope that teachers, counselors, and administrators keep alive despite budget cuts, apathetic parents, and frustrated, angry kids. I am humbled by many of the people I meet on tour. They sacrifice to help kids. I am also infuriated by others who choose a career in education because it offers long vacations.

What's going on in our schools? What are we doing right? What are we doing wrong? Why are there people who don't even like kids being hired as teachers? How do you know if the superintendent in your district is a caring leader committed to his vocation or a political climber using your school district as his staircase to the top? When the large glass doors close and the first bell rings, signaling the beginning of a new school day, why do some children face peril and uncertainty while others sail through, coming home with smiles on their faces, good grades, and bright futures?

Have you ever been the parent seeking your school's help, only to be told after countless empty promises, "Well, there's nothing we can really do"? Or perhaps you've been the parent who's had the opposite experience. When you reach out to a teacher or an administrator on your child's behalf, they help with understanding and compassion, making sure your problem is resolved. How can you motivate that kind of response from your school, and where can you turn if, no matter what you do, you face indifference?

If you're a student struggling with a serious peer-pressure issue or other challenge, how do you approach the school without fear of recrimination from your classmates or even from a teacher or counselor? How do you come clean with your parents about what is eating you up inside? Is there an escape from this condition called adolescence?

If you're a teacher, counselor, or administrator who wants nothing more than to empower kids, but you're confronting obstacles you *never* imagined, where can you seek assistance? What are your options? How do you hold on emotionally when you feel as if an entire system is working against you, when all you want to do is help a student in crisis? How do you communicate with a parent in denial, and temper the rage of a parent in fear? How much responsibility should you take on as an employee of the school district, and what do you do when you know that there isn't anyone else who's likely to fight for this student as you would?

I never thought I'd be sought after by tens of thousands of people as the expert who could answer these questions, let alone become a nationally recognized anti-bullying activist. I was now a survivor who was turning her pain into purpose, and none of it would have been possible if I hadn't gone public with my story. And it's not just peer-abuse victims and their teachers and families who reach out to me. Often, bullies come up to me after I've given a talk. The response from these kids can be overwhelming, their tears so affecting that I can hardly believe I have the opportunity to help them.

I cannot help but marvel at how exquisite life can be in its unpredictability. I remember a time when I used to dread the unexpected. Now I relish it, because it was through the unexpected that my whole world turned around. Yes, I had an exciting career as a publicist, but I cried myself to sleep because I was empty inside. For some of us, change doesn't come gradually. It hits you like a tornado, completely rearranging your life. I went from the entertainment industry, a world where glitz and glamour are often camouflage for some of the darkest truths about human nature, to school gyms and lunchrooms, where those same dark truths exist, only in infant form. In some ways, the school arena and the Hollywood arena are not so different. Both are ruled by the power of the popular crowd. Both are teeming with betrayal of innocence, backstabbing, loneliness, and hurt. The difference is that with love, patience, and wisdom, the situation in our schools can improve. I doubt that the realities of the casting couch or the tabloids ever will.

I've been recounting professional changes. Now let me tell you about the personal changes. My mom is still in a state of delighted disbelief. As I said, I don't want to ruin the ending if you haven't read my memoir yet, but I will tell you this. Mitch and I are still together. The story of what has happened to my dreams of marriage and my hopes for a family make up the background to my new professional mission. I know that those of you who read my first book will be keeping your fingers crossed for me.

Since the release of my memoir, I've gone from a swinging single in silk business suits and high heels who attended movie premieres and Hollywood parties to a card-carrying member of Sam's Club and a part-time mom to two adorable girls, their two very large dogs, and a pair of French bunny rabbits. I used to host champagne and caviar parties for heads of state. Now I host slumber parties, featuring such delicacies as peanut butter sandwiches (no crusts of course), blue push-up Popsicles, and Domino's cheese pizza. I used to escort Academy Award–winning actors to banquets in their honor. Now I cart kids to dance class, cheerleading practice, and poms. I also used to come home to emptiness. Now I come home to the love and comfort of family. Mitch, his daughters, the dogs, the bunnies—they're my anchors. Their love gives me the strength and the grounding I need to help save kids in crisis.

Sometimes, in quiet moments, Mitch or the kids will ask me if I miss my old life. My answer is always the same. *Never.*

And the bullies from school? Many of them are now my friends. It turns out that some of their children were getting bullied at school and they asked me to help. I did, and the result was unlikely friendship. The very people who made me run as far away from my hometown as possible twenty-two years ago are now the people who convinced me to move back. As my favorite movie character, Dorothy, in *The Wizard of Oz* realized when she woke up after the tornado, I discovered that "there's no place like home."

Now that you know how my life has changed, let me tell you a little about the book you're about to read. When *Please Stop Laughing at Me . . .* came out, I received so many wonderful letters that I've put some of them in this book. I'm always touched when someone takes the time to communicate with me, and I try to respond to each and every correspondence. I noticed over the last two years that the same questions keep coming up. Parents and teachers want practical advice on how to prevent bullying, how to help both the victim and the bully, and what schools can do to curb the problem. My teen readers want advice, too, but they're also curious about my personal life. "Are you still with Mitch?" they ask. Are we getting married? Do I ever talk to any of the famous actors and athletes I used to work with? And adult survivors, who endured peer abuse like me when they were young, want to know how they can overcome the residual pain and insecurity from those lonely school years.

I decided that this new book should pick up where the first one left off. It's time to offer solutions. I've been on the road learning the inner workings of the American school system. From wealthy suburbs and rural communities to small towns and major cities, I've held the hands of thousands of hurting kids and listened as they poured their hearts out, entrusting me with knowledge that I know can help you. Teachers, counselors, and administrators have opened up to me with their valuable insights. Adult survivors have confided their deepest fears in me. I'm going to share all this with you, because you must remember, whether you're a kid who's lonely and frustrated, a teacher, counselor, or administrator at your wit's end, a worried parent, or a survivor still haunted by the past, you are not alone. I am here with you, just as I was before, when you read my memoir. The only difference is, now we're joined by so many others from all across the United States. We're a force to be reckoned with, a community of courageous individuals whose wounds have made us stronger, smarter, and ready to end the plague of peer abuse. By now, you probably know that I don't hold anything back when I write. All my windows are open. I'm going to tell you all about my personal life, too. Because all of us are a combination of elements — we are an embodiment of the people we love and those who love us, the jobs we perform, the children we raise, and the lives we touch and who touch us. For those of you who read *Please Stop Laughing at Me . . .*, welcome back. I'm honored to spend quality time with you again. For those of you who are just finding me now, it's a privilege to meet you.

It's time to stand up and be heard. Please, won't you join us?

chapter one

The Wounded
Healer

October 2004

I don't think I can do this anymore. *What was I thinking going public with my story?* When I wrote my memoir *Please Stop Laughing at Me . . .*, chronicling my years as the school outcast and how I survived, all I wanted to do was give kids hope and adults insight. Now, two years later, the reality of what I've gotten myself into is beginning to dawn. . . .

I'm standing in front of the mirror putting on makeup in a hotel room in a town somewhere in California whose name I can't remember. I'm scheduled to speak at a middle school in one hour. The rock group Styx calls asking me to be the publicity consultant for their historic comeback tour. For a moment, I'm tempted. I'm drained and disoriented. This is my fifth speaking engagement in a week. Three thousand thirteen-year-olds, half a dozen camera crews, and several newspaper reporters and photographers will be jammed into a gymnasium for my ninety-minute presentation, followed by a thirty-minute Q&A. Immediately after, I have another student seminar, an afternoon teacher workshop and autographing, several hours scheduled in between for one-on-one sessions with students in crisis, and then a family seminar in the evening that's open to the public, after which I'll likely have families who will want to talk with me privately. I'm often asked why I stay past midnight holding parents' hands, why I don't leave. It's because I remember the hell that my own mom and dad suffered, and what they would have given for advice from someone who had been there before and had answers.

I wish this day was over. I've been on the road for twenty months, reenacting my worst memories of being tormented and shunned by my peers simply for being different. I don't recount my past. I *resurrect* it, letting audiences experience with me the hurt and humiliation my classmates put me through. The technique is effective. In gyms and auditoriums all across the country, lonely, ostracized students, many of whom have also isolated themselves from adults, are finally asking for support. School bullies come forward after they hear me speak, seeking forgiveness from their victims and promising to reform. For me, that's the ultimate triumph.

It's so satisfying, knowing I'm getting through to these kids, but I'm worried that it's taking too much of a toll on me personally. I try to visualize a box. Sealed inside it are the darkest emotions from my adolescence. Immediately before every speech, while I'm waiting offstage to be introduced, I say a prayer. *God, what I'm about to do is hard. Please don't let it be for nothing. Help me get to those who need this message the most.* Then I rip open the box and unleash the toxins inside. When my talk is over, I take a deep breath, suck all that rage and fear back into the box, and put it away until next time. . . .

I understand that what I'm doing is a form of emotional suicide. But these kids trust me because they recognize that my experience is authentic, that I'm not some adult up there faking it, pretending to understand but not having a clue. As I continue putting on my face, I realize the person staring back at me in the mirror isn't the confident forty-year-old woman I've worked so hard to become but that insecure sixteen-year-old girl I used to be in 1980. I thought I had laid her to rest two years ago at my twentieth high school reunion. It appears she has returned with a vengeance. My stomach is in my throat, because I'm scared I'll get hit with another dead pig in biology class. I'm worried those girls from gym will beat me up in the parking lot. What if the boys sitting in the back of the school bus dip the spitballs in glue like they did on the field trip?

It's as if I'm having one of those dreams where you know you're dreaming but you can't wake up. And yet it all *feels* so real. I must remind myself that today is Friday, October 14, 2004. Those things happened twenty-five years ago. My mind is just playing tricks on me, blurring the line that separates the past from the present.

If I keep on dredging up bad memories for a living, I'm damaging myself. But if I take the easy route and walk away, what about all the kids I might have been able to help who will continue to be damaged, or worse? What kind of a choice is that? No matter what I decide, someone loses.

Where is my sense of self-preservation, not to mention what I'm doing to my family and friends, and to Mitch? I've waited my entire life for a great guy like him. It'll kill me if I lose him. But how can I expect Mitch to put up with someone who's always out of town, and who's strung out emotionally the little time she *is* home? So far, I only get these flashbacks when I'm in the middle of a particularly intense tour week.

It's like being abducted by my past. When it does occur, I'm held hostage for only short periods. But what happens when these unpredictable episodes linger even after I've returned from the road? I love Mitch, and it's not his fault that we're former classmates. But seeing his face when I'm in that vulnerable state makes me scared for both of us. I've already gotten glimpses of it running toward Mitch at the airport, then hesitating before I fall into his arms. How can our relationship grow under those circumstances?

I feel like the recovering rape victim/advocate who has to talk to strangers all day long about being raped and then go home and make love to her husband, with that vivid reminder present in their bed. It would be impossible for something like that not to affect a person. Though my purpose is noble, it's depleting having to constantly relive all that pain.

I can't do this anymore. I'll end up a shadow of myself. Besides, who says I have to save the world? Other people turn a blind eye once in a while and lead perfectly normal lives. They don't beat themselves up because they pretended not to see that stray dog while they were driving home, or convinced themselves that it probably wasn't lost anyway, and even if it was, someone would find it. They don't lose sleep because they laughed at a joke in the office that was made at someone else's expense. No. They just live their lives. They watch the news and feel bad just like everyone else when they see the footage of mothers mourning their sons killed in battle in Iraq, or the images of starving children in some godforsaken place that they couldn't even find on a map. Why can't I be like *them*? I don't want to be me anymore. I don't want to have to choose between saving someone else and saving myself. I'm tired of having all this stupid compassion. Why can't I shut it off?

> *"Hey, Jodee, he likes you the best. You do it," A.J. demands.*
> *"No way. We'll get caught!" I cry, desperate to wiggle out of this one.*

It was the middle of seventh grade. I was the new student. I hadn't fit in at my previous school, or the one before that. I was terrified of being rejected again.

> *"There's still five minutes before he returns from break. Come on," everyone urges.*

The bell was about to ring. We were waiting for our teacher, Mr. Bufert, to walk through the door. Mr. Bufert had a chronic skin condition that made his scalp flake. He was self-conscious about it and only wore white shirts to school so the dandruff would be less noticeable. Shy and awkward, Mr. Bufert was a loner who bore the scars of someone who had been laughed at most of his life. The only place he felt that he belonged was in his classroom working with his beloved students. His face would light up every time he saw us.

> *"Jodee, it's just a prank. It's no big deal," Jim prompts, his eyes twinkling.*
> *I can do this, I think, trying to convince myself. Mr.*

Bufert has a good sense of humor. His feelings won't be hurt. Stop feeling so guilty. Remember what Jim said: "Nobody likes a wuss."

"A.J., I'll stand lookout in the hall, and you do it," I whisper, the knot in my stomach belying my confidence.

Realizing that time is running out, A.J. agrees.

Five minutes later, our deed done, A.J. nonchalantly addresses Mr. Bufert as he enters the room. "Do you have our papers from last week? I'm anxious to see my grade," she gushes.

"Certainly, A.J. I wasn't going to pass them out until the end of class, but since you're so eager, we can do it now," he replies, pleased to see such enthusiasm over a homework assignment.

As he reaches into his briefcase, he suddenly stops, looking puzzled. Giggles explode from the back of the room.

"I can't stand the suspense," A.J. whispers in my ear, excited. *I want to throw up, but just keep right on smiling. . . .*

"What's this?" Mr. Bufert asks, shaking his head, holding up the blue-and-white bottle of Head & Shoulders shampoo. "I give you people extra credit if you bring a joke into class, not for making a joke out of someone," he says, his voice weak with humiliation and shock. He suddenly realizes that his beloved students don't adore him at all—they disdain him.

I wanted to crawl inside a foxhole and die. Everyone in class thought I was so cool. Why couldn't I just revel in it? The truth stank. It was either be liked by everyone but hate yourself, or respect yourself and be hated by every-

one. I didn't know how much longer I could keep up this charade. Eventually my classmates would figure out that my "coolness" was an act. I was so tired of pretending to be someone I wasn't but it was still better than being the school outcast again. Life was a balance. Finding that balance was proving to be an arduous proposition.

What's different now? The truth still stinks! If I do what's right and continue this personal crusade against bullying, I'll be doing harm to myself, but if I don't, I'll end up hating myself. What if there is no balance to be found? Is this the paradox of every victim turned activist, always being torn between wanting to change lives and needing to survive your own? Does the battered wife who opens a shelter for other abused women, the recovering alcoholic who becomes an AA sponsor, or the breast cancer survivor who dedicates her life to fighting for a cure ever become burnt out? Are any of them wondering if they made a mistake, too, and that they're paying too high a price? Or do they accept the course of their destiny and somehow find the strength to continue? What if I don't have that ability?

I try to focus on some of the wonderful moments I've had on the road: seeing a bully apologize to an outcast as I'm walking past on my way out of the building; receiving a hug from a teacher who confesses that she was going to quit today but changed her mind when she overheard the most popular girl in her class invite her loneliest student to a sleepover; having a mom approach me after my evening seminar to thank me for helping her to understand more deeply what her child is going through; meeting a lunchroom attendant who tells me she was stunned this afternoon when a group of students from the "cool" table walked around the cafeteria asking kids who were sitting alone to join them. Her words remain etched in my memory: "Everyone is still talking about it."

"Your book has given so many students hope," commented one tearful mom at my family seminar last night. "I made all the mistakes you talked about, and now I finally know how I can help my kids," a school counselor whispered in my ear as I signed a copy of my book for her. "My daughter insisted that I come," said an emotional father. "This is the first time she's wanted me to be with her for any kind of event, let alone one at school."

How did I get into this mess? I understand boundaries, but I don't know how to erect them. Every time a lonely, confused child opens up to me, all I want to do is comfort them, and love their confusion away. That would be OK if it was only a few kids here and there. But I'm dealing with thousands of kids every week. And it isn't just bullies and their victims who reach out to me on tour. Victims of domestic abuse, molestation, incest, and other acts of cruelty confide in me, often admitting that I'm the only adult they've ever opened up to. Sometimes, at the end of a day, my shirt is damp with students' tears. A reporter once asked me why I wear so much black. It's because it hides the makeup stains.

I close my eyes and envision Barb. It was one of the first schools I ever spoke at. I had just finished my eighth consecutive student seminar that day when this beautiful, lanky brunette approached me in tears.

"Please, can I talk to you for a minute?" she asked, looking down.

"Of course," I responded.

"Thank you for coming today," she said. "You helped me see things so differently. Since my mom died, I haven't had anyone to really talk to."

By now, she was crying hard. I felt helpless. I wrapped my arms around her, holding her as tightly as I could, letting her know that everything was going to be all right. Then I gave her my e-mail address and encouraged her to stay in touch. Later that afternoon, one of the faculty members at the school came up to me. She explained that she was Barb's homeroom teacher and that she saw Barb and me embracing earlier.

"It appears your talk really touched my student," she commented.

"I know what it's like to be rejected and teased, and I was honored to give her that love and support," I said.

"Rejected? You think Barb is an *outcast*?" her teacher asked. "She's in the popular crowd, and one of the worst bullies at school. I'm stunned you were able to reach her."

※

I've got to pull myself together and stop being such a *martyr*. I've worked hard to get to this point. I should be overjoyed at everything that's happening, not having second thoughts.

Why can't I snap out of this? Eileen, my manager, is going to be here any minute to pick me up and I'm a wreck. How am I going to get through today? I'm still trying to erase yesterday's memories.

"I knew I shouldn't have done it," said the petite blue-eyed blonde. A high school junior, she had requested time alone with me.

"What did you do?" I asked.

"I never got invited to anything. I was so lonely, and he promised if I gave it to him he'd bring me to events and stuff, and get all the popular kids to warm up to me. I wanted to believe that he could like me," she said, crying.

"Honey, look at me," I said, grabbing hold of both her hands, and squeezing them tightly. "Tell me what you gave him."

"My virginity," she answered, avoiding looking directly at me. "When his parents were away for the weekend, I went over to his house. He had candles lit and music playing. It seemed perfect. Then, while we were, you know, in the middle of it, I heard somebody in the other room. Suddenly, a bunch of his friends burst in and started laughing at me, yelling, 'Stupid slut, like any of us would ever hang out with you.'"

My heart ached for this girl. I wanted to scream until there was nothing left in me. "Do your parents know?" I asked.

"No. I'm too ashamed to tell them, because they've been so proud that I'm a 'good girl.' I'm afraid this will just destroy them."

"How can I help?"

"They're coming to your seminar tonight. Can you help me tell them?"

Another student, at another school later in the day . . .

"I'll blow this school up," he said, enraged. Comely, with piercing blue eyes and wavy blond hair, he looked more like a California surfer than a high school student.

"Why are you so angry?" I asked. "Why do you want to destroy the school?"

"I think I might be gay. There's a few of us here—you know, gays and lesbians? We take so much abuse, and not just from other kids but from adults, too. It sucks. I asked the principal if we could start a Gay and Lesbian Club. They have one at my cousin's school. Anyway, the principal said we couldn't and to keep my filthy secret to myself."

"I'm sorry." I responded. "That principal was wrong. I'll talk to him. But you know that violence will only make this worse. Do your parents know you're gay?"

"Yeah, right— *my* dad? No way. I want to tell my mom, but she's already dealing with so much. She's depressed, takes these pills for it, but they make her kind of out of it, you know? Can I maybe just e-mail you once in a while, when I need to talk?"

"Sure," I answered, handing him my e-mail address. By now, a throng of kids had gathered, and were waiting in line to see me. Some wanted hugs, others a sympathetic ear, others specific advice. It was the same at every school. Their parents were either too wrapped up in their own lives or had stupidly concluded that bullying was just a normal part of growing up. How could anyone assume cruelty is normal? As I was talking with the kids, I noticed the principal standing at the other end of the gym, patiently waiting. As soon as the bell rang and they dispersed for class, he approached.

"I see you've made an impact here," he observed.

"Yes, I think so."

"I saw you talking to that gay kid earlier," he said. "I hope you didn't encourage him. I know he gets teased a lot here, but maybe it'll do him some good, make him rethink things."

I couldn't believe what I was hearing.

"You need to get out of the dark ages," I said. "You cannot allow a student to be tormented by his classmates for any reason. Your personal opinion is irrelevant. Bullying can damage people for life. *I know.*"

"I appreciate your concern, Ms. Blanco. But I have this under control. Now, about your teacher workshop today . . ."

As snippets of these conversations tumble through my mind, I am jolted back to the present by a knock on the door. "Housekeeping," says a perky voice.

"I'll be out of the room in a minute."

I glance at the clock. Eileen is probably downstairs in the lobby waiting for me. We're due to arrive at our first school today in twenty minutes. I toss a lipstick and a pack of peppermint gum in my purse, walk out the door, and make my way to the elevator.

I wish I could hide.

chapter two

The Rebirth

October 2002

If anyone ever says one night can't change your life, they're wrong.

Tonight was my twentieth high school reunion. I was frightened. I relived every detail of those horrible years during the writing of *Please Stop Laughing at Me . . .* It was only one week ago that I turned in the manuscript to my publisher. Doing that book was like sticking my finger down my throat. I was still raw. I didn't think I was ready to see all those people again. I sat in the parking lot of the banquet hall for over an hour, fighting the nausea as memories came rushing to the surface.

"Come on, Jodee, you can do it," Jacklyn says. She and several of her friends had stopped me in the hall near the main entrance to the school. It's between second and third periods, and we're on our way to class.

"No, no I can't. I don't want to kill that innocent little cricket," I cry, hoping no one else would step on it, either.

"Why can't you be normal for once in your life?" Jacklyn remarks. "It's nothing but an ugly old bug."

"Step on it, you wuss, or one of us will," Clarke demands.

16

*"No! Don't! Leave it alone!" I shout. "It's got feelings,
and none of you have any right to take its life."*

*"Oh, yeah?" Tyler challenges, stomping his foot down
on the hall floor.*

*"Help me, help me, please, my itty, bitty limbs," Clarke
cries, mockingly. Everyone bursts into laughter.*

*"Please, stop," I plead, realizing as I look down to see
if the small critter is OK, that it has crawled under the
heating pipe.*

*"You're such a freak," Jacklyn hisses. "It's your own
fault everyone hates you."*

*With that, she and the others, having had their fill of
fun, turn and walk away.*

*Relieved, I bend down, scoop up the tiny creature in
my hands, and take it outside, where I place it under a
bush. As I watch it scamper away, I can't help but wonder why I got stuck with a heart that had to care about
crickets. Why couldn't I be normal like Jacklyn and her
friends? Every day, I hate myself more.*

The longer I sat in the car, the more convinced I became
that I should turn around and leave. It was bad enough that
I had to revisit the past on paper. Why would I want to put
myself through the torture of doing it in the flesh? I was torn
between my dignity, which was telling me to confront my
fears, and my sense of self-preservation, which was warning
me to get the hell out of there. Meanwhile, snippets from my
years as the school outcast kept racing through my head like
movie trailers being projected onto a screen, beckoning my
attention.

"Nadia, are you and Mark sure you'll be able to get the beer?" Sharon asks.

"No problem," Nadia replies confidently. "Mark's brother is twenty-one, and he promised he'd pick up the kegs for us."

"Cool," Sharon responds, "I can't wait for Saturday. This is going to be the best party. Everyone's coming. Clarke's parents are out of town the whole weekend. They left his sister in charge. What a joke. She's a bigger partier than he is!"

Listening to Nadia and Sharon chatting by the lockers, I ache to be included in their world. "Hey, it sounds like Clarke's party is going to be amazing," I remark, hoping I don't sound too eager.

"Are you going?" Sharon inquires.

"Are you serious?" I ask.

"Yeah, we could even pick you up," Nadia says.

I can't believe my ears. They want me to come to the party. Maybe Mitch will even be there, I think. No one knew I had a crush on him. I'd probably end up taking that secret to my grave.

"Oh, my gosh, that would be great, you guys," I reply.

"Damn, there's only one problem," Nadia says, stifling a giggle. "I just remembered, Clarke said no dogs or freaks allowed! Too bad. It would've been so nice to hang out with you."

Crestfallen, I turn and walk away. Later that day, it was all over school how gullible I was.

By now, my hands were clammy, and there were beads of perspiration on my forehead. "Concentrate," I told myself. "Those things happened a long time ago. Focus on who you've become, not who you were." I shut my eyes and tried to envision my current life, dancing with famous actors at movie premieres, sipping champagne with ambassadors and rock stars. But the harder I tried to force the old images out of my head, the stronger they became.

The stench of rotten food stuffed in my book bag. The snipping sound of my grandmother's scissors as she cut spitballs out of my hair. The thump of a softball deliberately crashing into my leg. The snickering whenever I raised my hand in class. The hot pain of a lit cigarette burning my wrist. The gravel scratching my arms and legs as I was dragged across the parking lot by a group of giggling assailants. The pretending that everything was fine so doctors would stop pumping me with meds.

The yelp of the neighbor's dog as my classmates pelted it with hunks of mortar from a nearby construction site, until I stopped them, and they turned their attack on me. The stomachaches from wolfing down Snickers bars in the girls' bathroom for lunch, day after day, because no one would let me sit with them in the cafeteria. The wounds inflicted by my classmates' words, like razor blades slashing my skin.

"You suck, bitch!"

"Hey, who wants to take the mutant to the prom?"

"Too bad you weren't a miscarriage so we wouldn't have to look at your ugly face all day!"

"Don't be nice to her. She's gross."

"You better watch your step or you're dead meat."

"If I kiss you, will I turn into a toad?"

"Relax and breathe through your nose," I kept repeating to myself. "You can do this. It's going to be OK." Finally, the memories began to subside. Exhaling, I climbed out of the car and reluctantly made my way across the parking lot to the front doors of the banquet hall.

That was hours ago. In a moment, it will be sunrise. I can barely contain my excitement as I pull into the driveway of my mom's house. I can't wait to see the look on her face when I tell her what became of my fears.

"Mom, wake up!" I shout, bolting up the stairs to her room.

"Honey, what is it, what happened?" she asks, trying to hide a familiar dread in her voice.

"No, Mom, it's OK. In fact, it's a miracle," I respond, plopping next to her on the bed. "They don't hate me! They never hated me." I'm ashamed that a roomful of virtual strangers have the ability to make me feel this giddy. I'm even more ashamed of how frightened I was to attend the reunion in the first place.

"Tell me every detail," Mom says.

"It was surreal. Everyone seemed so happy to see me. I was stunned. Jacklyn was even nice to me."

"You're kidding."

"She asked about my career and told me everyone has heard about the book and is impressed. Isn't that something? And she looks good. In fact, the women aged well in general. Most of the guys didn't. Clarke and Tyler look middle-aged. They're definitely not the sexy bad boys they used to be. They were flirting with me like crazy," I add, smiling. "I know it's silly, but I loved it."

"I bet they were kicking themselves for not going after you when they had the chance!" Mom says.

She's beaming, and I can't help but feel guilty. I remember countless weekends, during those awful years of crying myself to sleep. It never occurred to me then how my mom ached for a moment like this—me returning from a date or a dance, cheerful and eager to share the details with her. Instead, she had to cope with a frustrated, lonely teen. I wish I could have given my parents more joy when I was growing up. I know my accomplishments have always been a source of pride for them, but being proud of your child's achievements is different from being fulfilled because they're happy.

"Didn't any of them wonder if they were in the book?" Mom asks.

"Jacklyn did. When I told her she was, she winced."

"Did you let her know that you changed all the names?"

"Yes, of course. I also explained to her that most of the characters are composites—combinations of different individuals—and not one specific person. Not only was she cool about it once I reassured her, but she said if there's anything she can do to help, to give her a call."

"Do you think that was a guilty conscience talking?" Mom says.

"I think that sells us both short. I doubt Jacklyn and her friends understood the damage they were doing. They believed what their parents taught them—that kids will be kids. Now that she's a parent herself, she sees things differently."

As I'm talking to Mom, I realize how much of an effect my classmates had on me. I feel like the sixteen-year-old girl I once was has died, and I'm channeling her re-awakened spirit and she's not letting go. Intellectually, I'm aware of how ridiculous that sounds, that to any sane person I'm making a big deal out of something that was nothing more than a great party. But I can't shake this feeling that my high school reunion was a portal that I had to walk through, and now I'm struggling to make sense of where I am.

Mom and I make our way downstairs to the kitchen, where she puts on a pot of coffee. I remember so many mornings like this, except then I had to go to school. She and I would be tense — her not wanting to send me but knowing she must, me hating the pretense of it all. We'd go through the ritual. Mom drank her coffee black. I went light on the milk, heavy on the sugar. We never drank in silence. There was always chatter, its purpose being to distract both of us from the inevitable. I would have to board that school bus. I would have to face those kids. She would have to endure another day of uncertainty, of not knowing the condition her daughter would be in when she returned home from school, and wondering how much more of this she could take.

Now here I am, in the kitchen with my mom again, drinking coffee, each of us knowing that this is one of those mother-daughter moments we had always hoped for but never believed would come. Though I'm trying to keep what happened tonight in perspective, I can't resist enjoying this feeling.

"Did you bump into *her*?" Mom asks, taking a sip of coffee.

We both know who she means. A.J. was goddess of the cool crowd. We were classmates from seventh grade through high school. If you played by A.J.'s rules, you earned acceptance, perhaps even popularity. But if you chose to be your own person you were at her mercy. I tried to fit in early on, hiding my independent nature like some deformity I was ashamed of. After a while, I didn't have the will power to pretend anymore. I couldn't stand the way A.J. and her friends treated people. They thought they were better than everyone else, and wallowed in the pain they inflicted on others. Their cruelty made me sick. When I began speaking up for their victims, A.J. realized she couldn't control me, so she made me her scapegoat. For years, I put up with her abuse, because my parents and my teachers told me to "ignore the bullies, don't give them the satisfaction." Today, I think of all the adults who give kids the same advice. I still don't understand the logic. We preach to our children not to be bystanders, that if you see someone getting picked on, stand up and defend that person, but if *you're* the one who's being harassed, ignore it. Isn't that a mixed message? It always made me wonder, why was I less worth defending than someone else?

"Angel, you seem a million miles away," Mom says.

"I'm sorry," I respond. "Yes, A.J. was there. She approached me by the bar when I was talking to Jacklyn."

"You used to have nightmares because of what that girl did to you," Mom recalls, tensing.

· "It's funny, Mom, but I'm not angry at her anymore, and I don't want you to be, either."

"What *happened* between you two tonight?" Mom asks.

Speaking about this with Mom, it dawns on me that bullying really does damage a person for life. How many of you were in the same boat as I was tonight, itching to see everyone from school and confirm how far you've come since graduation, yet scared stiff at the idea of being reminded of all that insecurity and rejection? How many of you tonight, in how many towns, also sat in cars in the parking lots of hotels and banquet halls, battling with yourselves over whether or not to attend your reunion, too? Part of you wants to prove to yourself that none of it matters anymore, but another part of you longs to finally be accepted by the cool crowd. You may not have fit in all those years ago, but if you can fit in now with your former classmates, it will give you precious closure. The problem is that if you attend and get disappointed, then what? That's what was going through my head as I watched A.J. walking toward me.

"It was weird," I explain. "I felt like a fan who was about to meet her favorite celebrity. Part of me was nervous and self-conscious. Another part was disgusted that I cared at all. I kept saying to myself, 'I have friends who are *actual* celebrities. Why does A.J. have such an effect on me? Why can't I get past high school?'"

"Oh honey, I can imagine how tough that must have been," Mom remarks, shaking her head. "How was she with you?"

"She was all smiles, as if we had always been friends. It was so bizarre because it was sincere. We talked about the book, and she said she was proud of me for writing it. But here's the kicker. When I told her how scared I was about coming tonight, she said she couldn't understand why, because everybody liked me back in school!"

"That's probably how she remembers it," Mom says.

"Did you say anything to her, or did you just let it pass?"

"I reminded her that I was the outcast at Calvin Samuels."

"What was her answer?" Mom asks.

"She said that maybe other people made fun of me, but she never did, and that she honestly liked me back then. When I described to her some of the things she did to me, she felt horrible. Then she said something that really struck a nerve."

"What was that?"

"She asked me why I took so much abuse, why I didn't fight back. In some ways, she was right."

"That's my fault," Mom says. "If I had to do it again, I would have handled things so differently."

"It's OK, Mom. You and Dad did the best you knew how. I'll tell you one thing, though. When my book comes out, I'm going to use it to educate parents about those clichés that never work."

"So what else happened with A.J.?" Mom asks.

"She said that she was scared to come tonight, too," I continue. "I told her I couldn't believe it, since she was so popular in school. She said a lot has happened to her since then, and that she was never the confident person everyone thought. Mom, she was near tears. We hugged for a moment, and then she apologized for making me think she and every-one else hated me. 'We never hated you,' she insisted. 'We just didn't understand you.' I'm still in a state of shock."

"Does that help you?" Mom asks tenderly.

"Yes. I thought I was the only one who was pretending back then. I used to fantasize about hurting A.J., and now I can't help but think how ironic life is, that maybe, we could have been friends. And guess what else? A.J. and Jacklyn asked if I'd join everybody at Skinny Jim's after the reunion. I know that being invited to hang out with them shouldn't have meant so much to me, but I'd be lying if I said it didn't. It felt like the past, the present, and the future were colliding into each other, rewriting the history of everyone who was there. It was as if I had woken up in a parallel universe where the sun came out at night. My reality wasn't my reality anymore. I felt disoriented and enlightened all at once."

"That's wonderful, sweetheart. You've waited so long for this. We both have."

Mom is fighting back tears. As much as I hungered for the acceptance of my former classmates, I'm beginning to realize that my mom needed it as much as I did. I used to think that the only person held hostage by my past was me. How stupid not to understand that my mom was a prisoner of it, too.

"I wish your dad were here," Mom says.

"Me, too," I answer, reaching for her hand. Though Mom tries to hide her sadness from me, I can see how much she still misses my dad, who died tragically ten years ago. I decide that now is the best time to tell her the other big news.

"Mom, I met a guy!"

"Who?" she asks, unable to contain her enthusiasm.

"His name is Mitch. He was hot in high school, but he looks even better now. I nearly flipped when he began flirting with me. I swear my knees went weak!"

"I don't remember you ever mentioning him," she says.

"I always liked him, but he had a girlfriend. Besides, he seemed out of my reach."

"Tell me what happened," she says. "I'm floating on air right alongside you."

"I was on my way to the buffet table when this gorgeous man asked if I remembered him. No girl at Calvin Samuels could ever forget Mitch. We chatted for a bit about our lives since graduation. He's in the process of getting a divorce, but it's amicable, he says, and was a long time coming. He's got two daughters — Amber, who's nine, and Val, who's seven. He runs a family business with his stepfather."

"Sounds like he has his act together," Mom says.

"He's really appealing. The more I stood there talking to him, the more it all started coming back to me, the crush I used to have on him. I felt like Cinderella at the ball, who finally got noticed by the prince."

"Then what happened?" she asks.

"We both ended up going to Skinny Jim's. I wasn't sure I'd see him there. All of a sudden, he walks in. My heart fell to my stomach. There I was, sitting at a table with the most popular kids from school, and I wasn't scared anymore. Mark, Nadia, Tyler, and Clarke were all at the table. I fit in with everyone, Mom! The club started playing music from our era. Mitch and I danced all night. Jacklyn and A.J. joined us on the dance floor. All those school dances, they danced with the guys I dreamed about. Now *I* was the one dancing with someone *they* were fantasizing about! We were laughing so hard that all four of us fell onto a heap on the floor. It was the prom night I never had."

"Oh, angel, I'm so happy for you."

"All those years I thought that I was a freak. Tonight, I realized there was never anything wrong with me."

"No, honey, there wasn't. Your father and I tried to make you see that, but you had to learn it for yourself."

"You haven't heard the best part," I tell her, beaming. "After we left Skinny Jim's, Mitch walked me to my car. I gave him my number and then he kissed me! I know this sounds sappy, but oh my God, can he kiss! Do you think he'll call today?"

"Of course he will," Mom says. "Why don't you take a nap before he does? You haven't slept yet!"

"Oh no, Mom, I'm too excited. I'm going to rewrite the last chapter of *Please Stop Laughing at Me . . .*"

"Rewrite it? I thought the book was already in production."

"It is, but the last chapter is based on my grammar school reunion, because my high school reunion hadn't happened yet. I have to write about last night, because it changes everything. Last night, I forgave my former classmates for hurting me. I realized that it wasn't as simple as it seemed back then. More important, I forgave myself for believing all those horrible things they said to me, even after all these years." I give Mom a hug, then run to call my editor. When I relay to him the events of the evening, he's more excited than I am about the new last chapter.

"Don't worry, Jodee," he says. "Every editor secretly longs for that one moment in his career when he gets to say, 'Stop the presses!'"

As I sit at the computer, furiously typing away, for a moment I'm stumped. How can I confess in the book that I had a crush on Mitch all along? It'll make it look like the only reason I want him now is that I couldn't get him then. I can just hear the gossip: "She was the outcast, he was the hottest guy at school. That's the only reason she's dating him now." The truth is, it wouldn't matter to me who he was when we were kids. It's the man he is today that I think I could fall for. I decide to keep my little secret for now. When the time is right, I'll tell the world! I could never have anticipated the impact of that revelation.

As I put the final touches on the new last chapter, the phone rings. I pounce on the receiver. "Hello?"

"Jodee, it's Mitch. I had such a good time last night. I was wondering, would you like to go to Navy Pier with me this afternoon? We could have a late lunch and watch the sunset."

Oh, my God, is this really happening? "I'd love to," I answer, trying not to gush.

"Terrific. Give me your mom's address and I'll pick you up at three."

I hang up the phone and run downstairs, where my mom and my cousin Jeanine are chatting. "Mom, he called! He wants to spend the day with me. I'm so excited!"

"Thank goodness," Mom says, smiling. "I thought he'd call, but until that phone rang I wasn't going to leave the house."

It's a dream come true. There's only one problem. What happens when the book comes out? Though I've changed all the names, will that be enough? It's one thing for my former classmates to say they're supportive of the book. It's another when they're faced with the truth of their behavior for everyone to see. Am I just opening a keg of worms? Why resurrect the past and jeopardize my future when the present finally feels so good? But what about my reason for writing the book in the first place, to help kids? How can I turn my back on them now? What have I gotten myself into? Thank God I can't see what's coming.

chapter three

Learning to

Walk in

Different Shoes

November - December 2002

The days are growing cooler. Most people dread the coming of winter. I've always loved it. As a teenager, I used to spend hours imagining my first winter with a boyfriend — how he'd kiss me in the snow, help me decorate the Christmas tree, teach me how to ice skate, or snuggle with me in front of the fireplace listening to Journey and Styx albums. On weekends, we'd hang out with our friends, lost in our own world. For years, I held on to that fantasy, cosseted it like a tiny baby bird that I wanted to protect until it was ready to fly. Then, one morning I woke up and my adolescence had come and gone. Reluctantly, I placed the dream inside a cage and put it away. Every once in a while I would feel it stirring, wanting to be free, but I made a promise to myself never to let it out. Over time, it grew silent and died.

When Mitch asked me to go to Navy Pier with him the day after our reunion, that baby bird started fluttering its wings again, desperate to fly. As I stood there on the boardwalk kissing the boy who used to make my knees weak when he passed me in the hall, the sound of waves lapping against the pilings beneath the dock, I realized that my dream hadn't died at all. It was only sleeping. "Come on," warned the rational adult in me. "Don't you think you're going overboard here? Shouldn't you be more circumspect?" But the teenager in me, summoned out of hiding by the high school heart-throb, wouldn't let her get a word in edgewise.

Mitch and I went out every night that week. I'd always had this thing about *The Wizard of Oz*. As a child, I believed that Judy Garland, who played Dorothy, was my guardian angel. Some kids had imaginary friends. Dorothy was mine. Now, as an adult, whenever I see a rainbow or something associated with that film, I interpret it as a good omen, a sign from the universe that I'm on the right track. On my second date with Mitch we saw a huge vintage poster of *The Wizard of Oz* hanging in the foyer of the restaurant. Two nights later, when we stopped for a drink at a bar that had just opened in my hometown of Pason Park, Illinois, we overheard the couple next to us talking about an ornate hand-painted collage on the back wall near the dance floor. Curious, we decided to take a look. In the center of it was an image of Dorothy staring at a rainbow. Mitch nearly fell over.

I was still living on the East Coast. I had delayed my return to New York for a week and my clients were getting restless. I was the primary public relations consultant on a live stage show, a major film project, and several corporate accounts. My schedule was full, and I couldn't put off going back to work any longer. Mitch and I decided that our last evening together would be a romantic dinner. On the way back to my mom's, after a wonderful meal, it started to storm. We turned on the radio, hoping to hear a weather report; instead, the station started playing this whimsical and haunting version of "Over the Rainbow" from the Hawaiian Islands. Mitch looked at me, rolled his eyes, and we both started to laugh.

That night was magical. Mitch was the one. I knew that he was falling for me, too. How ironic, after twenty years of living all over the world, searching for Mr. Right, I finally found him at my high school reunion. I dreaded going back to New York. I didn't want my life there anymore. It had grown empty and meaningless. I knew that if I moved back to my hometown everyone would assume it was because I was smitten with Mitch. Our budding romance would make the transition easier, but that wasn't the reason I wanted to come home. I realized how much I'd missed my family and my roots. I vowed that when I got to New York I was going to make the break with that life. Consulting was still my primary source of income, and I could easily set up an office near Chicago.

As Mitch and I kissed, I luxuriated in the fullness of it. After a moment, he pulled back and looked at me. "What's wrong?" he asked.

"Nothing, it's just that I hate to leave," I answered. "This has been like a fairy tale."

"It's only for ten days," he responded. "I'll see you when you get back."

The way he said it unnerved me. "Is there something you're not telling me?" I asked him.

"No, why?"

"I don't know. Something in the tone of your voice."

"Everything's fine," he answered.

I would discover two weeks later that my instincts were right. When I returned from New York, I couldn't wait to see Mitch and called to let him know I was back. He was distant on the phone. He asked if he could see me later that evening.

I was confused by where he wanted to meet. It was a tavern with no atmosphere, just good, strong drinks. I considered it more of a place where you'd hook up with a buddy after work, not a date. He also didn't offer to pick me up. That wasn't like him. OK, I thought. It's his busy season, and he's probably exhausted from work. I ignored that annoying little voice in the back of my head that sounded like the robot from *Lost in Space*: "Warning, Will Robinson! Warning! Danger!"

When I walked into the bar, I cringed. It reeked of cigarette smoke and cheap aftershave. What was going on? Normally, Mitch would never bring me to a place like this. He was one of the classiest and most considerate men I'd ever known. He was also running late, another sign that something was amiss. I ordered a glass of white wine. It came in a plastic bottle with a screw top. I waited, trying to ignore the sinking feeling in the pit of my stomach. About twenty minutes later, he arrived. I'd never seen him like this. He had huge circles under his eyes. He was unshaven, and his shirt was wrinkled, as if he'd been sleeping in it.

"What is it?" I asked.

"Jodee, there's something I've got to tell you," he said.

"What?" *No, please don't take this dream away.*

"Remember I told you that after Deana, my ex, and I separated, I met this young woman from Cancun?"

"Vaguely," I answered. "You said you hung out with her a little bit while you were on vacation."

"Yes, well, when I was there I invited her to visit me in Chicago, and she's arriving next week."

"For how long?"

"That's still up in the air," he said.

"Why didn't you say anything to me about this before?" I cried.

"I told you about her."

"Mitch, you *mentioned* her in passing conversation, but you never even hinted that it was anything more than a casual flirtation. How could you lead me on like this?"

"Jodee, I never meant to lead you on," he said. "You've got to believe that. But I never anticipated you walking into my life, either, and when you did, I was so overwhelmed by what we were both feeling, I didn't know what to do. You're right. I should have told you, but I never thought she'd take me up on my offer to come here. When you were in New York, she called to 'surprise me with the good news.'"

I wanted to pummel him. I felt like Dorothy when she first arrived in the Emerald City. The guard, not yet aware of who she was, shut the gate in her face. I could almost hear her as I sat there getting dumped. "I was so happy," cried Dorothy. "Now I'll never get home." That's what being with Mitch was like — it was as if I had finally found home. I told myself how ridiculous this was, that we'd only been dating a short time, and I was behaving like a melodramatic sixteen-year-old. But my self-talk was falling on deaf ears. I had been waiting my whole life for this guy, and I couldn't fathom losing him now.

"Are you in love with her?" I asked, not sure I wanted to hear the answer.

"Let's just put it this way. At one point, I thought it was a question worth exploring. Since meeting you, I'm not so certain. But I started something with her and I have to see where it goes."

"You have to see where it *goes*? What about where *we* were going?"

"I know, and that's why this is killing me, but I can't just tell this girl to take a hike. She's sublet her apartment and taken a leave of absence from work."

"Are you scared of your feelings for me? Is that it? Is that why you're doing this?"

He didn't answer. I wanted to scream. I knew the only thing to do was to let him go. If it was meant to be, he'd come back. If it wasn't—

"Jodee, I realize I can't ask you to wait for me, but—"

"Look, just do what you have to do," I told him, fighting back tears. "I just wish you had been more honest in the beginning."

"Jodee, please try and understand. I never meant to be dishonest. I didn't tell you because I was feeling the same way you were. I still do. But I just can't turn my back on this other person."

"No, but you'll turn your back on me."

"I'm so sorry," he said.

What an idiot, I thought to myself. He knows how good we could be together. He's not even denying it. Though I was hurt and angry, I couldn't help but respect his integrity. If I was this other girl, I'd expect him to follow through on his promise, too. I asked him to walk me to my car. He wrapped his arms around me and kissed me. But this time, instead of it filling me up, it deflated my spirit like a raft whose plug had just been pulled.

All the energy I'd been flying high on since the reunion began to evaporate. In the following weeks, I would pick up the phone, start to dial Mitch's number, then stop. I would write him letters, then stuff them in my closet. Everyone thought I was overreacting. I felt like I was living some twisted version of the Cinderella story. The prince, after searching near and far throughout the land, finally finds me. Gazing dreamily into my eyes, he slides the glass slipper onto my foot. Then he turns and starts to leave!

"Hey, wait a minute!" I cry. "What are you doing? The frickin' slipper *fits*."

"I know, dear lady," he says. "'Tis true that destiny has chosen for us to go off into the sunset together happily ever after."

"Then why, oh handsome prince, are you running for the door?"

"Well, um, there was this other lass I sort of made a promise to who lost a ruby slipper . . ."

My thoughts are interrupted by my cell phone. I look at the caller ID window, hoping it's Mitch. It's Gary, my publisher, calling to see if I need his office to ship me additional bound galleys, advance reading copies of the book.

"I know you were sending some to your former classmates," he says. "How many do you have left from the original fifty?"

"Actually, they're still on the floor in my mom's office," I tell him. "I haven't opened the carton."

"Why? I should think you'd be anxious for your classmates to read it. What's the saying, 'Payback's a bitch'?"

"Come on, you act as if I did the book to get even. You know that's not why I wrote it."

"I was only kidding," he replies. "Besides, I thought you

said everything was great and that you've all been hanging out together since the reunion."

"I know. I'm just a little worried that the book might offend some of them. Even though the characters are composites, they're bound to see themselves in these portrayals. At the very least, they'll recognize the incidents they perpetrated. My confidence is so shaken by the breakup with Mitch, how am I going to handle it if they walk out on me, too?"

"That guy you were seeing? I'm so sorry. I'm assuming you didn't give him a galley yet, either."

"No, but I will. Imagine the look on Mitch's face when he discovers he's the hero in the last chapter? It's not his reaction I'm worried about. It's everyone else's from our class."

"Jodee, you've done nothing wrong here," he says. "They wronged *you*. The only thing you're guilty of is telling the truth, and it's not even for your own gain; it's to help others. If your former classmates don't have the grace or dignity to reconcile themselves with it, that's their failure, not yours."

Dear God, what's happening to me? It's as if my strength of character has been put into reverse and I'm becoming less than who I am. I barely recognize myself anymore. When I went to school with these people, I never cared about what they thought. As desperately as I wanted their companionship, if it meant hurting someone else or jeopardizing my self-respect, I always found the courage to do what was right. How could I have possessed that kind of backbone with my classmates then and be losing my nerve now? And it was harder when we were kids. School is pretty much your whole world at that age. My classmates and I were together eight hours a day, five days a week. We couldn't escape each other. I knew the laws of the kingdom called adolescence: bend to the sovereignty of the cool crowd and enjoy the riches of peer acceptance, or oppose their imperial rule, as I did, and be cast into exile. After all these years, I'm finally a welcome guest at the royal palace. As much as I long for my book to be published, the reality that it might mean banishment again has me wondering if it's worth the risk.

"I guess you're right, Gary," I reply. "What's the worst that can happen? My former classmates read the book and decide they don't want to play with me anymore?"

"That's the spirit!" he says.

Though I may have convinced my publisher I'm as gung ho as ever, I wish I could make myself believe it. The truth is, I'm enjoying every moment of my new-found acceptance and am saddened by the possibility of losing it.

My life has been such a whirlwind these past couple of months. Despite the disappointing turn of events with Mitch, I'm still determined to move back home, and have been operating my consulting business out of my mom's office while I look for a condo in the area. I've been spending more and more time with my former classmates, too. It's as if the last twenty years have evaporated, except now I'm not the outcast anymore. I'm also grateful for their company, because it's a welcome distraction from missing Mitch.

I keep thinking there must be something wrong with me. I was never a silly, giggling teenager even when I *was* a teenager. But since the reunion I'm like a high school girl who's willing to do almost anything to protect her new-found social status. What happened to the confident, sophisticated thirty-eight-year-old businesswoman who took pride in her willingness to stand up and be heard? Every time my former classmates include me in something now, whether it's the latest juicy tidbit of gossip or a girls' night out, the old Jodee, the one I secretly want back, goes into hiding and this giddy teenybopper with "Oh, please don't stop liking me" pasted across her forehead takes over.

On the other hand, I spent my entire youth crying myself to sleep, aching to fit in. I just want to enjoy how good this feels for a little bit longer. Who knows what will happen when my former classmates read the book? At least I'll be able to say that I got to experience a dream, however fleeting. *That's right, Jodee. Keep on trying to tell yourself this is normal and healthy.*

I don't know it yet, but I'm far from alone in my inability to shake off the primal hold the popular crowd from school still has over me. In fact, I will soon discover that there are millions of others who are just as ashamed and embarrassed about it as I am. We work, we dream, we marry, have kids and grow old, and rarely does anyone ever suspect the truth. Our classmates put a hole in us, and our self-esteem keeps falling out. We're constantly scooping the broken pieces off the floor and stuffing them back inside, like the scarecrow in *The Wizard of Oz*, hoping no one notices.

We could be your doctor or lawyer, your favorite actor, or the homeless guy on the street. No matter what we've become since graduation day, we still see ourselves as outcasts, freaks, misfits, *rejects*, those labels having been burnt into our being long before we were old enough or wise enough to understand that they weren't true.

We were the ones who always walked to class with our heads down, got picked last in gym, and sat alone at the far end of your lunch tables, pretending to be reading. We had stringy hair and pimples. Some of us were fat. Some of us were so skinny that our ribs stuck out. Invisible people don't care about their appearance. Despite how successful some of us may seem to you now, we're still hollow inside, unable to see ourselves clearly, because we can still hear your voices at the edge of our subconscious, calling us names, putting us down. Everyone needs to feel that they belong. When you denied us that, you stole something that we have spent our entire lives trying to get back. We want to hate you but can't, because we need your acceptance in order to complete ourselves.

We are *Adult Survivors of Peer Abuse*, a ghostly population of individuals struggling to break free of your influence. And the worst part is that most of you never meant to hurt us. You probably don't even remember making fun of us. Every time you rolled your eyes as we passed you in the hall, snickered at our attempts to win your approval, or made us the butt of a joke, you may have believed it was all in good fun. And when you see us today at the mall or the grocery store, you smile and make small talk, unaware of the damage you've done. The bully never remembers. The outcast never forgets.

As I continue my silent tirade, it's dawning on me that if I feel this way, and I'm only one voice, imagine what would happen if thousands of other adult survivors could be persuaded to share their stories and join me in my crusade to prevent school bullying? I will learn firsthand the meaning of the phrase, "Be careful what you wish for."

Suddenly, it's as if lightning were surging through me, renewing my strength and sense of purpose. Handing out the galleys to my former classmates doesn't seem so scary anymore. I'm willing to accept it if they turn their backs on me once they read the book. I take a deep breath, grab my car keys, and head for the office. As I'm driving into the parking lot, my cell phone rings. It's Shelly, inviting me to join the gang for dinner this evening — "the gang" meaning the old jock crowd from high school. They try to get together every couple of weeks. Shelly is the heart of the group, the one who plans most of the social outings and makes sure everyone stays in touch. An ebullient redhead with a warm, affable disposition, Shelly was a beloved cheerleader at Calvin Samuels. Though she wasn't as striking a beauty as some of the other girls on the squad, Shelly had such energy and team spirit that no one in those bleachers could keep their eyes off her.

I always admired Shelly. She reminded me of a young Bette Midler, with her quick wit and infectious personality. Whenever I saw her in the hallway or by the lockers, I'd smile and say hello, wishing I could wave a magic wand and make us friends. I remember so many times standing next to her and asking a question or making a comment that I hoped would give us something to talk about. It never worked, and I couldn't understand why. When my parents had clients or business associates over for dinner, I could converse with them easily. Yet, whenever I opened my mouth at school, I'd get an awkward look from my classmates, as if to say, "What on earth are you talking about?" It was like we spoke two different languages.

Sitting here now, chatting with Shelly, I'm barely able to recall the uncomfortable exchanges of our youth, and I can't help but shake my head.

"We all know how bummed out you are about Mitch," Shelly says. "We think a night out is just the medicine you need! So, are you in?"

"Sure," I answer.

"Cool," she says. "We'll see you at Skinny Jim's around seven."

As the evening draws nearer, my mood begins to brighten. I'm looking forward to seeing everyone. It'll also be a perfect opportunity to give some of them a galley. The sooner they read it, the sooner I'll know if my fears will be realized or not.

Skinny Jim's has always been a favorite hangout of Calvin Samuels graduates. The only bar in town that still plays classic rock, it's usually packed, especially on weekends, where seventies and eighties diehards dance to the songs of their youth. Most of the patrons are trying to recapture something they've lost. I'm trying to experience something I never had. I tell myself it's nothing more than an innocent escape, that I'm attaching too much importance to the power and allure of this pretend time tunnel.

Skinny Jim's is already hopping when I arrive. Despite how much I enjoy coming here, it can be unnerving being in a place where the past feels more alive than the present. AC/DC's "You Shook Me All Night Long" is blaring from enormous loudspeakers. I see Shelly and Clarke waving at me from a table in the back. As I make my way toward them, the music pounding in my ears, part of me wants to turn and leave. They were both so rough on me in school, especially

Clarke. I keep hearing his voice mocking me on the way to class. If someone had told me then that, years later, Shelly and Clarke would not only want to make amends for how they treated me but also reach out to me in genuine friendship, I would have said, "Yeah, *right!*" I guess the saying is true: "Never say never." Then I remember the galleys I've brought and realize that I'm carrying a time bomb in my purse. As I tighten my fingers around the strap, I wonder, if it goes off, could I survive the blast? By the time I get to the table, Shelly's ordered me a white wine. I sit down, hoping she and Clarke don't notice how nervous I am. No such luck.

"Hey, Jodee, what's wrong?" Clarke asks. "You seem edgy."

Tick.

Tick.

Tick.

"I've brought the galleys of my book and I'm worried you guys are going to wig out after you read it."

"Well, that's a good way to put us at ease," Shelly teases.

"No, I'm serious," I reply. "You may not see yourselves in the story, but you may recognize things you did."

"Jodee, we know the characters are composites," Shelly says. "You've explained it to us fifty times. I wish you'd stop worrying already."

"Where are Mark and Nadia?" I ask. "I brought a galley for them, too."

"They had to go to their son's basketball game," Clarke answers. "But I'll see them this weekend." I hand him a galley, and he tucks it under his jacket.

"Hey, that reminds me," Shelly says. "Didn't Noreen

want to read it? I thought you said you were going to call her about tonight. Is she coming?"

Noreen and I were friends during our freshman year at Samuels. We were kindred spirits brought together by our hunger for peer acceptance. By the time we both realized that I was becoming the school outcast, she had already begun to pull away. I hadn't seen her since graduation. Then we met at the reunion. The girl who was once shy and unsure of herself, who hid behind excess weight and too much eye shadow, had metamorphosed into a striking, confident woman, impeccably dressed with grace and style. She was married, with a young daughter and a successful business career. We'd been staying in touch ever since the reunion.

"That's her just walking in," I reply. Clad in tailored jeans and a gray blazer, Noreen is the epitome of elegance and self-assurance.

"I'm so sorry I'm late," she says, sitting down and ordering a drink. "My daughter had a rough day at school."

"What happened?" Clarke asks.

"She wore her new glasses and some of the kids made fun. We had a good talk, though, and I think she'll be OK."

"My daughter Leah got hassled at school today, too, and it isn't the first time," Shelly says, shaking her head. "She's a freshman at Samuels and some of the girls in her class are brutal. Last weekend they invited her to a sleepover. Leah was thrilled. Then in the middle of the night she calls me begging to be picked up. It turns out these girls wanted her there so they could humiliate her for their own amusement. It was awful."

For a moment, Noreen has this look on her face like she's

just swallowed a bug. I will discover before this evening is over that Leah's story sparked a memory for her in a way none of us could ever have expected.

"Noreen, I can't get over how much you've changed since high school," Clarke says.

"We've all grown a lot since then," she replies. "I guess you could say I was a late bloomer."

"Jodee, I think you're the only one who hasn't really changed," Clarke observes.

"Really? I think I've changed a lot."

"No, Jodee, it's true," Shelly agrees. "You're the same person you were when we were kids. We just had to grow into you. Remember how you used to protect the underdog at school? You didn't even like seeing someone step on a bug! You'd tell them that they had no right to kill something that tiny and helpless, and then you'd scoop it onto a piece of paper and take it outside. Who else at our age *did* stuff like that? Of course, we thought you were weird. And you're still the same. The only difference is that now we admire you for it."

"Wait a minute," Clarke says, grinning. "Speak for yourself. I still think it's a little weird!"

This is all so new to me. My former classmates are laughing with me instead of at me. After all these years, they've accepted me for who I am. The evening passes quickly, and I nearly forget, until I hear the bartender announcing last call.

Tick.

Tick.

Tick.

Reaching into my bag, I pull out three galleys and hand

one to each of my companions. The bar is dimly lit, and I watch them squint as they try to read the cover copy.

Four.

Three.

Two.

One.

A familiar panic rises in me.

"I'm going to have to pry it away from my daughter's hands first," Shelly says, flipping through the pages. "What about you, Clarke—aren't you eager to read it?"

"Jodee, was I mean to you?" he asks.

There it is, the tacit denial. I don't know if I feel happy because that means his recent fondness for me is genuine and isn't motivated by a guilty conscience, or upset that he sincerely doesn't recall how he treated me.

"Clarke, just because you may have been the inspiration for a character doesn't mean that character is actually you," I reassure him. He shifts uncomfortably in his seat. I don't know who feels more trapped right now, him or me. "Clarke, it's the love and respect you give me now that counts, not how things were in the past," I say.

I watch his body visibly relax. I never thought I'd see the day when he was worried that *I* might reject *him*. I should be experiencing a sense of vindication, but instead it's making me feel embarrassed, like when someone takes you out to dinner and his credit card is declined—that awkward moment when you're not sure how best to preserve his dignity. It's as if I've just discovered that Clarke is human. When we were in school, I put him on a pedestal because he was part of the cool crowd and I wasn't. Like most kids who were always on the outside looking in, I bought into the mythology of popularity and worshipped its false gods. As I look across the table at Clarke, I wonder if I'll ever get used to seeing him as humble and vulnerable. I ask myself what I'm trying to hold on to here and which is more real, my friendship with these people now or my idealized version of them from high school.

"Noreen, is something wrong?" Shelly says. "You seem preoccupied." *So she did notice.*

Noreen looks directly at me. "You don't remember, do you?"

"Remember what?" I say.

"God, I feel terrible," she says. "I should have apologized long ago."

"For what? What are you talking about?"

"It was right around Thanksgiving freshman year. That's when Sharon and Jacklyn had taken me into their clique. They knew you and I were friends earlier in the semester and, I swear, I never saw it coming."

Noreen's shoulders begin to slump as she continues. She is no longer looking at me.

"Jacklyn asked me to find out if you'd be up for a sleep-over. You were so excited, and you asked your mom if we could do it at your house. The following Friday, Jacklyn, Sharon, and I came with our pillows. Your mom went to so much trouble, making pizza and brownies. She was beaming, because you were so happy that night."

Noreen is near tears. I can't imagine what she's about to tell me. I honestly don't remember anything about this slumber party. "It's OK," I interject. "Go on."

"We were all sleeping on the floor in your room. The closet

light was on, in case anyone had to go the bathroom. I wish now that room had been dark. Then we couldn't have done it."

"Done what?" Clarke asks. "How much damage can a few fourteen-year-old girls do with a parent present?"

Noreen closes her eyes, as if trying to shut out the memory. "A lot," she answers. "Around 2:00 A.M., Jacklyn and Sharon woke me up and asked me to go downstairs with them to the kitchen. They raided the cabinets until they found a can of flour. Then they opened the refrigerator and grabbed the ketchup and mustard. I couldn't understand what they were doing. I begged them to tell me but they just kept on giggling. Next, Sharon told me to take out my make-up. 'Come on,' they whispered. 'This is going to be so cool!' We tiptoed back to your room. Then Sharon opened up the can of flour and started covering your face with it. I tried to deter them by telling them they were going to wake you up. Jacklyn just rolled her eyes and squeezed a big glob of rouge onto her finger and rubbed it into your cheeks until you looked like a clown. Then she smiled and said, 'Your turn, Noreen.' Jodee, I knew it was either play or pay. Not knowing what else to do, I opened the eye shadow and caked it onto your lids. Jacklyn and Sharon were jubilant. That's when I saw it. While they were quietly high-fiving each other, I noticed your eyes flicker open. You had been pretending to be asleep! You knew what we were doing, but I guessed you were so used to being excluded that this was better than not being included at all. I wanted to tell Sharon and Jacklyn that we needed to stop, but I was afraid if I did they'd turn me into an outcast like you."

Noreen is crying now. Clarke reaches over and touches

her shoulder.

"Next, Jacklyn began smearing the lipstick all over your mouth. When she was satisfied, she opened the ketchup, then the mustard. Holding one in each hand, she pointed the plastic bottles downward and squeezed. Suddenly, the bedroom light was on. We turned, and there was your mom, standing in the doorway. I'll never forget the look on her face. 'Mom, don't get them into trouble, they didn't mean anything,' you pleaded. I felt sick. Your mom took you to the bathroom and told us to go downstairs and wait for her in the living room. When she came down, it was clear she had been crying. She told us she couldn't believe anyone could be that cruel. When Shelly told us earlier what happened to Leah, it reminded me how we humiliated you that night, how horrible it must have been for your mom. Now that I'm a mom, it really hits home. Jodee, I'm so sorry. I plan on apologizing to your mom, too. I wanted to mention something the night of the reunion, but you were having such a good time. But hearing Shelly, well, I couldn't keep silent any longer."

I don't know what to say to Noreen. The mind has a funny way of protecting itself. I must have blocked out what happened. Even hearing it tonight, it still doesn't feel familiar. What else have I buried in my subconscious, and how safe is it for me to use my own pain to help bullied kids if there are secrets like this hidden inside me? It's scary enough that I have to wrestle the demons that come with the memories I *do* have. What about those lurking beneath the ones I *don't* yet have?

"Jodee, I'd apologize to you on national television if that's what it takes to show you how sorry I am."

"Noreen, it really is OK," I say. "Your friendship now is what counts. That goes for all of you. The only reason I'm dredging up our past with this book is so I can help kids. Otherwise, I wouldn't put any of us through this."

Shelly is visibly shaken. "I didn't realize how bad it must have been for you in school," she says. "I'm so sorry. If I had known, I want to believe I would have done *something*."

"All right, girls, enough emotionalism for one night," Clarke says. "Instead of feeling bad about things we've done, let's talk about the good things we can do now. Jodee, who else are you giving a galley to?"

"I sent one to Tyler, Sharon, A.J., and, of course, Mitch. That's it so far."

"I'll give Mark and Nadia their galley this weekend. If you get me the date of your book-signing, I'll e-mail everyone I know and insist they attend. I'll make 'em an offer they can't refuse!"

"I love you for that, Clarke," I say. "But don't you think you should read the book first?"

"No book is going to change my respect for you."

Though there is conviction in Clarke's voice, I see doubt in his eyes. I know there is nothing I can do in any of this but wait.

Tick.

Tick.

Tick.

chapter four

The Adult
Survivor?

January - March 2003

The holidays were quiet and uneventful. Every once in a while, my mind would drift to Mitch, and I couldn't help but wonder how he and Kathy were spending Christmas. Did they huddle by a cozy fire clinking champagne glasses and professing their love for each other? Did they bundle up on a blustery winter afternoon, their boots crunching in the snow as they walked through rows of Christmas trees until they found just the right one? As far as my imagination was concerned, she was living out my Yuletide fantasy, the one I thought I'd forgotten until Mitch's kiss reawakened it that afternoon at Navy Pier.

Mitch and I spoke several times the week between Christmas and New Year's. He had called to thank me for the galley and to tell me that he was looking forward to reading it. He didn't mention anything about Kathy, and I didn't bring it up. I was itching to ask him what was going on, but I didn't want to appear too anxious. By the time we got off the phone, my stomach was doing flip-flops.

That was over a month ago. I finally heard from Mitch again last week. He called and said that he'd read the galley and was wondering if we could meet for lunch. When I walked into the restaurant, he hugged me, burrowing his face into my neck. Neither of us wanted to let go. Then he gently pulled away and looked at me. "I was stunned by your book," he said. "I couldn't believe you made me the hero in the last chapter. After how I've treated you, I felt guilty."

"You shouldn't. You gave me the prom night I never had, and for that I'll always be grateful no matter what happens."

"I'm so sorry about what you went through at school. I remember that some of the people in our class gave you a hard time, but I had no idea how bad things really were. Why didn't you come to me for help?"

I didn't know how to answer when Shelly and Clarke asked me that question either. How could I explain to them, without hurting their feelings, that it never would have worked, that their compassion now is the result of an adult looking back in retrospect and not the reality when they were kids? I know they want to believe differently. I do, too. It reminds me of this old proverb that my dad used to tell me: "Better to remain silent and be thought a fool than to open your mouth and remove all doubt." No one will ever know for sure if they would have stood up for me, because I didn't ask, they never offered, and in the long run perhaps that's best. This way, all of us can still have faith that, had I turned to them for help, they would have been there for me, just the way they'd want their own children to behave.

As Mitch and I were leaving the restaurant, I mentioned my book signing the next week and invited him to attend. He said he'd be there, and would try to bring his daughters. "I've told them all about you, and they're eager to meet a real author," he said, smiling. Up until that moment, I was proud of myself for resisting the temptation to ask him about Kathy.

Finally, I couldn't hold back any longer. "Mitch, I have to ask, how are things with Kathy?"

"OK, I guess," he answered.

Something in his voice told me there was still room for hope.

In addition to a renewed sense of optimism about Mitch, I was beginning to get encouraging feedback from my former classmates about the book. Tyler and A.J. called me over the weekend to let me know they'd read it and were supportive. When I asked Tyler how he felt about my including what he did to me hours before graduation, he said if it prevents just one kid from doing something that awful today he was glad I wrote about it.

People do change. Tyler transformed from the cool, tough, Marlboro-smoking king of the party crowd to a serious-minded business executive and dedicated family man. He confessed to me during our telephone conversation that he remembers almost nothing from his teen years and that he went through most of high school in an alcohol- and drug-induced haze. He credits his wife with getting him sober and keeping him sane. His life still isn't easy. His youngest son suffers from Asperger's syndrome, a disorder similar to autism that affects one's ability to socialize and connect with others. "To his classmates, he's 'weird,'" Tyler says. "I wish they could understand that underneath my son's odd stares and nervous tics is an intelligent boy desperate for friendship."

I never thought I'd say this, but Tyler is a good man. I wish I could have seen beyond his meanness when we were kids. I was so busy trying to protect myself from who he was pretending to be that I never allowed myself a peek at who he really was. Every time I talk to my former classmates about our shared past, I always end up pondering the same disturbing question: What part did I play in the drama of my own ostracism? And how many other kids today are coming home from school as I did, confused and in tears, desperate to unravel the mystery of why, no matter how hard they try, they don't fit in? The victims of bullying always want to believe that it was never their fault, that they were shunned and tormented simply for being different. But *is* it that simple? Before I started hanging out with my former schoolmates, I always used to wonder why they didn't understand me. But what about what *I* didn't understand about *them*? I'm not making excuses for Tyler, Clarke, A.J., or anyone else who has ever been a school bully. Cruelty can be forgiven, but it can never be undone. However, the more I explore how I may have unknowingly contributed to my own fate as the outcast, the more I'll be able to help kids dealing with the same problem today. I'm beginning to realize that the bully and the victim are flip sides of the same coin. Both are incomplete in their own way, searching for something outside themselves to feel whole. Before Tyler and I hung up, he told me he wished he could take back all the unkind things he did. Me, too, I wanted to cry out.

Tyler isn't the only one who pleasantly surprised me with his support of the book. Jacklyn and A.J. both sent congratulatory e-mails. But it was Noreen's response that bowled me over. ABC TV's *Good Morning America*, with Diane Sawyer, contacted my publisher inviting me to appear on the show. *GMA*, as it's referred to in the publishing industry, is one of the best showcases for publicity. One appearance can make or break a book's success. The network's only caveat was that they wanted someone who bullied me to appear on the show with me and admit live on the air what they did and how they feel about it now. I told the producer that I couldn't imagine anybody willing to put themselves in that position, let alone on national television, and I begged her to reconsider. But ABC insisted, saying that, unless I could persuade one of my former classmates, they wouldn't put me on at all. When Noreen heard about this, she immediately volunteered.

"No, Noreen, it's too much to ask of anyone," I said.

"But you're not asking," Noreen replied. "I'm offering."

That was over a month ago. I couldn't write a story more compelling than the one unfolding right now. What began as a three-minute interview segment evolved into a two-part piece on school bullying. ABC has asked Noreen and me to work with the producer on assembling a panel of bullies, victims, and their parents. Though Noreen would never say anything, I know the sacrifice she's making. She's already stretched to the limit with the demands of family and career, let alone baring her soul in front of thirty million people.

I still haven't heard from Mark or Nadia. And, oddly enough, I had dinner with Clarke and Shelly the other day, and they avoided any mention of the book. I don't even know if they've read the galley. What if they did and they're angry at me? There it is again, the insecurity. It's like an old injury that keeps flaring up without warning. And it isn't the only thing that's bothering me lately.

My former classmates often admit that they would

change their behavior if we could go back in time, but they never tell me if they would change anything about mine. I know it's out of love and respect, that they feel the least they can do after all that's happened is take full responsibility for it now. But I need to know whether if I hadn't followed the insipid advice of all those well-meaning adults who told me to just ignore them and walk away, things might have been different. They say that hindsight is twenty-twenty. Who better to assist in my quest to find answers than those who once tormented me? Some of them will help me save lives. Others will hide. One person in particular will unearth something so disturbing that it will inspire me to dedicate my life to changing the disciplinary policies of the American school system.

The last couple of weeks have been a blur. It's midafternoon and I'm at LAX, rushing to catch a flight to New York to meet Noreen. Tomorrow we're going on *Good Morning America*. She and I have been turning our lives upside down to accommodate the network's every request. Though I've been upbeat for all our sakes, underneath I'm uneasy. Too much is riding on this one interview. If anything should go wrong, my publisher and I will end up bearing the cost of a major promotional tie-in with thousands of bookstores nationwide, which I had to move heaven and earth to make happen; the investment of those additional printings of the book in anticipation of heightened sales, and most of all, my credibility. I'm the one who persuaded everyone to believe in this project. When every major publisher rejected the book, I was able to secure a deal with a small independent house only through sheer will-power. If *Good Morning America* doesn't fulfill everyone's expectations, it'll be me who will pay the penalty.

As I make my way through the crowded terminal, chewing Tums to quell my nervous stomach, I keep thinking about an old Broadway musical I saw with my parents when I was a kid, starring Sammy Davis, Jr. called *Stop the World—I Want to Get Off.* That's exactly how I feel right now. In addition to the prospect of having my childhood excavated for public consumption, this is my fifth airport in less than four days. I've been traveling from one end of the country to the other, breaking my back trying to stay on top of everything: teaching at New York University, dashing back and forth to the Windy City to give seminars at the University of Chicago, squeezing in last-minute trips to Boston for meetings with my publisher, flying to DC in between to follow up on endorsement leads for the book, preparing for a nationwide author publicity tour, and working day and night to keep my consulting clients happy. That was the reason for this trip to Los Angeles, to reassure my clients here that my performance on their accounts wouldn't suffer during the book launch. Most of them smiled through clenched teeth and told me that if I didn't start making them a priority again soon, they'd cancel their contracts. I'm panicked because their business is still my primary source of income.

Though I'm kicking myself for not planning ahead better, it's hard for me to walk away from any opportunity because when it leads to accomplishment I'm able to satisfy my need for a fix of self-esteem. This is a familiar scenario for many Adult Survivors of Peer Abuse. You either grow up to be a compulsive overachiever like me or you become the opposite, someone who never reaches his potential. Both can drive you to unhealthy extremes. Over the past several years, I became so obsessed with achievement that I never thought about what I'd do if each of the avenues I was pursuing all came through at once. Soon I will meet thousands of other adult survivors who've been where I am. I will come to understand that many of us are gifted in ways we can't appreciate because our classmates did such a good job of convincing us that we were inadequate. Unable to recognize our own potential, we try harder to make others see it and, as a result, often manifest more than we bargained for. It's like an accidental garden that sprouts from a spilled packet of seeds you never knew you had. You feel responsible for it, but you don't know how you're going to keep it up. I find that it's usually the people who are scorned for being different who possess the ability to make a difference in this world, and those who refuse to change in order to fit in when they're young who change the world the most when they grow up.

I still have a few moments before boarding, so I decide to call the hotel to let Noreen know I'm on my way. I'm told by the front desk that the reservation has been canceled. "There must be some mistake," I reply. "Can you check again? What about something under the name Blanco?"

"Ma'am, I'm very sorry, but that room has been canceled, too."

While I'm fighting back a wave of nausea, I see Noreen's home number flashing across my cell phone window. "Noreen? What's happening? Why aren't you in New York?"

"Jodee, I've been trying to reach you all day. Didn't you

get my voice mails?"

"I'm sorry. I've been in meetings since early this morning and haven't had a chance to check my messages. What's going on?"

"*Good Morning America* cancelled our appearance."

"*Why?* What happened?"

"Haven't you been watching the news?" Noreen asks. "Everyone's saying that President Bush is going to declare war on Iraq. That's why ABC canceled us. The producer said the White House has scheduled a press conference and the network is bumping any stories not related to the Middle East."

I knew this whole Good Morning America *thing was just too good to be true. I knew it!*

"Jodee, are you OK?"

"Not really. Any books being published now, unless they're about the Middle East, are going to be lost in the shuffle. I know how selfish and awful I must sound to you. Here we are facing the prospect of people actually dying in a war, and I'm worried about my book. But it's more than that. What about the wars being fought in our schools? What about the millions of kids who can't even go from homeroom to study hall without being humiliated or worse, and who cry themselves to sleep every night out of loneliness and despair? I've put everything I have into getting out there to help them, and this book was my vehicle."

"I'm so sorry," Noreen says. "Why don't you tell all this to the producer? Maybe she can reschedule us."

Though I love Noreen for her optimism, I'm not as hopeful as she is. After we hang up, I call the network to try and negotiate a solution, only to be told that it's impossible. Crestfallen, I start to dial my publisher to break the news to them, then hang up. Why ruin their night? I can just as easily tell them in the morning. Moments later, I hear the airline announcing the final boarding call for my flight. At least I don't have to fly all the way to New York and can get off at the stopover in Chicago.

The next morning, Mom, who thought I was in L.A., is shocked to find me making coffee in her kitchen. I explain what happened, and she wraps her arms around me. "And it isn't just *Good Morning America*, Mom. By the time I got in last night and checked my voice mail, I had more than twenty messages from producers and reporters canceling their interviews with me 'until further notice.' The stores are going to return all their stock to the publisher. How can I help even one kid if no one knows I exist? This is a disaster."

"Angel, it's always darkest before the dawn," Mom says.

"Why do you always do that? Why can't you just let me be miserable if that's what I need to feel?"

"Because I think you're jumping the gun," Mom replies. "I have a good feeling about this."

I realize that Mom means well, but her Pollyanna attitude makes me want to scream right now.

"Don't you roll your eyes at me, young lady! I've been right before."

I dread calling my publisher, and decide that I need to get my emotions in order before I talk with anyone. I turn off my cell phone and head upstairs to escape for a while into the numbness of sleep.

"Honey, everything really will be all right," Mom calls out

as I shut the bedroom door.

When I awaken in the afternoon, I steel myself for the task at hand and begin dialing my editor's number. Before I can complete the call, I see his name on my caller ID.

"Hey, Gary."

"Thank goodness I found you. Are you sitting down?"

"Yeah, I'm sitting." *Oh God, it's worse than I thought.*

"The bookstores have been calling me all day. They say you were amazing on *Good Morning America. Please Stop Laughing at Me . . .* is flying off the shelves."

Did I hear him right?

"I'm so sorry I wasn't able to catch your segment myself, but I'll watch it on my TiVo tonight."

"But, Gary . . ."

"Hold on, I'm not finished yet. Are you ready for the *really* big news?"

I wonder if now is the time to pinch myself. . . .

"Jodee, are you there?"

"Yes, yes, I'm here. Go on."

"Your book made the *New York Times* bestseller list."

"What? Oh, my God, you're *kidding*!"

"No, their office notified me this afternoon. This is the first title we've ever published to become a *New York Times* bestseller, and to think it hit the list within forty-eight hours."

"Gary, I just don't see how any of this is possible."

"What do you mean?"

"I wasn't *on Good Morning America* this morning. I haven't even done one media interview yet. They were all canceled because Bush has declared war on Iraq."

"That only proves one thing: certain books strike a nerve. Listen, we'll talk more later today. Right now, I have a meeting with my marketing and sales departments. I have a feeling we're in for quite a ride."

That would be the understatement of a lifetime.

After I tell Mom the incredible news, she asks how it's possible for the book to make the list without any publicity or reviews. I explain to her the Zeitgeist of modern publishing: "If you have enough books in stores, which we did, and there's something in the air, people talk. There's been a buzz about this book among booksellers for weeks. They're the ones who have reached the readers. It's being hand-sold in independent stores and the chains have moved it to their front tables. The book is selling on its own."

"Angel, it's all beyond me, but it's completely wonderful," Mom says.

Before I call Noreen to tell her the bizarre twist of events, I notice a voice-mail message. My euphoria quickly turns to nausea as I listen to it. "Hey, Jodee, it's Clarke." I can tell by his tone that something is wrong. "I thought you'd want to know about this as soon as possible. I bumped into Mark earlier today, and he said Nadia is furious about the book. And, Jodee, it isn't only her. A lot of other people are upset, too. Call me as soon as you get this message, OK?"

Oh, my God.

chapter five

The Real

Versus

The Surreal

March 2003

I hear locker doors clanging, girls giggling and gossiping, and the sound of rubber soles squeaking across a gym floor. The bell just rang signaling the beginning of first period. I want to cover my ears, but I can't because my arms are loaded with books. As I make my way to social studies, I begin trembling. I didn't do last night's homework, or the assignment the night before that. I'm behind in all my classes. I've missed entire weeks of school. But I had to go to work. My clients scheduled meetings, and threatened to fire me if I didn't attend.

I must talk to the principal. I am running across campus toward the administration office. To my horror, I realize that with each step my legs are growing heavier and heavier, as if the lower half of my body is part of a film being projected in slow motion. The harder I try to move forward, the more paralyzed I become. I am on my knees now, dragging myself across the hall. I finally reach the office. Nobody is there. I am frantic. "Where is everyone?" I cry. A secretary with pasty, wrinkled skin and vacant black eyes emerges from the back and sits down at the reception desk. She asks why I'm not in class. "But I don't belong here," I answer.

"Let me check the files," she says. Then she opens drawer

after drawer, shaking her head as she rummages through rows of old, yellowed folders. After what feels like an eternity, she pulls one out, bends down, and hands it to me.

"There must be some mistake!" I say. "I'm thirty-eight years old. I was a student here at Calvin Samuels, but I graduated. I know I did. You have to believe me!"

Just then, Clarke and A.J. walk into the office. They are sixteen years old. A.J. is wearing skintight jeans and a Cheap Trick "Live at Budakon" concert t-shirt. Her hair is feathered like Farrah Fawcett's, and she's carrying a fringe purse with a Bonne Bell lip gloss peeking out of the side pocket. Clarke is in his blue-and-gold football uniform, and holding his helmet. A canvas book bag is slung over his shoulder, with the words "Party Hardy" written in marker across the front flap. Finally, I tell myself. They'll tell this crazy secretary that we've all graduated.

"Clarke, A.J., tell her this is ridiculous, that we don't belong here," I say.

"What are you talking about, Blanco?" A.J. replies.

"Come on," I say. "We were just at our reunion. A.J., you're married with kids."

Suddenly, Tyler, Shelly, and Noreen walk in. They look at A.J. and Clarke and grin. Then they form a circle around me and begin to chant:

Freak.

Freak.

Death to the freak.

"No, listen to me," I plead. "We don't go here anymore. I can prove it!"

Freak.

Freak.

Death to the freak.

"Clarke, we had drinks at Skinny Jim's before Christmas. Don't you remember?"

Clarke rolls his eyes and they all begin to laugh. The secretary is laughing now, too. I panic and start to scream. It is then that I usually wake up.

I experienced similar dreams during the writing of the book. I thought they had run their course. I was wrong. If anything, they're worse now. It's probably because of the roller-coaster ride I've been on these past few weeks. After I received that distressing voice mail from Clarke, I called him and we met for lunch. He was delighted to hear about my book making the bestseller list, but despite his enthusiasm I could hear the trepidation in his voice when I asked about Nadia.

"She says the mean cheerleader character resembles her physically."

"But the characters are—"

"Composites. Yes, I know. I tried to explain that to her. But she says it doesn't matter, that some people will still think it's her anyway, and she's concerned that her kids are going to be made fun of at school because of it."

"Maybe she should have thought of that before."

"Come on, Jodee, you don't mean that."

"You're right. I'm sorry. I do feel terrible that she's worried for her children. I would never want anyone to go through that. My mom did, and it still haunts her. I'll talk to

Nadia."

"I'd wait if I were you. She's pretty upset. That's one of the reasons I wanted to reach you right away. She told me she's going to your book signing."

"You think she'll try to confront me?"

"Honestly, I don't know. But at least now you'll be prepared if she does."

"Clarke, I see the look on your face. What is it that you haven't told me?"

He is silent.

"Please, I want to know."

"Nadia says she doesn't remember you ever being abused the way you describe. Several other people have said the same thing."

"What did you tell them?"

"I was honest. I told them I've forgotten almost everything about school, but I do remember what we were capable of back then, and that's why I know you're telling the truth."

"What did they say?"

"Nothing. What could they say? They're not stupid people. Why would you exhume the remains of your childhood as a lie? They know that they hurt you. They're just angry because your book is making them examine parts of their own youth they'd prefer to keep buried."

"Thank you. Your support means a lot."

That was a week ago. In a few hours, I have my first book signing. It's at the Borders bookstore in Pason Park. The store has asked me to give a one-hour talk before the autographing and discuss some of my experiences as the school outcast. My emotions are all over the board. One moment I'm biting my nails, worried that no one will show and I'll be standing at the podium, microphone in hand, looking out at a sea of empty chairs. A second later, I'm pacing the floor in a state of panic over what will happen if everyone does attend. The store manager said he sent hundreds of invitations to faculty, administration, and parents in the local school district and he's confident the turnout will be strong. I wish it was tomorrow morning and I was drinking coffee, reflecting on the events of the night before, instead of having to face that night right now. After the book signing, Mom is throwing a huge party to celebrate. Shelly and Noreen are coming over later to help her set up for the caterer. As evening nears, my jitters intensify.

How am I going to get up in front of the people in my hometown and relive the worst memories of my life as I'm looking into the eyes of those who were responsible for much of it: teachers and counselors who turned their backs on me, former classmates who want to believe I'm a liar, my mom, who, though she tried her best, often made things worse? How will I avoid feeling swallowed by this audience, many of whom will have come tonight for the same reason people slow down when passing an accident on the highway? How will I keep it together, knowing that I'll be alone and naked up there, my wounds exposed and vulnerable to ridicule? What will I do if a familiar face attacks my credibility, or a teacher at Samuels says that nothing like I described ever happens now, and how dare I sully their good name after all these years? What will I do when I search the crowd for Clarke and Shelly and see them leaving the store with the rest of my long-awaited friends, who will never accept the truth of their actions?

What if someone accuses me of revenge? In some small way, could they be right? I'm still unnerved by my reaction when Clarke told me Nadia's fears about the book. For a split second, I felt a sense of satisfaction before my empathy for her kicked in. It was so fleeting that it seems I could have imagined it. But, deep down, I know I didn't. Am I making too much of something that merely proves I'm human, or does it make me less of a human being?

I've got to stop with all these "what ifs." I'm working myself up to the point of becoming unhinged, and I've got less than an hour to get ready for tonight. I remember that Judy Garland once asked just before a performance to be reminded to breathe, because her mind was racing so badly at the time, she was afraid she wouldn't notice if her lungs weren't getting air. I never thought I'd be able to relate to how she felt that day, until now. It's as if I need earplugs to block out the noise from my own head. Not getting any sleep for nearly a week isn't helping matters, either. I look like a raccoon, the circles under my eyes are so dark.

As I pull out my makeup to begin the arduous task of operation camouflage, I spot an envelope tucked inside my cosmetic case. It's a good luck card with a photo of a droopy-eyed old bulldog with big, fat jowls wearing a pair of angel wings. Handwritten inside are the words "Angel, break a leg tonight. I'm so proud of you. Love, Mom." Mom's been so supportive of the book, and I know it can't be easy for her, having to revisit those awful years. I gave her a copy of the manuscript months ago, so in case she was uncomfortable we could address it before galleys were printed. I'll never forget her response. She asked me to come over for a glass of wine. Her eyes were swollen and red when I arrived.

"I think it's beautiful," she said, hugging me.

"Really? I know I was brutally honest in some parts."

"Jodee, I wouldn't want it any other way. The honesty in these pages will save lives. I'm sure of it. Imagine how much it could have helped us if there had been a book like this when you were in school?"

"You're sure you're OK with me dredging all this stuff up again? I don't want to embarrass you, but I do want to talk about some of the mistakes I think you and Daddy made, as well as all the amazing things you did right."

"I want you to. I think it's important for parents to hear. I'll even join you on some of your talks, if you like, and share my point of view as your mother."

Yes, I tell myself. I have one remarkable mom. "I'd really like that, and I'm sure audiences would, too," I said. "Thank you."

While Mom went to the fridge to make us a snack, I mustered up the courage to ask her the one question I'd been avoiding. "Hey, Mom, was there anything about the book you didn't like? Tell the truth."

She placed the tray of cheese and crackers she was carrying onto the coffee table, then sat down next to me. For a moment, I thought she wasn't going to answer. Then, she quietly took my hand, and began to speak.

"There were sections that were very painful for me to read, because there was a lot I wasn't aware of, like how desperately alone you truly felt. Oh, honey, I'm so sorry, I —"

"Mom, it's OK," I said. "No one can live inside another

person's psyche, not even their child's."

"But I should have been more aware."

"You did everything possible. You couldn't force my classmates to like me."

"No, but I could have been more aggressive with those clueless teachers and principals who said you were being overly dramatic, that what you were going through was just a normal part of growing up. What was wrong with me? Why didn't I—"

"Mom, stop torturing yourself! There are lots of things we'd both change if we could go back, but we can't. I know you and Daddy loved me. That's what matters most."

"I'm so happy you feel that way," she said.

After we finished eating, we curled up on the couch, turned on the TV, and watched reruns of *Bewitched*, my favorite show from childhood. As I snuggled in close next to Mom, both of us giggling at Samantha and Darrin's conundrums, I couldn't help but wonder, my school years were hell and I had loving, supportive parents. What about the bullied students who don't have a caring family? What happens to them? Where do they go for help? I would soon meet some kids who would show me how disturbing the answers to those questions could be.

The doorbell rings and it pulls me out of my haze. *The book signing* . . . I hear Mom greeting Shelly and Noreen. I slip her good luck card back into its envelope and put it in the shoe box on the closet shelf where I keep my precious mementos. Then, taking one last look in the mirror, I tell myself that everything will be OK tonight, and I go downstairs. My mom is sitting in the kitchen, laughing and chatting with my friends. Her joy is palpable. I pause by the door and quietly watch the three of them, trying to ignore the lump in my throat. If only I could have given Mom one moment like this when I was growing up.

"There you are," Shelly says. "I just got off the phone with Clarke. He says he's at the store now and you won't believe how many people have shown up for the signing. He says it's standing room only!"

"You guys go ahead," Noreen says. "I'll stay here until the caterer comes and then I'll meet you there."

I realize, when Shelly, Mom, and I arrive at Borders, that Clarke wasn't exaggerating. The store is packed. "There must be something else going on here tonight," I suggest. "These people can't all be here for *me*."

"I think you're wrong about that, Jodee," Shelly says. "Take a look over there."

There's a podium with a microphone in the center of the store. Behind the podium is a huge blow up of my book cover with a bright red banner hung across it that reads "*New York Times* bestseller." To the right is a long table with one chair. Atop the table are a box of black markers and a vase of beautiful fresh-cut flowers. To the left is another table with a display featuring hundreds of copies of my book arranged in a perfect pyramid. In front of the autographing area, there are row after row of occupied seats fanning out toward the back of the store. There are people sitting on the floor. Those who couldn't find a place to sit are standing.

"Oh, my God. Can you believe it, Mom?"

"It's almost too much to comprehend," she replies. "My daughter, the *author*. Your dad would be so proud. I know he's here, grinning from ear to ear!"

As I make my way to the podium, the manager of the store comes up to greet me. A young man with an infectious personality, he tells me that this is the largest turnout they've ever had for a book signing. "You must be very popular," he comments, unaware of the irony. Just then, I notice Nadia's husband, Mark, walking in the door with a small group of my former classmates. None of them are smiling. *Oh, dear God, please let me get through this. Give me a sign that it's going to be all right.*

Suddenly, as if on cue, I hear someone calling my name. I turn and see Mitch standing there with his two daughters. "Perfect timing," I say, giving him a hug.

"Yeah, I saw who just walked in. Are you OK?" he asks.

"Now I am," I reply. Mitch squeezes my hand and briefly introduces me to the kids. Amber, who's ten, is precocious and astute, and I know right away that I will have to work hard to earn this child's respect. Val, two years younger, is quieter and more the wise observer. When you look into her eyes, you know that you're staring at the face of an old soul.

"You better get up there," Mitch says. "Everybody's waiting."

I take a deep breath, step up to the podium beside the store manager, and gaze out into the audience while he gives his official welcome. I feel as if there's an electrical current charging through my body, making me vibrate with energy. Everyone is here, including many people I never expected: Mitch's parents, classmates I haven't seen since grammar school, friends and neighbors I'd lost touch with years ago, family members who came in from out of town to surprise me, colleagues and co-workers, and dozens of others. The room is also full of parents with their kids, teachers from schools as far away as Michigan and Indiana, clergymen and police officers. I can hardly believe they have all come to hear me speak.

Then I notice Mark and his entourage standing in the back near Clarke. They appear edgy and uncomfortable, whispering to one another. It occurs to me that Nadia is nowhere in sight. Could it be she's planning a grand entrance? I shudder and try to cast the thought out of my mind, when one of them shoots me a withering glance. I am immobilized. Images from the past begin flickering across an invisible screen. I see hands shoving me into lockers, faces mouthing threats in the hallway, food flying at me in the cafeteria.

I've got to get out of here.

"And now, ladies and gentlemen, Jodee Blanco."

Gathering every ounce of resolve, I begin. I am surprised by the strength in my voice. It's as if I'm listening to someone else speaking:

"Hello, everybody. I am honored that you've come this evening. I'm going to talk to you about what happened to me from fifth grade through the end of high school, simply because I was different. I was the kid whom everybody made fun of, the one who always got picked last for gym, who sat alone at lunch every day, who never got invited to hang out with anyone, and who cried herself to sleep every night. The harder I tried to fit in, the more I got rejected, and the worse I hated myself. And the sad part was that the kids who were doing this to me honestly didn't understand how badly they were hurting me. In their minds, it was just joking around. Tonight, you're going to learn that it's *not* just joking around, that bullying damages people for *life*, and I know, because I stand before you as damaged goods." I catch several of my former classmates looking at each other uneasily.

"By the time I was a freshman in high school," I continue, "I was suicidal. By sophomore year, I was so angry at my classmates, I tried to sneak a knife into school, and if it wasn't for my mom finding it before I left the house, I don't know what might have happened." The room is still. Some people appear shocked by what I've said, others sympathetic. I see a few parents watching their children intently, trying to interpret their expressions.

As I recount stories from my troubled youth, the fear I'd been experiencing earlier begins to melt away and is replaced by a surprising resiliency. The more I reveal, the more I feel the audience opening its heart to me, giving me the courage I need to continue. I share how for years I would sneak into the girls' bathroom every day at lunchtime and wolf down candy bars because no one would let me sit with them in the cafeteria. I describe how I'd often steal into my mom's room after school and apply her concealer to my shins and arms in an effort to hide where I'd been kicked, or worse. The memories are pouring out of me now, loosed by a need for catharsis. I realize the effect I'm having as I see one woman quietly begin to weep. And it isn't only other Adult Survivors of Peer Abuse like me who are reacting emotionally. Some of my former classmates who brought their children with them because they're being bullied are visibly shaken and near tears. The irony of that is hard to grasp. Others are squirming in their seats, looking for an escape.

My mom is sitting there, smiling. I can't imagine what

she must be feeling right now. When I finish my talk, I ask if anyone has a question. A little boy with large brown eyes raises his hand.

"What's your name?" I ask.

"Kyle, and I'm in fifth grade," he replies.

"OK, Kyle, what would you like to know?"

"Everyone picks on me at school. They even hit me sometimes. I was wondering if maybe you could help me figure out why I'm no good."

There is a sense of hopelessness in his demeanor that makes my heart ache. I walk up to Kyle and wrap my arms around him. Then I cup his face in my hands and tell him, "There is nothing wrong with *you*. It's everything that's *right* about you that makes them single you out. Don't change for anyone, Kyle. It is those who are mean to you who need to change."

He politely thanks me, then reaches over and hugs his mom who is sitting next to him. "I'll be OK, don't cry," he tells her. Many in the audience are wiping their eyes. Another small hand gingerly goes up, and then another, each child with a story almost identical to Kyle's. The loneliness and sadness in their tiny voices has everyone visibly shaken.

There's a palpable stillness. Then a mom sitting in the back stands up, barely able to speak she's so emotional, and confesses her fear and frustration because her daughter is being taunted and ostracized at school. Next, a teacher speaks up about the bullying problem at her school, asking what to do, because the principal cares more about his golf game than he does about his students. Pandora's box has been opened. The room becomes a sea of hands beckoning for recognition. The store manager finally intercedes and requests that everyone get in line so that I can autograph their books. I'm so caught up in the excitement that I begin giving out my personal e-mail address and cell phone number to anyone who asks for it. I could never fathom that this book signing in my hometown would mark the beginning of a national grassroots movement, or that Kyle, the extraordinary boy who was brave enough to raise his hand first, would save many lives in the not too distant future, nearly sacrificing his own to do so. After I sign the last book, I see Mitch walking toward me. In that moment, I know that nothing will ever be the same in my life again.

"Come on, Jodee, it's time to celebrate," Mitch says.

When we get to my mom's, the house is already bustling with guests. As I make my way to the bar for a drink, I see Mark with several other of my former classmates assembled in the kitchen, chatting. I am not sure what to think. The one who'd cast me the dirty look earlier in the evening is warm and ebullient, all traces of her previously dour demeanor erased. Mark spots me standing there and smiles. "Congratulations," he says. "We're really proud of you."

Could I have heard him correctly?

"Thanks," I reply, stunned. "But I thought some of you guys weren't too thrilled about the book. I was told Nadia was furious."

"My wife can be overly dramatic. I wouldn't worry about it. She'll come around. We all did."

"A toast," Clarke says, holding up his beer. "To Jodee, the coolest person in our class." As we clink glasses, I feel Mitch come up behind me and put his arms around me. Though I don't know this now, my friendship with these people will grow richer in the coming months, in ways none of us could have predicted. And Shelly, Mitch, and Clarke will become three unlikely musketeers providing moral support in my crusade to save kids.

While I'm soaking up every single second of this remarkable evening, Lissy, my old business partner, and a PR whiz who has begun handling the publicity for the book, comes racing into the kitchen, flushed with excitement. An effervescent woman with an infectious laugh and a great sense of humor, she tells me she's about to burst over the news.

"What news?" I ask.

"Remember how we were so bummed out because the media was canceling on us?" she says.

"Yes, why?"

"It looks like the tide is finally turning. I just got a message from *Teen Newsweek*. They want to do a cover story on you. And NBC called, too."

Hours later, after everyone has gone home, I go up to Mom and thank her for hosting such a wonderful party for me. "Angel, seeing you happy is the best thanks of all," she says.

The next day my publisher calls. "I heard that was some signing last night," he said. "It must have been, because the *New York Times* just contacted me. Your book climbed three notches on their list."

Who would have thought it could happen because of one

book signing in a town nobody ever heard of—the same town I tried to run away from years ago, which had now welcomed me back with open arms, eager to make up for the sins of the past? Mom always used to tell me, "The worm will turn." How right she was.

chapter six

Out of
Control

March 2003

Did you ever do something without thinking because you were caught up in the moment? That's what happened to me at the book signing. Thrilled to have gotten such a response, I started giving my cell phone number and e-mail address to scores of lonely kids, worried parents, frustrated teachers, struggling adult survivors, and even curious shoppers who happened to overhear my talk. It never occurred to me that handing out my personal contact information to hundreds of potentially desperate strangers might cause a problem.

Word spread over the Internet, and within days I started receiving hundreds of e-mails and phone calls from across the country. I've been so busy trying to answer them all that I've practically had to put my life on hold. It's midafternoon, and I'm on my laptop at Mom's frantically poring over the latest pleas for help, when I hear my cell phone ringing. It's a distraught mother in Oregon, Susan, who says her sixteen-year-old daughter, Crystal, is being brutalized by a group of classmates for always defending the underdog.

"They throw garbage at her, call her names, even threaten her physically," Susan says. "It's gotten to the point that Crystal is refusing to go to school, and I don't know what to do."

"Have you talked to the principal about any of this?" I ask.

"Yes, my husband and I met with him. His solution is that Crystal needs to back off. He told her that even though her compassion is admirable, no one can save the world. Can you believe that! Why is it that the sensitive, caring students always seem to be the ones who end up being told not to practice what they believe in?"

It is a pattern I'll see often, and one that I discover can have a direct link to student violence.

"I couldn't stand seeing anybody getting picked on, either, when I was in school," I reply. "I'd march right up to whoever was doing it and stop them just like Crystal. Everyone turned on me, too, even the kids I stuck up for all the time."

"Did your parents know?"

"I was afraid to tell them. I'd already transferred schools twice, and I didn't want them to see me as the misfit again."

"What finally happened?"

"After a while I couldn't take it anymore, and went to the principal near tears, asking for help."

"What did he do?"

"Pretty much the same thing Crystal's principal did. He patted me on the shoulder and advised me not to be so sensitive."

"God, what's wrong with these schools?" Susan cries.

This is a question I will hear often and risk everything to answer.

"Jodee, I know it's a lot to ask, but would you talk to my daughter? She's reading your book right now, and I think it would be a lifeline for her. She feels so isolated."

I hang up with Susan, promising to call Crystal first thing in the morning. I won't discover until it's too late that because of the wounds Crystal has already sustained, she will soon exhibit a dangerous psychosis, one with consequences that will push me to my breaking point.

As I return my attention to reviewing e-mails, I notice the message indicator on my cell phone beeping. It's a voice mail from a lonesome, bullied sixth grader in Minnesota named Selena, wondering if I would give a talk at her school. "Please help me," she says. "I don't want them to hurt me anymore." I can tell by the tremor in her voice that she is doing her best not to cry. "I sent you an e-mail, too," she adds hopefully. I scroll down the list until I locate hers.

> Dear jodee, my name is Selena. I read your book. Please can I meet you? I'm an outcast like you were and cry a lot too. I wish I could live in heaven with Grandpa instead of staying here. Here is a picture of me. PLEASE come soon!!!! I need you. Love and kisses, Selena, P.S. I left a message on your phone too!

Every day I receive more requests from troubled youngsters like Selena, imploring me to fly to their rescue. One was from a boy living in a foster home. Then there are the kids desperate for companionship, constantly sending e-mails, instant messaging me when I'm on line, and telephoning at all hours. How do I make them understand that I can't fill that void? All of these children already loathe themselves so much that, unlike their peers who *make* mistakes, they believe they *are* mistakes. What if I fail one of them? Will a child being chronically rejected at school and misunderstood at home end up feeling abandoned by me, too?

I download Selena's photo. She is standing in her backyard with her dog. Her hair is short and curly, falling about her face in tiny, matted ringlets. Her eyes are an arresting shade of green and contain more sadness than her years on this earth should permit. She is also morbidly obese. I reach out and touch my computer screen, wishing, perhaps in vain, that somehow she could feel my hand on her forehead, willing her to have faith that life can change, that she won't be lonely forever, that one day this duckling will become a swan.

I need to go to this girl. I e-mail her back that I'd love to visit, and ask for her mom's phone number. Perhaps it's emotional exhaustion from weeks of resisting the impulse to go to all of these children that's driving my decision. Maybe I don't believe I'm doing enough for any of them, and that if I can hug Selena and make her feel special it will make me feel better about myself. I continue going through my in-box, skipping ahead to the essentials of the most desperate messages.

Hi, this is Courtney and I live near Detroit. I'm in eighth grade. I heard about your book online and am saving up to buy it. Why I'm writing to you is everyone at school hates me. They call me ugly pig and mock me all the time. My mom says they're right, that I'm not pretty, and I should just accept it and focus on my other qualities. Please, would you be my friend and hang out with me? Or could we at least be pen pals?

I'd like to slug that mother. Why would she say that to

her own child? As I begin typing my reply, I envision myself wrapping my arms around this little girl and hugging her tightly, whispering in her ear how beautiful she is, and that her mom is wrong. Then I move on to the next e-mail, and the next, praying, as I respond to each one, that I'm helping these kids in some small way.

> Dear Jodee, my name is Linda. I'm thirteen years old and I am a cutter. I get called a slut and a whore every time I walk into my school for no reason at all. I cut my arms with safety pins and I also cut my breast by the bone. I am alone and I cry very often and I cry every day. I can't take it anymore.

Another child in another state, this time a boy named Ely . . .

> I am being bullied at school and they won't do anything about it. Will you help me?

An adult survivor scared of attending her reunion . . .

> Dear Jodee, I was a tomboy and a reject. School was hell. I got made fun of, called horrible names, and spent every weekend by myself, waiting for the phone to ring. While I loved my parents dearly, my mother's response was always "Well, maybe if you didn't make yourself stand out as much they'd accept you." Counselors at school would say the same thing. As an adult, I struggle to make friends. I'm paranoid they are just putting up with me. My high

school reunion is coming up, and I'm terrified. Could I talk to you about it?

I can't be there for all these people. I'm only one person.

I was tormented all through school just like you. They used to call me "the maggot." My daughter is going to the same high school I did, and now it's happening to her. I've gone to the principal, even the superintendent, and they say I'm overreacting. Is there a time we could talk by phone, or if you're coming to Seattle, perhaps we could meet. I don't know where else to turn.

I feel like I'm alone on a boat in a storm. Water is gushing in and I'm bailing as fast as I can, but all I've got is a single bucket.

It's my son. He just did time in prison for drugs, and I'm worried he'll never get over what happened to him in high school. He was an outcast like you. Will you be in Detroit anytime soon? I think if he could meet you it would help him so much.

I think I'm bulimic. I'm afraid to tell my parents, and I don't have any friends at school. I feel so alone.

Hi. My name is Donna and I'm in seventh grade. The kids at school make fun of me because I look like a boy. They call me "dyke" and spit at me. I'm scared my parents will find out and tell the principal. I really want to talk to you in person. Would that be possible?

On and on, child after child, parents, teachers, adult survivors, all crying out with the same pain, like streams flowing into a single, raging river . . .

> Hello Jodee, my name is Jill. I'm fifteen. Every morning before school, I think if I could just fall down the stairs or slip in the shower I'd have to go to the hospital, but I wouldn't have to go to school. On the bus, people throw anything at me they can find. At lunch, they put hair in my food, and laugh when it makes me cough. I get hit and kicked too. I can't tell anyone or things will get worse. Thanks for letting me tell you.

I urge Jill and every child confiding in me to turn to their parents or another trusted adult. I beseech them to hang on, emphasizing that they're not alone, someone *does* understand. I wish I could offer more. The public sees only the surface of what's going on in our schools. The media does the occasional story when there's a dramatic or tragic angle that justifies the airtime. The government gets involved only when the threat of bad press leaves it no choice. But as I'm going through these e-mails, I'm starting to realize that not even I fully understood the extent of the problem. I believed what happened to me was extreme. I'm finding out now that it wasn't. Based on what I've heard these past few weeks, my experience was *typical.* How is that possible? And why are so many kids telling me they're afraid to go to their parents? What's wrong with everyone?

My name is Erin and I want you to know that I think you're a hero.

I have thought about killing myself. I'm going to a counselor now, but I still feel like no one knows what I'm going through. Bullying at my school is bad. Earlier this year a boy brought a gun to school because of being bullied, and a year before that a girl brought a knife cause of the same reason. So, now I'm scared one of my classmates or I would be the next one to bring a weapon to school. I was hoping, if you have time, could you come here to Virginia? I feel like my life is very close to how yours was. Please e-mail me back as soon as possible.

I'm not ready for this.

I'm a seventh-grade teacher. The bullying in my school is bad. I feel powerless. My students feel powerless. Is there any way that we could talk?

I notice that many of the teachers and parents e-mailing me were victims of severe bullying themselves. I can't help but wonder, does that make them better equipped to deal with the situation, or the potential facilitators of a disaster waiting to happen? I will learn that the answer is both.

I'm an educator in a large school district. Bullying in my classroom seems to be getting worse each year. These kids see nothing wrong in being downright cruel to some-one, and their parents are even worse. I have one student

I'm very worried about. Will you be coming to Wisconsin? I would be so grateful if you could give a talk at our school.

I start printing out all the e-mails that seem most urgent, the ones that hint at suicide or violence. Some are ten and fifteen pages long. As I'm dividing the letters into piles, the phone rings again. It's my publisher.

"Gary, I'm so glad it's you," I say. "I'm getting swamped with calls and e-mails. Would your office be able to help me field some of them, at least for a little while until I have things under control?"

"Jodee, our office is getting deluged, too. That's why I was calling *you*, to find out what contact info you wanted me to give these people so we can send them directly to you."

"Gary, I can't keep up as it is. Can't you guys help me out? Some of them are schools asking if I'd come and speak. Could you call a few and book me? It would be great promotion."

"I think you should hire an assistant."

Though I reassure Gary that I'll try to find someone, it's not that simple. My consulting clients are still my primary source of income. Most of them have decided not to renew their contracts, and I won't see a royalty check for the book for months yet. I can't possibly afford an assistant right now. But I also can't afford not to help these kids. I couldn't live with myself if anything happened and I didn't intervene when I had the chance.

I'm dizzy trying to cope with all of this. If karma exists — and I believe it does — I experienced mine the night of my high school reunion, and the course of my life has been rewriting itself ever since. I'm not the same person I was five months ago, or even five days ago. Part of me feels blessed to be on this journey. Another part is struggling with the transition.

I'm also coping with another challenge. I keep trying to tell myself that it's just the pressure I'm under, but I think it may be more than that. Mitch and I have been seeing a lot of each other, now that he and Kathy broke up. *Hooray!* Last weekend, we were on a date when suddenly I couldn't distinguish emotionally between the past and the present, and I saw Mitch as the popular guy from high school and not as my boyfriend today. Even though intellectually I was fine and enjoying our conversation, psychologically, I felt unnerved, like I had gone back in time. And it's not just when I'm with Mitch. Sometimes it happens out of the blue when I'm socializing with former classmates. When it does, I'm gripped by that familiar fear of walking down the halls at school that used to make my throat close. I experienced something similar at the reunion, but I thought by this time I would have gotten past it. Though I'm not aware of it now, these odd episodes will enable me to motivate a skeptical mental-health community to reexamine their position on school bullying and its effects.

I look out the window and realize it's grown dark. My neck and shoulders ache. Just a few more e-mails and I'll quit for the evening, I tell myself. Then the phone rings again. It's Kyle's mother, the little boy who brought nearly everyone to tears at the book signing. She says that Kyle is becoming suicidal and that he he'll only talk to me. "Please," she says, "can you get here right away?" We decide to meet at a nearby restaurant. Exhausted, I drag myself into the shower and then throw on some fresh clothes. As I'm walking out the door, Mom stops me, saying she overheard me talking to Kyle's mom and asks if I'd like her to come along. Relieved that I won't have to face this alone, we leave together. When we get to the restaurant, I see Kyle, his mom, Debbie, and stepfather, Daniel, sitting at a table in the corner. All three of them look as if they have been through a war.

"What's going on?" I ask, hugging Kyle as Mom and I sit down.

"I don't know what to do anymore," Debbie says. "He's coming home every afternoon in tears. He's afraid to go to the bathroom at school because a bunch of boys have been threatening to beat him up."

"Kyle," I say, turning to face him. "Is all this true?"

"Yes," he replies. "At recess today some kids started calling me bad names. When I told them to stop, they knocked me down and kicked at me."

"Hey, Blanco, want to play Red Rover with us?" ask several of my classmates.

I shake my head.

"Aw, come on. Don't be a chicken! It'll be fun!"

"OK."

"Ready?" they say, linking hands together and forming a chain.

"I guess."

"Red Rover, Red Rover, let Jodee come over."

I take a deep breath. All I have to do, I reassure myself, is run into them hard enough to break their wrists apart. I take off, willing my legs to move as fast as they can. The space between us recedes quickly. With less than a foot to go, I lunge forward, hurling my body at them. Suddenly, I feel a sharp pain as a knee smashes into my groin, doubling me over.

"Jodee, is something wrong?" Kyle says. "You look so sad."

This child is an old soul. He's compassionate and perceptive way beyond his years. Some adults never reach his level of awareness. I will meet others like him on this remarkable journey. Each, in his own way, will open my eyes to the one trait we all have in common and lead me to a startling conclusion that will challenge the conventional wisdom about why certain kids always get bullied.

"No, honey, I'm fine," I say. "I was just remembering something and got distracted for a moment. Sorry about that. Let's focus on you right now, OK?"

"It's because I'm mature for my age, isn't it?" Kyle says.

"Yes, I think that could be a large part of it," I answer, astounded.

"What if I change, and learn to like kid things, except mud — I'll never like *that*."

His parents look at each other and smile, shaking their heads.

"Kyle, remember what Jodee told you at the book signing about not changing who you are?" Mom says. "You shouldn't have to force yourself to like something just so others will accept you. That doesn't sound as if it would be too much fun."

"I don't know what else to do," he replies.

"I think we need to get you involved in activities outside

of school, so you can make friends with kids you have something in common with," I suggest. Kyle immediately brightens upon hearing this.

"Can I ask you one more thing?" he says.

"Sure."

"It might be a long time before those bullies at school grow up. Until they do, how can I keep them off my back?"

I tell him I have some suggestions, and we set a time to meet the following week. Mom also arranges to have lunch with Debbie, encouraging her to reach out whenever she needs a sympathetic ear. As we're getting into the car, I thank Mom for being so helpful.

"I'm glad you came," I tell her.

"Angel, it was therapeutic for me. I used to feel so helpless when you were going through it. Tonight was like a gift. And this is only the beginning."

"Mom, do you really think I can make a difference?"

"I think you already have."

I realize there are clinical experts who might scoff at me for trying to give comfort and guidance to bullied students, because I'm not a licensed psychologist. But if you were stuck in a deep, dark hole and two people offered to help — a geophysicist who had studied the dynamics and properties of holes but had never actually been in one himself, or someone who had been trapped in that very same hole that you're in, discovered the way out, and survived — whose help would you want?

I'm not saying that the caring, committed men and women with careers dedicated to learning how and why children behave as they do aren't vital to the prevention of peer abuse. On the contrary, their contributions save lives every day. Those who make it harder on all of us are the battle-weary professionals in a system where compassion has been eclipsed by cynicism. Disillusioned with their jobs, they use the same tired old psychobabble on students, who then respond by shutting themselves off even more from adults.

These are the kids who are turning to me, and they deserve more than clichés and empty promises. Looking back on my own life, I know exactly where things went wrong: the innocent but costly mistakes my parents, teachers, and other adults made and how to avoid them; what I could have done differently to improve my situation; why the schools I attended were a breeding ground for peer abuse; what all those therapists who were treating me never understood, and what many doctors still don't understand about their adolescent patients. I have insights, answers, real solutions that only a survivor can know. But will people listen?

chapter seven

The Little General

April 2003

Winter turned to spring without a prelude. It was as if we looked out our window one morning expecting to see the ground still under a blanket of white, discovered flowers blooming, and were forced to tend to our gardens before we could put away our snow blowers. They say that a person's life is composed of passing seasons. I feel like whichever one I'm in now is ahead of itself and I'm scrambling to adjust. In a few hours, I've got the first of several high school speaking engagements that my publisher has arranged this month. All of them are in response to requests that Gary's office has been scheduling until I can hire an assistant, which, according to him, had better be soon.

My mom has always told me that God only gives you what he knows you can handle. As I'm rushing through baggage claim at the Philadelphia airport, cell phone ringing in one hand, a half-nibbled Slim-Fast bar in the other, frantically searching the crowded terminal for my friend Eileen, I sure hope Mom was right.

Thank God for Eileen, who's worked with me on several consulting projects in the past and lives nearby and has kindly volunteered to be my all-around girl Friday while I'm in town. I'm scheduled to give two 90-minute talks this afternoon, each for an audience of a thousand students. Teenagers are unpredictable. What if I can't hold their attention that long? The superintendent of Marron High School, where I'll be speaking, said that bullying has become such a problem in their district that I shouldn't be surprised if I encounter some hostility. Apparently, they've brought in other experts on the subject, none of whom were effective, and now there's a general attitude among the student body that adults "just don't understand." Later, I'll discover that it's not only the kids at Marron who feel this way. I'll spend years proving to students all across America that there *is* an adult who understands. What I don't realize now is that being this adult will come with a price no one should have to pay.

I glance at my cell phone screen. Fifteen missed calls, nine voice mails, and the thing is still ringing. I won't even think about e-mail. Deep breaths, I tell myself. Then I hear my name being called. I turn and see Eileen waving at me from the coffee kiosk. I smile and make my way toward her.

I've never known anyone quite like this woman. Cherubic and petite, with shiny silver hair and curious blue-gray eyes, she has the heart of a fairy godmother and the will of a Marine general. I often think the wire-rimmed glasses she wears must be endowed with some magical power that allows her to see right through people. She can spot a phony in seconds. I've seen her in action, and she may look harmless but her appearance is deceiving. Beneath her unassuming demeanor is a friend, wife, and mother of two who's a force to behold if someone she cares about is being threatened.

For years, she juggled a business career and her responsibilities as a homemaker. From PTA outings, school bake sales, dance practice, drama club rehearsals, track meets, and church volunteer work to sales reports, business trips, staff meetings, conferences, and conventions, she never stopped to think about her own professional goals. Actually, she never stopped, period. When we met last year, she and her husband were just becoming empty nesters. Bored with corporate America and ready for a new challenge, she's told me that she's looking for herself and her purpose. Today will lead her in a direction neither of us could have predicted, one that will not only change both of our lives but the lives of thousands of others.

"Hey, kid, how's my favorite author," Eileen says, hugging me. I have to chuckle whenever she calls me "kid." I'm seven inches taller than she is, and with the heels I've got on right now, probably a foot.

"I bet that's all you've eaten today, isn't it?" she observes, shaking her head.

"Well, yes, but—"

"No buts, Blanco! You can't speak to a bunch of teenagers on an empty stomach. I've packed you a lunch. You'll eat on the way."

As we walk toward the car, I can't help but think that Mom was right again. God does provide. I would feel alone today if Eileen weren't here. She makes me feel safe and at ease, though it is odd having someone else take over. When I was a publicist, I was always the one responsible for taking care of the talent. My clients did what I told them to because they knew it was in their best interest. Now I *am* the talent?

And Eileen is a loving, supportive friend with whom I can be myself. Imagine if I was being accompanied by an actual publicist. That would definitely take some getting used to.

"Damn," I exclaim, as I begin furiously riffling through the contents of my purse.

"What's wrong?" Eileen asks.

"The directions to Marron High School—I must have left them on my desk. I have no idea how to get there."

"Already taken care of," she says. "I printed them out last night, along with some information about the district. I thought it might be helpful. You can review it on the ride there."

"You don't miss a beat, do you?"

"Someone has to be in charge," she says, handing me half a sandwich and a bag of trail mix. "You concentrate on helping these kids. I'll worry about the rest." She doesn't know how prophetic this moment will turn out to be.

The drive is pleasant. Eileen and I exchange girl talk. She brings me up to date on her daughter Jillian's newest romance and her progress choosing a college. Eileen beams whenever she talks about Jillian. I can't help but wonder if I'll ever get to experience that feeling. I never thought much about motherhood until I started spending time with Mitch's daughters and realized that there was an empty part of me I ached to fill.

"You have to meet Jillian's boyfriend," Eileen says. "He's captain of the swim team and so adorable. Speaking of boyfriends, what's going on with that guy Mitch you've been dating?"

I share with Eileen how much has happened these past months. "This is the first time I've ever been in a relationship that I could envision going the distance."

"I'm so happy for you," she says. "Is it ever weird for you, though?"

"What do you mean?"

"The whole scenario, I guess, dating one of the most popular guys from high school, hanging out with people who used to treat you so badly. How are you able to put the past aside so easily?"

Her question is unnerving. Though I keep telling myself that the flashbacks and recurring dreams are nothing more than the result of my life changing too quickly, and that once I adjust they'll stop, I know there's more to it than that. I will soon find out just how much more.

"We should be there in about forty minutes or so," Eileen informs me. "Have you thought about what you're going to say to these kids?"

"No, and I don't want to until I'm onstage. I don't like to prepare speeches. If I have to prepare, I don't know my stuff enough. I plan on speaking from the heart. Whatever happens after that, I'll take it as it comes."

"That sounds like a plan," she says, smiling and turning on the radio. The rest of the trip, we ride in comfortable silence accompanied by classic rock. Then the song "Subdivisions," by the old seventies group Rush, starts playing. The anthem of the alienated, it's about the pressure to conform and what can happen if you don't. "Be cool or be cast out," admonishes the haunting refrain. When I was writing the book, I listened to it often, along with recordings from Cheap Trick, AC/DC, Styx, and other bands of the era, using them as a staircase to the past. It became a form of self-hypnosis that allowed me to travel back in time, and just when I thought I would scream from the flood of memories being resurrected by the music, I would start typing.

Sitting here now in the car with Eileen, hearing that song by Rush, it's having a similar effect. I can feel myself being carried to that dark, scary place of my adolescence. This is good, I tell myself. It's putting me in the right frame of mind for my talk. I'm going to have to relive my past in front of these kids anyway — do onstage what I did when I was writing the book. Part of me is grateful to the radio station for jump starting my psyche. Another part is squirming. It's not being onstage that has me rattled. I've been in dozens of plays, and I've given many professional speeches. I'm not uncomfortable talking about my past to an audience. I got over any jitters about that when I did the presentation at Borders in Pason Park. No, whatever is making me nervous and uneasy now is something else that I can't identify.

Eileen lets me know that we're less than a mile from the school. Not wanting her to see my growing anxiety, I shift my attention outside the window, gazing at the tree-lined streets of this quaint Pennsylvania town. Most of the homes are substantial, built at the turn of the century. Main Street is flanked by specialty shops and exclusive boutiques. Within moments, we're pulling into the parking lot at Marron. An imposing gray structure of concrete and stainless steel, it looks more like a modern office complex than a school. If it weren't for the football field, we might have driven right past it.

There are students gathered by the front of the building, waiting for the first-period bell to ring. I watch them interact. Adolescence is timeless. A group of cheerleaders are huddled together by the main entrance. Several feet away, a painfully thin girl with long, unfashionable hair is standing alone quietly watching them. *They're probably gossiping about that poor girl behind her back. I bet that later today they'll pass around a nasty note about her in class and then wait for her to burst into tears so they can laugh. She'll try to pretend it doesn't bother her, that she's above their abuse. She may even ignore them and walk away, because that's what her parents told her she should do, and being the good girl that she is, she would never question the wisdom of adults. She will go home tonight and when everyone in the house is in bed, she will sob into her pillow, praying for God to take her in her sleep so that she won't have to endure those cheerleaders again tomorrow and wish she didn't secretly ache for them to like her.*

"Eileen, I can't do this," I say.

"Come on, Jodee, I've seen you speak before. You're going to knock 'em dead!"

"No, Eileen. I'm serious. I can't go in there."

"Oh, my God, you're trembling," she observes.

I must pull it together. Marron is expecting me to inspire students with the story of my survival, and I'm letting myself be kidnapped by the past. What if I'm terrorized by ghosts every time I walk into a school?

"I'm sorry, Eileen. I'll be OK in a minute. It's just that I haven't been anywhere near a high school since I graduated, and being in one again is conjuring up a lot of bad memories."

"Tell me how to help so we can get you through this."

I don't answer. I have no answer. I feel ashamed that this is happening, but powerless to stop it. For a moment, Eileen is silent. Then she grabs hold of both my hands. "Look at me," she says. "Those kids out there are not your classmates. They can't hurt you."

"I'm afraid."

"I know you're afraid, but you can do this, Jodee."

"How can you be so sure?"

"Because you're not the type to give in to fear. I've seen you go up against consulting clients that were tougher than this and you didn't run then, and I'm not going to let you run now."

We get out of the car and walk across the parking lot to the main entrance. Despite my determination, when we reach those large glass doors I hesitate, terrified. Eileen puts her hand on my shoulder, then stands on her tiptoes so that she can reach my ear, and whispers, "You can do this. There are people depending on you." The confidence in her voice is clear and strong.

"You're like a little general sending a soldier into battle," I whisper back, smiling.

"Yes," she replies. "And this is a war we can win."

The foyer of the school is bright and sunny, with big red couches near the windows. The walls are decorated with a montage of student artwork and the occasional poster warning about the dangers of everything from alcohol and drug abuse to teen pregnancy. I wonder if anyone ever reads them. I know I never did. I think schools put them up to make parents feel better. Immediately to our left is the administration office. We're greeted warmly at the reception desk by the school secretary, who hands both Eileen and me a security pass for the day. A moment later, Diane, the principal, an attractive woman impeccably dressed in a black blazer and cashmere slacks, comes over and introduces herself. I'm immediately impressed by her energy and enthusiasm.

"It's wonderful to meet you," I reply. "Thank you for inviting me."

"We're honored you could come. I loved your book, and I think our kids are going to benefit enormously from hearing your story.

"We have a couple of minutes before we need to go to the gym," Diane says. "Could I ask you a few questions about the presentation? I'd also like to give you a heads-up on some specific bullying problems we've been having lately."

As we're talking, I realize how dedicated this educator is to her students. She will be an exception to the norm. Though I could not predict it now, I will encounter many deadbeat principals who don't take bullying seriously and bring me in only because they're getting heat from the school board or the PTA to address the issue. They'll make a big fuss about getting me there, but when I take the stage many of them won't have read my book or know a thing about me other than what was written on the requisition form they signed. I understand that a lot of them are legitimately overworked, but if you were the one responsible for the welfare of a school full of children, would you give some author whose work you never read or whose background you never reviewed the opportunity to influence their lives? I'll even meet principals whom after a perfunctory hello upon my arrival, I never see again. How will they reinforce to the students a message that they weren't there to hear? Some don't attend my seminar for teachers and administrators.

I will soon discover that there are a frightening number of principals who are preoccupied with the wrong priorities and disconnected from their students. While they may be well-intentioned, like my grandmother always said, "The road to hell is paved with good intentions." Judging by some of the schools I'll visit on what will evolve into an all-out crusade against bullying, that road is becoming well traveled. In future, I'll learn how to identify administrators who see what they do only as a job and those who embrace it as a vocation. The latter, who live to help kids, will become my courage and inspiration and change how I see the world. The ones I meet who don't give a damn aren't going to know what hit them by the time Eileen and I are finished.

After a few moments of conversation, the principal suggests that we move to the gym. As the three of us weave our way through the throng of students rushing to first period, I feel suffocated by the familiar sound of voices laughing and shouting, lockers slamming, high heels clicking on linoleum, and, somewhere close by, the incessant popping of bubble gum. I shiver and cover my ears, struggling to stay in the present. But as my nostrils fill with the aroma of cheap institutional food wafting from the cafeteria and the sickly sweet smell of someone's strawberry lip gloss, a wave of nausea sweeps over me, and I can feel my mind succumb to the pull of its memories.

They're getting meaner. My parents say I need to ignore them and they'll leave me alone, but it never works. When I walked into science class this afternoon, a bunch of them started shoving their fingers down their throats, making gagging noises. Then one said they all wished my stupid mom had had an abortion so they wouldn't have to look at me every day. Why do they hate me so much? I never did anything to them. The worst part is that no matter how awful they treat me, I still wish they would like me. I heard them talking about a party this weekend at Tyler's house, and all I could think about was how much I wanted to be invited. God, I hate myself.

"Here we are," the principal says, snapping me back to the present. Eileen will later tell me that for several moments she was prepared to hold me if I turned to run.

As we're escorted into the still of the empty gym, all I keep thinking is that I made a promise to myself twenty years ago that I would never step foot inside one of these places again. It's as if I'm betraying the girl still living inside me, who wishes I would protect her. She feels naked, standing here in the center of the basketball court under the glare of fluorescent lighting flanked by dozens of rows of bleachers on either side. She wishes that, instead of doing a sound check right now, she could run to the nurse's office and call her mom to pick her up. Unfortunately, she is at the mercy of the rational adult who has come to this school for a purpose.

"Wow, it really filled up in here," says the audio technician, a sweet kid in his senior year at Marron.

I look out into the audience and see wall-to-wall teenagers, with more still filing in. Some are fidgeting; others are busily chatting. Most seem bored and eager to get this over with. A group of newspaper reporters and several television news crews have just walked into the gym and are setting up their equipment. Eileen is talking to one of the guys from NBC, handing him a press release.

"Are you ready?" Diane asks.

"Yes," I reply, clipping the microphone onto my sweater.

chapter eight

It's Not Just Joking Around!

April 2003

The principal introduces me and a hush descends upon the gym. I gaze out at the sea of faces in the audience. A group of kids in the back are laughing under their breath, brimming with attitude. Their smug superiority makes me seethe. I can only imagine how they treat their classmates. Several other students are looking at them and shaking their heads, as if no matter what I talk about today it won't make a difference. I have to resist the impulse to march into those bleachers and grab them all by the shoulders, make the bullies see the reality of the pain they inflict, and those kids watching them realize that I know exactly what they're going through! Suddenly, I can feel a voice inside me desperately wanting to let loose.

"How many of you are familiar with the tragedy that took place in Columbine, Colorado?" I ask. To my surprise only a few students raise their hands, and I realize that no one here has taught these kids anything about the Columbine shooting. It should be required learning in every social studies class in this country if we want to prevent similar disasters in the future. Marron will not be the only school I encounter with this bewildering void in its curriculum.

I briefly describe to everyone the events that precipitated

that fateful April day, starting with the chronic abuse that the shooters took from their classmates, how school administrators turned a blind eye, and how it eventually led to murder-suicide that could have been prevented. As I'm relating the details of the story, it occurs to me that probably no one in this gym has ever heard the Columbine story told from the perspective of a former outcast. . . .

I'm going to scream! Listen to all these insipid fools on TV being interviewed as experts who never experienced bullying in their lives. They're all missing the point! What happened today wasn't about neo-Nazi Web sites or the need for better gun-control laws. If somebody had tried hard enough to reach out to those alienated and troubled boys, they wouldn't have descended into a dark world for a sense of belonging. They didn't go on a rampage because they were able to access guns! What they needed that they couldn't access was a school that didn't have its head up its butt. Look at those teachers and students in tears talking on camera outside the school, trying to "make sense" of it all. Could they be any more in denial?

Dear God, what's wrong with me?

What kind of a monster am I?

I notice Eileen watching me, appearing concerned. "Are you all right?" she silently mouths. I give her a subtle nod, trying to ignore the volcano bubbling up inside me.

"Something inside those two boys finally snapped and they decided that they couldn't take it anymore," I continue.

"One day, they came to school armed with guns, shot and killed twelve fellow students, a teacher, and put another classmate in a wheelchair for life. Then they shot and killed themselves."

I hesitate, paralyzed by sudden uncertainty. Should I do it? I ask myself. Should I tell them what was really going through my mind that day? I swallow hard, knowing I have to be honest.

"Though I'm ashamed to admit it, when I first heard about the shooting at Columbine, my heart didn't go out to all those innocent victims. My heart went out to the killers."

Murmurs of shock ripple through the gym and several teachers cast me disapproving looks. Undeterred, I press on, sensing that there are students listening to me right now who are experiencing a similar desperation. My instincts will prove frighteningly correct.

"Not that I condone violence or murder," I emphasize. "I don't! But I *understood* why those two boys did what they did! I understood why they were so frustrated, so lonely, and so desperate that they saw no alternative. Why did I understand? Twenty years earlier, I tried to do the same thing. The only difference was that my weapon wasn't a gun, it was a butcher knife."

Feeling sick to my stomach being so exposed, but knowing I'm starting to get through to these kids, I lock eyes with one student at a time, as I survey the length of the gym, scanning their faces for a reaction. The empathy coming out of some of them both touches and frightens me. Others appear as if they've just seen a ghost, and I suspect it is guilt that motivates this reaction.

"I was so tired of being called 'ugly' and 'bitch,' of always being left out, of walking to class alone, eating lunch alone, of being laughed at and spit on day after day simply for being different, that I decided to cut out the hearts of everyone who was breaking mine. So one morning while my mom was still in the shower, I grabbed a knife from the kitchen drawer and dropped it into my book bag. When she came downstairs to see me off to school, she saw the blade sticking out. She wrestled the bag away from me, threw the knife into the sink, and then brought me to the hospital, where I spent the afternoon in a tiny room with padding on the walls talking to doctors. I was fifteen years old and a sophomore in high school." I pause for a moment to let them digest all this. "And I know that there are kids sitting in this gym right now who are being bullied and shunned just like I was. And *you know* there are, too."

Dead silence. Confident, I forge ahead.

"How often are you hanging out by the lockers with your friends when someone who you don't think is cool passes you in the hall? You and your friends look at each other and roll your eyes, perhaps even snicker. I know that you're not trying to be mean," I explain. "You're just *joking around,* right?" Heads begin to nod. "Wrong!" I shout. "To that person, it's *not* just joking around. When you ridicule, bully, exclude, or ignore someone on purpose, treat that person as if you wish they didn't exist, you're damaging them *for life,*" I exclaim. "I know because I still carry the scars."

I determine that I must take this audience back in time and allow them to experience my pain for themselves. Otherwise, I'll just be one more speaker who briefly got their attention, but whose words will be forgotten the second she's left the building. As I struggle with that little girl inside me who doesn't want to relive all those horrible memories, a rare joyous moment from my adolescence bursts forth. In eighth grade, my drama coach entered me in a statewide speech competition. He gave me five monologues to recite from *Spoon River Anthology*, in which I portrayed five different ghosts, each standing over her grave, looking back on her life. I took first place for my performance, and it was a high-light of middle school.

Just as I did on that stage so many years ago, I bow my head, close my eyes, and inhale deeply, knowing that when I lift my head and open my eyes I will be someone else. Only this time, instead of fictional characters, I am the people from my own past, teenage versions of us all. As I channel my past, I switch around the names and places to honor my promise to my former classmates that I'd protect their privacy.

I become Nadia, the beautiful auburn-haired head cheerleader, the instigator of acts of cruelty and the most popular girl at school; Jimmy, the handsome star of the wrestling team, voted "most likely to succeed"; Jerry, one of the most well-liked guys at school, the class smart aleck with a secret that would haunt all of us three decades later; Tommy, the former wimp turned body-builder and quarter-back of the football team, a boy determined to do to others what had been done to him; Roger, the sweet special-ed student with Down's syndrome and the butt of every joke; Mr. Blatt, the overzealous biology teacher, who cared more about his students liking him than learning from him; Tyler, whose addiction to drugs and meanness to the underdog were con-tagious to the cool crowd; and, of course, the one and only

Mitch, the high school heartthrob.

As I morph into each character, reliving painful scenes from my youth, I can feel the connection between me and the audience deepening. It's as if these stories are now taking on a life of their own. I reenact the morning I find Nadia, Jimmy, and Jerry, along with eight other kids, throwing dirt into Roger's face. Though Roger's eyes are bloody and red, and he keeps rubbing them to stop the burning, he's smiling, because he's thrilled to be receiving attention from the cool crowd and is too innocent to comprehend what's really going on. I describe how I try to stop his attackers, only to become their next target.

"Later that day," I continue, "I find rotten food and garbage stuffed inside my locker, with a nasty note calling me a 'retard lover.' Then, after school, while I'm waiting for my mom to pick me up, I hear footsteps coming down the hall. I could have been on the school bus on my way home already, but my parents and I had decided earlier in the year that it was best if I didn't take it anymore. I don't know what the buses are like here at Marron, but I can tell you how they were when I was in school. The really popular kids sat at the back of the bus. The medium-popular kids sat in the middle of the bus. And then there were the students like me. We didn't belong to any clique, and got stuck at the front of the bus. You can't imagine how cruel those kids at the back of the bus could be to us." Dozens of students nod their heads knowingly.

"As much as I hated the school bus, that one day I wished I could have taken it. As the footsteps draw nearer, I turn and see the kids who were tormenting Roger coming toward me. They open the large front door, push me outside, and slam me onto the pavement. There had been a snow-storm several days earlier, and the ground is caked in white. Jimmy, who had called himself my best friend all summer, pins me down with his leg here." I point to my left shoulder. "Jerry, puts his knee here," I explain, touching my right shoulder. "Then Tommy puts his hand here," I say, indicating my chest. "The rest of them scurry out into the parking lot, returning with fistfuls of snow, which they then begin to shove in my ears, and down my throat. And what do you think they're doing during this entire time?" I ask.

"Laughing," cry out the same students who were nod-ding their heads seconds earlier.

"And you want to know something?" I respond. "In their minds, I'm sure they really did believe this was all in fun. How often are you hanging out with a group of friends when sudden-ly everybody starts ganging up on one person? Nobody thinks anything of it, because to all of you it's nothing but a joke. Speaking as that person, it's no joke. You're hurting us."

I see a glimmer of guilt flash across several faces. Encouraged, I continue the story. "After a while, there was so much snow and ice in my throat, it became difficult to breathe, but everyone was laughing so hard they didn't real-ize I was struggling for air. Then Jimmy says, 'Hey, I think she might really be choking.' Jerry just shrugs his shoulders, and the next thing I know all of them walk off and leave me there, shivering, on the ground."

The audience gasps. One girl with deep-set brown eyes and long dark hair sitting toward the front, the one I saw staring wistfully at the cheerleaders in the entranceway of the school when I first arrived, is in tears. A boy wearing all black several rows behind her is furiously writing in a journal. I make a mental note of where they're sitting and what they look like so I can ask the principal to let me visit with both of them privately afterward. There will be many more by the time I conclude this talk.

"Not long after the incident in the parking lot," I continue, "I found my favorite pair of shoes floating in the toilet in the girls' bathroom, this time with a note that read, 'We hate you, freak. Go to another school.'

"In that moment, something inside me went dark and I knew that I could kill," I reveal. "Standing there in that lavatory stall, I closed my eyes and said a prayer, and it was the same prayer that I would say every day until high school graduation: 'Dear God, please give me cancer because if I have cancer, my parents won't be mad at me when I want to be absent from school.'"

Out of the corner of my eye, I see the principal watching her students intently. Her face is expressionless, and I can't tell if she's worried about them or angry with me for bringing all these emotions to the surface. I feel a momentary twinge of insecurity, and quickly remind myself that this is what I came here to do, tell the truth no matter what. Now she's speaking in hushed tones with some of the faculty. *Just block it out, Jodee, and focus on the students!*

"The girls who did that to me probably had fun planning it!" I exclaim. "I'm sure that everyone was passing notes back and forth about it, giggling and excited, so caught up in the thrill of being in on the joke that it never even occurred to them how it would affect me.

"How often," I ask, "have you or someone you know done

something similar to a classmate, perhaps on a blog like MySpace? You weren't trying to be cruel, but did you ever once stop to think how that person would actually *feel*? It's not just joking around! You have real power over each other's lives, and what you do to each other now will affect all of you long past graduation."

I continue reliving scene after scene from my past . . .

Begging Mr. Blatt to understand that I couldn't dissect a pig with the rest of the students in biology class because I loved animals too much, and pleading with him to let me write an extra-credit paper instead, only to be laughed at and told I'd be flunked if I didn't participate. "I stood up, looked him straight in the face, and said, 'Mr. Blatt, with all due respect, sir, I can't desecrate this innocent creature. I'm sorry if you feel you have to flunk me.' Then I got up and walked to the principal's office. And what do you think I heard the whole time I was going down that hall?" I ask the audience.

"Laughter," shout several students.

"And some of those kids weren't laughing because they didn't like me or because they were trying to hurt me. They were laughing for the same reason that some of you have been snickering ever since I got here today."

As I say this, I pause and stare at the kids in the back of the bleachers whom I saw laughing under their breath earlier. Then I continue talking, letting my gaze sweep across the rest of the audience.

"I did something intense that day in biology class just like what I'm doing now, and it's making some of you squirm. You don't want to react in a way that your friends wouldn't think is cool, so, not knowing what else to do, you laugh because you're nervous. But it doesn't matter why you laugh at someone. Being laughed at stinks! And, just like those kids in biology class who hurt me twenty-five years ago, those of you who have been laughing at me now are hurting me, too. And if you can hurt me, an author who's only here for a few hours, imagine how you're hurting the feelings of your classmates whom you laugh at every day?"

By now, all is quiet in those back bleachers. Satisfied that everyone has gotten the message, I look at those kids again and smile warmly, so they know I was never angry, only determined to gain their respect.

"The principal was cool," I continue. "He told me I didn't have to dissect as long as I did an extra-credit paper. The next day when I got to class, Nadia and her friends were waiting. 'Hey, Blanco, want some bacon for lunch?' Nadia then walked over to the specimen table, grabbed a partially dissected pig, and threw it at my face. Everyone started laughing. I know that some of those kids who were laughing felt bad about what had just happened, but they were afraid that if they didn't laugh everyone would laugh at them. It's bad enough if you laugh at someone of your own free will, but it's even worse if you do it because everyone else is doing it. That makes you a coward. So next time you find yourself in a similar situation, instead of showing your classmates how small you can be, why not show them how big you are and stand up for that person rather than helping to bring him down?" Whoops and hollers fill the gym, and I hear someone yell, "You go, girl!"

"I finally got through middle school and began high school," I continue. "I thought things would be different.

There was this girl who let me sit at her table every day as long as I promised not to talk to her or her friends. Can you imagine how hard that was? Every day I'd listen to them chatting about the parties they were invited to, what they would wear, and how they would do their hair and makeup. I ached for one of those girls to turn around just once and say, 'Hey, Jodee, do you think I should wear my blue sweater or my black one?' No one ever did. Then, one afternoon, one of them gets up and tells me that I can't sit there anymore. 'It's not like we hate you or anything,' she says. 'It's just that everybody else does, and we don't need them to start giving us a hard time, too.' I begged them to reconsider, explaining that no one else would let me sit at their table. 'Look, Jodee, it's nothing personal.' I then began what would become the most humiliating journey of my life, going from table to table begging people to let me sit with them."

At this point, I walk out into the bleachers, approaching members of the audience as I reconstruct this scene from my past. "Hey, could I sit with you guys?" I ask a group of girls, pretending that they're my former classmates and we're in the cafeteria. "Get out of here, freak," I respond, quickly switching characters. Momentarily taken aback, they stare at me in shocked recognition. For a split second, I see Noreen sitting with them. I blink away the memory as I move toward another group of students in the bleachers. "Please, could I sit here?" I ask. "Yeah, like any of us would want to sit with a loser like you," I hiss, changing characters again. Then, dripping with sarcasm, I say a loud and embarrassing "Goodbye" while waving my hand mockingly.

It is then I realize the room is starting to spin. *This isn't*

Calvin Samuels. The mortification I'm feeling right now isn't real. Taking deep breaths, I will my body to relax until the dizziness subsides, and continue my dramatization with several more students. I notice, as I'm walking through the bleachers, that dozens of kids are now in tears. It is all I can do not to hug them, and I add their faces to my growing list of whom I'll want to talk with later on.

"Eventually, I ran out of the cafeteria and into the bathroom and cried," I say. "But if a teacher had gone up to any of those kids and said, 'Hey, you guys, I just saw Jodee weeping in the lavatory, what did you do to her?' they would all have responded, 'We didn't do anything.' And they would have been telling the truth! Bullying isn't just the mean things you do," I say. "It's all the nice things you never do! Letting someone sit alone at lunch pretending not to see how badly that person wishes to be included? Bullying! Letting someone walk to class by themselves afraid to talk to anyone for fear of being rejected? Bullying! Always choosing the same person last whenever dividing into teams for gym or class? Bullying! It's *all* bullying!"

Despite how much I struggle to stay in the present and remind myself that I forgave my former classmates, every moment I spend talking to these kids is breathing new life into an old anger, and it's scaring me. I see images of Clarke and Shelly in my mind, and instead of experiencing a warm sensation of friendship I feel my fists clenching. Is what I'm doing a healthy catharsis, or am I resurrecting from the dead something awful that's going to stand on its haunches and devour me?

Shaking it off, I continue. "Think about the lunchroom

here at Marron," I say. "How many kids sit alone every day pretending to be reading because they're too ashamed to let anyone see that nobody will talk to them?" A homely, overweight girl in the front row turns away self-consciously as several students glance in her direction. Maybe it's the way they're looking at her, or how utterly alone she seems to be, but as I watch her shrink in her seat, eyeing the clock, I can barely contain my sadness. I think how much this girl reminds me of Selena, the sixth grader who e-mailed me for help.

The school is bright and cheerful. Some students are talking by the lockers, and others are getting ready for class before the bell rings, sharing last-minute homework notes and discussing assignments. As I walk down the hall with Selena's mom, who's surprising her daughter with my visit today, I feel the pressure Selena must be under, having to attend middle school here. It's like a midwestern Beverly Hills 90210. Everywhere I look, I see perfectly styled hair, French-manicured nails, Abercrombie clothes, and freshly glossed lips. Even I feel self-conscious among all these covergirl wannabes. I can imagine what Selena must go through here, having to face these people every day.

"She'll be so excited to finally meet you," her mom says, as we round the hallway to the main office. "All she talks about is your book, and how you're the only person who understands."

"I'm glad we could make today happen," I respond. "You mentioned that the principal knows this is supposed to be a surprise?"

"Oh, yes!" she replies. "Her first-period teacher will pretend she needs some worksheets from the office and send Selena to get them. Then the principal will keep her talking until we arrive."

When Selena sees her mom and me walk through the door, her face lights up and I can feel the lump in my throat. As I look at this sweet child coming toward me, arms outstretched to give me a hug, I'm aware of the irony of her self-loathing. Despite Selena's physical appearance—unkempt hair that refuses to stay tied back in her pretty blue bow, immaculate clothes that cling cumbersomely to her overly large frame—she radiates a spirited inner beauty that transcends anything I've seen at her school today.

"Hello, Selena, I'm so happy to meet you," I say, embracing her.

"I can't believe you're here," she says. "My mom said that she talked to you and you were too busy to come."

"We thought it would be more fun to surprise you," I reply.

"A lot of kids in my class have read your book and are talking about it. Are you going to give a presentation?" she asks, shyly.

"I'd be happy to, but only on one condition."

"What's that?"

"I'd like you to introduce me."

"Really? I'd love to," she says, beaming.

When we enter the classroom, the teacher greets us warmly and then turns the floor over to Selena. With the eyes of her abusers on her, fear flashes across her face, but then quickly disappears, and she introduces me with *a poise far beyond her years. "Yay, Selena!" someone shouts from the back of the room. "All right, Selena," calls another student. I look over at Selena's mom, who is watching her daughter, holding back tears. While I know this won't be the end of Selena's struggles with her classmates, I hope it can be the beginning of a new self-confidence for her.*

"Hello, everybody," I begin. "My name is Jodee Blanco and I'm here today in honor of a very special friend of mine, Selena."

It isn't only Selena who's swirling through my mind as I look at this lonely girl. I see myself, too.

"And I don't blame you for not wanting to invite kids like that to sit with you at lunch," I say to my audience. "Why should you? They're usually either overweight or have their face buried in a book. Typically, they don't dress fashionably or manicure their nails, and I bet they never even say hello to you, right? I mean, let's face it, they're weird. Why should you have to interrupt your time with your friends to be nice to somebody who makes you feel so uncomfortable? I understand, I truly do."

A few students glance at me curiously, and several teachers give me perplexed looks, as if to say, "Where is she going with this?"

"But did any of you ever wonder why those kids turned into people none of you would ever want to be caught dead hanging out with? I can tell you exactly why, because I *was* one of those misfits. But it was never a choice. My classmates chose for me, just as all of you are choosing for those people you've decided don't meet your standard of 'cool.' Why should we care if our hair looks nice or our clothes are fashionable if you look past us as if we're not even there? Why should we say hello and risk being rejected when none of you actually talk *to* us, you only ever talk *about* us? Why should we give a damn about our appearance when you treat us like we're invisible? We don't look in the mirror, because we don't feel worthy of a reflection. The very qualities about us that gross you out are the very things that you create by treating us the way you do. And the saddest part of all is that so many of us look up to you. When will you realize that we're human beings, too?"

There's a powerful shift of emotion in the gym. I think I've finally won over the skeptical teachers in the audience, too. I feel as if I've lifted a curtain that nobody knew had been closed. I see visible changes in people's faces and body language. Many students who were barely paying attention before are sitting forward now, listening and nodding their heads. A couple of the girls in the back row, who had been so arrogant earlier, are hugging and comforting one another. Apparently, I'm not the only one to sense something unusual going on here. The camera crews continue to shoot footage, and I see newspaper reporters quietly speaking to some of the faculty. I still feel naked, but it's a strong, dignified kind of naked, like skinny dipping in clear, cool water that makes you feel more alive than you ever have before.

"Later that day when I got home from school," I continue, "I snuck into my mom's bathroom, grabbed her foundation makeup, and slathered it all over my legs and arms to hide the cuts and bruises where I'd been kicked in the shins and slammed into the lockers between classes. Then, when my parents got home from work, I told them everything was fine at school, went up to my room, blasted my stereo, and screamed into a pillow. Sometimes I'd get lucky and my throat would become so raw from screaming that I could convince Mom I had strep and she'd let me miss school the next day. That particular night, I did something new. After my parents went to bed, I went into the kitchen and dumped three bags of stale Halloween candy bars into my book bag, the same bag that, less than one year later would hold the butcher knife. The next day at school during lunchtime, I snuck into the library, stole the hall pass, went into the girls' bathroom, sat on the sink, and wolfed down candy bars for lunch. And that is how I would have lunch almost every day until high school graduation. And yet everyone who rejected me in that lunchroom honestly believed it wasn't any big deal. What should they have understood?" I ask, taking several steps forward into the bleachers.

"It's not just joking around!" the audience shouts.

"*Yes*," I respond. "And I guarantee you that, twenty years from now, that same person who sits alone at lunch, who walks to class by herself, and who never gets invited to anything, could become a famous author or movie star, or even the principal of a middle school." The audience giggles. "But I promise you that when she gets home at night and is looking in the mirror as she takes off her makeup, she will not see the successful person she's become. She will still see that insecure outcast.

"And let me tell every one of you who are being bullied and excluded as I was: There is nothing wrong with you! It's everything that is *right* about you that makes you stand out! You are not rejected because you're beneath the crowd. You're misunderstood because you rise *above* the crowd! And don't you ever change for anyone. It's the people who put you down who need to do the changing!"

Hundreds of students jump up and start whistling and applauding. As the roar of excitement reverberates throughout the gym, I close my eyes and drink in this remarkable moment. Then I take a deep breath and begin recounting my last memory of high school, one that I had to fight with my editor to keep in the book because it's so graphic.

"It was my last day of high school, last class, last period, and all I wanted was one good memory," I say. "I was alone in the classroom when Tyler walked in." I describe Tyler as being similar in appearance and style to Kid Rock, explaining how Tyler was popular with the party crowd because he was rebellious but that he also gained favor with the athletes and faculty as the star of the track team. "This guy could do no wrong in anyone's eyes. He would treat me all right if we were alone, but if his cool friends were around it was a different story.

"I handed him my yearbook and asked if he would sign it. He agreed, and took out this huge black indelible marker and began making big, broad, sweeping strokes on the inside front cover. I was so excited! I thought, Finally, someone is doing something nice for me. This is an omen that everything will be OK when I start college. 'Oh, dear God, you can cancel the cancer request. We are so cool right now!'"

The audience chuckles.

"Then Mitch walks in," I say. "Let me tell you about

Mitch! He was the high school heartthrob, the guy every girl at school wanted." For the next several minutes, I reveal what I hadn't even disclosed in *Please Stop Laughing at Me . . .* the huge crush I'd had on Mitch since fifth grade, how I used to fantasize about him giving me my first kiss, taking me to the prom, perhaps even one day marrying me. There's something so liberating in finally talking about it that I have to suppress the urge not to start giggling like a teenager.

"I remember I was in a television studio with Mel Gibson —" At the mention of Mel Gibson's name, several female faculty members look at me with new appreciation. "And out of the blue he turned toward me and told me how beautiful he thought I was," I say. Those same teachers are now staring at me in wide-eyed disbelief. "And all I could think of when it was happening was why couldn't this be Mitch?" I say, shaking my head. "That's the kind of torch I carried for Mitch. I don't think I've ever told that to anyone before." Several smiles light up at me, and I feel glad that I chose this moment to let someone in on my secret.

I explain how Mitch was never mean to me, that he was always warm and kind, but that he had a steady girlfriend for many years and was very loyal to her. I also tell them how he was going through hell because his mom had died only several days before graduation.

"Tyler is still signing away," I continue. "Mitch peeks over his shoulder, and then he sits down and buries his head in his hands. I thought he was just grieving for his mom. As the rest of the kids start filing into the classroom, they look over Tyler's shoulder, and the laughter gets louder and louder."

As I'm reenacting this scene, tears are streaming down

my face. "By now," I go on, "everyone is laughing. I look over and see Mitch, who appears to be in pain. Grinning, Tyler hands me my yearbook. Written in black indelible laundry marker, all in capital letters are the words 'F–k you, bitch! Everybody hates you and always will. You're God's worst mistake.'"

There's an audible gasp from the audience, and as I look out into the bleachers I see more kids in tears. Others are glancing at each other nervously. A few are rocking back and forth, staring ahead. It begins to dawn on me that I'm tapping into something here that I may not be prepared for. Apparently, the teachers aren't, either. I see them shooting worried glances at one another as they realize they're going to have to deal with the aftermath. No one expected *anything* like this. All I keep asking myself is, *what* have I opened up?

I peek at my watch. Though it seems I've only been onstage for a little while, I see that nearly three-quarters of an hour have gone by, and soon the bell will ring, signaling that the students should go to their next class. I need to switch gears, I tell myself, bring all of us out of these dark memories and back into the light. I scan the room, searching for Eileen. I see her whispering to the principal.

"But my story has a happy ending!" I say. Then I launch into the night of my twentieth high school reunion, recounting the extraordinary events of that evening. Soon I can feel the audience rooting for me, and I know by the expressions on their faces that I've reached these students' hearts. When I get to the part about Mitch walking me to my car, there's a collective intake of breath in the gym.

"And there in the parking lot of the hometown I'd run as

fast and as far away from as I could twenty years earlier, I finally got the kiss I'd been waiting for since the fifth grade, and Mitch has been kissing me ever since," I reveal. The boys start to whistle and cheer, and squeals of excitement erupt from the girls.

"My story has a happy ending, but there are kids in this gym right now whose stories won't unless you do something about it. I want to let you in on something. I was really nervous when I took this stage," I confess. "It's hard for me to talk about my past as I did today. But I did it because I care about all of you. I think I've earned your respect, right?" I see dozens of kids nodding their heads in earnest. "I'm going to ask you to do something for me now. I want you to close your eyes and remember the worst moment in your life, a specific moment when someone you really care about either said or did something that really hurt you, that made you wish you'd never been born."

And then I take the audience back.

"I want you to remember every detail of this moment and relive it in your mind as if it's happening right now." I scan the faces in the audience, and I see hundreds of pairs of eyes tightly shut in concentration. Pleased, I continue. "I want you to open your eyes now," I instruct. I see large numbers of students bristling with emotion at the unexpected power of their memories. "How you felt in your worst moment is exactly how the person at school whom you let sit alone every day at lunch, never invite to anything, and whom you ridicule and bully feels. The only difference is you only had to feel that way once. The outcast feels that way every morning when he walks through the doors into this building."

The gym grows silent, and even the kids wh clowning around earlier have become quiet and introspective. Teachers are visibly shaken, too, and I will learn that this is a harbinger of things to come, that many educators were bullied when they were students, and that's why they're drawn to education.

Next, I ask the audience to do a homework assignment. "No one will grade you or check to see if you've completed it," I explain. "I want each of you to walk up to someone you've never been nice to before, someone who seems alone or whom you considered 'weird' before today, look at them, smile and say, 'Hi, how's it going?' That simple gesture of kindness could change their lives, and it could save yours. Because if someone had done that for me, perhaps I wouldn't have tried to sneak a butcher knife into school. And if you don't think Columbine could happen here, you're wrong."

I close the talk by offering advice.

"How many of you have been bullied, and when you asked adults for advice they told you to ignore the bully and walk away?"

Hand after hand is raised.

"While those adults mean well, they were wrong," I say. "Ignoring a problem will never make it go away. You have to look your tormentors in the eye and, showing no emotion or fear, tell them to stop. Then keep staring at them for several seconds, just long enough to make them squirm," I continue. "The first few times you try this, the bullies will become meaner because you're taking away their power. But after a while they will respect you. And even if they're such dense jerks that they still give you a hard time, at least you know that you defended your dignity. Always remember, standing up for yourself nonviolently is your human right. Seeking vengeance later on is the mistake.

"I also encourage you to join activities outside of school where you can make new friends. Contact the local park district, community center, or YMCA, and the public library. Ask them if they have any organized activities for teens. They'll send you lists of cool stuff they've got to do, from martial-arts classes and computer clubs to readers' groups and teen theater. The secret is to go one town over from where you live; that way, the kids you meet will be from a different school district and they'll be new faces. It may be inconvenient, but it's essential. This activity will give you something social to look forward to during the week, and the friendships you develop will make you feel more confident. And a confident person is harder to bully.

"And last, but most important, don't be like me, trying to hide what was happening from my parents. Confide in an adult you trust," I tell everyone. "They will want to help if you give them the chance." As my journey through the American school system continues, I will discover that, sadly, this is not always true, and that some of the worst impediments to the well-being of children will be parents themselves.

I thank everyone for listening to me, and then take a bow. The applause is gratifying. Hundreds of students stand up and whistle. Teachers nod their approval. The media is furiously writing and recording. As I step off the stage, I am swarmed by students.

"Please, can I give you a hug?" a sweet girl with glasses asks, her eyes red and swollen from crying.

"Hey, can I have a hug, too?" inquires a grossly overweight boy who's about fifteen years old.

"I need to talk to you, please. I need help," a girl with blue hair and a nose ring whispers in my ear.

I am bombarded by desperate need, and all I want to do is scoop each of these teens into my arms. Then, as I'm embracing one student after another, mascara stains all over the front of my pink sweater, which has now become damp from tears and runny noses, a group of kids approach me, sad and upset. I reach out to embrace them. "I know what it's like being the outcast," I say soothingly.

"Oh, no," one of them says. "We're not outcasts. We're, like, the most popular kids in school, and now we realize how mean we've been to some of our classmates. What should we do? How can we make it up to them?"

As I'm offering advice, I see Eileen inching her way toward me through the throng of kids. I give her a look that says, "Can you believe this is happening?"

Grinning, she shrugs her shoulders. "Well, kid," she says, "I guess there's no turning back now."

The principal approaches us, an anxious look on her face. "Jodee, dozens of students are begging for one-on-one time with you," she says. "Some of them have histories of violence and suicide. What do you want to do?"

I hesitate, unsure of how to respond.

"Give Jodee a conference room," the Little General says confidently. "Ask your counselor to sit in with her and we'll take this one child at a time."

chapter nine

Revelations

May 2003

It's been a few weeks since the event at Marron. I'm moving into my new condo in Tinson Park, about a mile from where I grew up, and my mom and my cousin, Jeanine, are here helping me unpack. As we're sorting through boxes, I'm also trying to sort through the enormity of what happened at that high school gym. I'll never forget the feeling of being besieged by that many needy kids, holding them and stroking their heads, whispering words of encouragement as I listened to them tell their stories.

Part of me was thankful to have gotten through to them. Another was freaking out. All those strangers hugging me, squeezing my hand, touching my arm, the mingling of perfumes and hair gels, adolescent sweat and pungent breath all at once, clammy hands, oily faces burrowing into my sweater. I never before experienced such a profound dichotomy: trying to reconcile the joy my spirit was feeling with the limits of what my body could physically endure.

I also had demands on my attention from students whose problems had nothing to do with bullying. Many of these kids were so starved for an adult to listen — not judge but actually *listen* — that they seemed unable to hold back. Hearing their cries for help was like getting drenched in a rainstorm where your vision is blurred and you can't really see where you're going. But as you're getting pelted with water you feel uncommonly alive and awake, humbled by the force of nature that's touching you in that moment. The pain some of these kids were feeling was just that, a force of nature. I couldn't help but wonder about their parents. If I had kids and found out they'd confided in a stranger before coming to me, it would wound me. I didn't know whether to feel sorry for these parents because their children were obviously shutting them out or infuriated with them for the same reason.

A sophomore confessed to me that she had been raped by the quarterback of the football team and was afraid to tell anyone because his friends warned her that she'd become an outcast if she turned on him. Another girl, whose dad was in prison, was struggling with an alcoholic mother and beatings by her boyfriend. I even had one student ask me if I would help her tell her mom that she wanted a sex-change operation. I thought to myself as I was witnessing their agony that this couldn't be happening, that America's youth couldn't possibly be this lost . . . *could they*? Not being a licensed mental-health professional, I was careful not to play the role of psychologist with anyone, but, rather, concentrated on being an empathetic and compassionate ear, offering whatever support I could.

I would later learn that anyone hired by a school is automatically considered a mandated reporter and is required by law to divulge all incidents of abuse related by students. Some of these kids were searching for a safe haven for their secrets and admitted that I was the first adult they'd ever trusted enough to tell. How could I honor my legal obligation without betraying that trust? I kept thinking that if I make any of these students resent that they opened up to me they'll never feel safe confiding in an adult again. Though I didn't realize it then, I got lucky at Marron. I was able to persuade every student in crisis to let me talk to their school counselor on their behalf so they could get the professional help they needed. But I will soon discover that straddling the precarious line between the law and a child's trust isn't always that simple.

By the time I saw the last person waiting to meet with me, I longed to get back to the hotel and take a shower. The weight of their familiarity was oppressive. Every person I gave my attention to that day filled and drained me at the same time, and I remember wondering how therapists and social workers keep their balance being exposed to all that human suffering.

"Honey, is anything wrong?" Mom asks. "You've been working on that same box since we got here."

"I was just thinking about that high school appearance in Pennsylvania."

"I know how rough that day was for you, but you're making a difference in so many kids' lives," Mom says. "You should be proud of yourself."

"I am, but I'm not sure I could handle that again."

"Angel, I believe what you're doing now was meant to be and that God will give you the strength when you need it."

"Come on, Mom, that's great, but what if you're wrong?" I say. "You don't understand how intense things got in that gym."

"What happened?" Jeanine asks.

"It was chaos after I finished speaking. And it wasn't only students rushing up to me in tears, wanting help. Teachers and counselors swarmed me, saying they needed to talk about how *they* had been bullied in school, and were still having trouble coping with it."

"You're kidding," she replies.

"No! Some of them would butt in front of their own students to get my attention. I had to ask them to step aside until all the kids had been taken care of."

"It seems you've unlocked some kind of hidden desperation in America," Jeanine remarks, ripping open the box marked "kitchen stuff" and unwrapping its contents.

"That's what scares me," I reply. "And I got thrown some other curveballs I didn't expect."

"What do you mean?" she asks.

As I tell Mom and Jeanine the rest of my experience at Marron, I can see the expressions of disbelief on their faces.

"Isn't anyone paying attention at that school?" Mom says. "And what about the parents of these kids? How can a child get raped by another student and not one adult sense something was wrong?"

"What was the principal doing while you were trying to deal with all of this?" Jeanine asks.

"She had her hands full, too," I reply. "The poor woman was frantic trying to assist her counselors, who where being overwhelmed by distraught students, contacting parents to let them know what was going on, on top of dealing with media that wanted to interview both of us."

"I can see why you feel that you may have bitten off more

than you can chew," Mom says.

"And it's not just the emotional component. Physically it was hard, too. Some of those kids smelled like they hadn't washed in days. I'd find myself breathing through my mouth when I hugged them. What kind of person lets a child leave the house like that?"

For a moment Mom appears as if something has hit her in the chest, then she quietly picks up a roll of tack paper and begins lining my kitchen shelves with it. By the time I realize what I've done, it's too late to take it back, and all I can see in my mind's eye is the memory of my filthy hair and dirty nails, and the sound of her voice pleading with me to care about myself.

> *"Honey, I made an appointment at the hairdresser for both of us, and we can have a manicure and pedicure if you like," Mom says, smiling.*
>
> *"Forget it, Mom. I know you mean well, but I really don't feel good."*
>
> *"Jodee, there's nothing wrong with you. We've been to the doctor and he says your symptoms are psychosomatic."*
>
> *"He's wrong! I'm exhausted all the time and I don't have any energy. I know I'm sick, Mom."*
>
> *"You're making yourself sick."*
>
> *"That's not true! What about the weight I've lost?"*
>
> *"The only reason you're losing weight is because you won't eat."*
>
> *"I can't eat."*
>
> *"And I suppose you can't shower or use deodorant, either?" The moment the words left her mouth, I could see*

the regret on her face.

"Angel, I'm sorry, I didn't mean that the way it sounded."

Mom didn't understand. No one did. Why should I give a damn about my outside when I was already dead on the inside?

It's odd how we remember certain things people say and, even though we forgive them, we bear a scar and are ashamed of ourselves for it.

"Mom, you did everything you could," I say, giving her a hug.

As we continue unpacking, my cell phone rings. It's Mitch wanting to know if I'd like to have dinner later this evening. "Why don't you see if Shelly and Clarke might like to join us," he says. "We can celebrate your moving back home!"

After promising to give them both a call, we chat for a few minutes and then arrange to meet at one of my favorite Italian restaurants.

"You're beaming," Jeanine says, smiling.

As my cousin and my mom help me settle into my condo, my mind drifts to my old life on the East Coast and the familiar world I left behind. I abandoned it so quickly that I didn't give myself the chance to contemplate what it would be like walking away from everything I thought I wanted for everything that I couldn't wait to escape. All those years in New York and L.A. working in the entertainment business was like being in Oz. There were the magical experiences I had dancing with movie stars at fancy parties, collaborating with famous people on fascinating projects. But I also had to walk through scary, dark places like the haunted forest, where nothing was as it appeared to be and enemies lurked, waiting to take what was mine. Like Dorothy, all I wanted was to go home. But when I discovered I could click my heels three times and it would whisk me back to the familiar, I was so excited to finally get my wish granted that I didn't think about how hard it would be to say goodbye. When Dorothy wakes up back in her bed in Kansas with all her loved ones around her, you're led to believe her adventures in Oz were nothing but a dream. I'm starting to wonder if the past twenty years of my life were nothing but a dream, too. For years, all I could think about was wanting a normal life with genuine friends, not jetting from exotic location to exotic location hobnobbing with the powerful and elite all day, then crying myself to sleep because it was just a job and, damn it, I wanted a *life*. Or was my old life the true one and this one back home just me pretending? Sometimes I miss my old friends in Oz, the adventures we had, and the unpredictability of that wild and wonderful place. I wonder, after Dorothy was back in Kansas for a while, did she long for that yellow-brick road? Did she ever wish for another tornado?

"Honey, your cell phone is ringing," Mom calls out from the kitchen.

You've got to stop thinking so much, I tell myself, answering the phone. It's Eileen. She's turned her home in Pennsylvania into a makeshift "command central," to respond to the tsunami of phone calls and e-mails that have been coming in since I spoke at Marron. You would never imagine that word of mouth could spread that fast. Parents of severely bullied students, teachers at their wits' end over ineffective zero-tolerance policies in their districts, and teen outcasts who are tired of being ignored have all heard about what happened at Marron and the requests for appearances have been pouring in. Eileen and I are learning that the American school system has a grapevine unlike any other. We will discover that sometimes the harvest can be both sweet and bitter.

I can't get over how reliable Eileen has been through all of this. It's bad enough that my life has been turned upside down since I embarked on this journey, but now hers has, too. The pace has been frantic. I'm still receiving dozens of pleas for help from the people who heard about what I was doing from the book signing at Borders in Pason Park. I don't want to take advantage of Eileen's kindness and generosity, but she insists that she's enjoying every minute of what she describes as "this incredible ride." She keeps telling me for years that she's been searching for something that would give her a sense of purpose and that she's finally found it.

"Hey, kid, how's the move coming?"

"I'm almost settled in," I reply.

"Don't get too comfortable. I'm in the process of trying to book you on a speaking tour."

Though I want to reach as many kids as possible, I gulp at the sound of those words. Having been a publicist for so long, I know that touring isn't pretty.

"How many cities?" I ask.

"However many I can get!"

Now wanting to dampen her enthusiasm, I bite my tongue, knowing it won't be as easy as she thinks.

"By the way, we have to discuss what your speaking fee will be," Eileen continues.

"I did Marron pro bono," I reply.

"You can't do all of them for free," she says. "How will you survive financially?"

"I still have consulting clients."

"Yes, but if you're on the road speaking you won't be able to resume that business, and so what will you do for income?"

"It's just that the idea of charging schools to help kids makes me cringe."

"I can understand how you feel, but you've got to be realistic. You're going to have expenses. And what happens when it's *thousands* of people trying to reach you, not just hundreds? You *can't* keep giving out your cell phone number and e-mail address! You'll need a Web site, an office, not to mention operating capital," she insists.

I can't deny that Eileen makes some valid, if scary, points.

"Whether you know it or not, you've just declared war on school bullying," she states. "Name me one war that was won without funds. Jodee, you must charge the schools when you speak."

Reluctantly, I agree.

"By the way, does this mean you'll let me pay *you* now?" I say.

"You're not in a financial position to do that yet," she replies. "Let's just wait a bit."

"Eileen, I can't take advantage of you."

"How about this? You pay me a percentage of every booking I get for you."

"Done," I reply.

Eileen officially comes on board as my manager and speaking agent. Those will be only two of the hats she wears in our quest to make America accountable for the emotional safety of its students. As she begins booking my first tour for the fall, she'll discover that it will prove harder than she anticipated. Many of the schools that contact us won't have the budget approval for anti-bullying initiatives. Some principals will be hostile toward her when she follows up on leads given by parents, teachers, and students themselves. Both of us will also confront a tremendous learning curve, her taking on many of the responsibilities that I had during my tenure as a publicist and me assuming the role of talent, which I wasn't nearly as ready for as I'd thought. Our friendship will be tested in ways neither of us could have predicted.

chapter ten

A Twist
of Fate

May 2003

I just returned from New York, where I spent the past several days tying up loose professional ends. The trip was bittersweet. The city that had been my home for more than twenty years, and that I could never imagine leaving, now seemed oddly unfamiliar. It was as if the invisible umbilical cord that had been keeping me connected to New York was now starting to wither and fall off.

As I was rushing down Sixth Avenue to my last meeting of the day, wishing I could hide from the sounds and smells that are a typical part of daily life in Manhattan, and that I once considered exhilarating, I realized that this wasn't me anymore. Part of me was grateful to begin a new chapter. Another was sad to end the old one. On the cab ride back to the airport, watching my beloved New York skyline fade into the distance, I called Mitch. Hearing his voice, I envisioned strolling through the mall in Pason Park, having coffee with my mom and Jeanine, driving past the landmarks of my youth, like Skinny Jim's and the ice cream parlor, things I could never do living so far away, and as sad as it was looking out that cab window and saying goodbye to New York, I felt relieved that I was finally escaping the rat race that I'd let define me for too long.

Since returning from the East Coast, I've been busy settling in. Mom surprised me with a beautiful, fully furnished office that she had decorated with *Wizard of Oz* artwork. When I picked her up for lunch the day after I got back, she asked me to retrieve a file for her from the "spare office," and when I opened the door I was stunned. It's a luxury being near Mom and knowing how good it must make her feel having her daughter working across the hall. We missed each other all those years I was in New York. I don't think either of us admitted to ourselves how much until now. The condo is coming along nicely, too, and for the first time since childhood I finally feel like I have roots again.

It's late morning and I'm at the office I share with Mom reviewing e-mails from kids in distress when the phone rings. It's Eileen. She says that my old high school, Calvin Samuels, called. They have an opening for a speaker for their teacher in-service day and want to know if I'm available.

"You've got to be joking," I reply.

"No," she says. "The vice principal, Dr. Collins, contacted me earlier this morning. Apparently, the person they originally scheduled canceled at the last minute and someone on her staff suggested you as a replacement."

"Do they realize they're the high school in my book?" I ask, still trying to process this.

"Dr. Collins knows you're a graduate, but as far as making any other connection, I don't think they have."

"If someone asks, you can be honest, but otherwise I'd rather make my entrance without the weight of their prejudice or fear."

"I take it that means you want to do it," she says.

"The only way to conquer a fear is to face it," I reply. "I was terrified to attend my reunion, and look how that turned out."

Though I may have convinced Eileen I'm making the right decision, when we hang up I'm trembling. I haven't been inside Calvin Samuels since the afternoon I walked out clutching my senior yearbook, the echo of my classmates' laughter ringing in my ears. Whenever I drive past the school, I get this Stephen King–like vision of a place in a horror movie, a gateway to hell where everyone is evil and unsuspecting teens are sucked up into the darkness, and then I feel my hands, clammy and cold, gripping the steering wheel and I have to blare the radio to blast the disturbing image out of my head.

"Daddy, did you talk to the principal?" I ask my father the second he walks in the door.

"Yes, honey," he replies, hanging up his coat and joining Mom and me on the couch.

"What happened?" Mom asks, handing him a glass of wine.

I can tell by the look on Mom's face that she's worried. The dean called her earlier today, telling her that if my absences continued, they'd have no choice but to turn my case over to the state truancy department. Though Mom doesn't know, when she was on the phone with him I was listening on the extension in my room.

"Dean Muldar, my daughter wants to be in school and the only reason she's not is because she's being terrorized by her classmates, and so far your office has failed to pre-

vent it," she says.

"Mrs. Blanco, as I've told both you and Jodee before, we've had repeated talks with the students she says are picking on her, but other than that there's not much more we can do."

"Not much more you can do? What about suspending them or putting their parents on notice that the school won't tolerate this kind of behavior!"

"Quite frankly, Mrs. Blanco, these are good kids who have always been a source of pride to the school," Dean Muldar replies. "They're very involved in our sports program and other extracurricular activities, and no one on my faculty has ever observed them behaving in a malicious manner toward anyone."

"That still doesn't change the fact that they're harassing my daughter! Jodee can't even go to the bathroom at Samuels without being afraid."

"Then perhaps you should consider contacting a therapist," Dean Muldar replies tersely. "We've done everything we can, and unless your daughter returns to school by Monday we will be reporting her to truancy. Now, if there's nothing else?"

That's when Mom hung up and called Dad.

"I told the principal how frustrated you were after your conversation with Dean Muldar," Dad is explaining to Mom.

"What was his response?"

"That he talked with Jodee's teachers himself and they all agreed with Dean Muldar. They can't imagine these students are capable of the cruelty Jodee describes."

"God, this is like a nightmare," I say, wanting to scream. "Why would I make all this stuff up?"

"You wouldn't, and I told your principal that," Dad says, putting his arm around me.

"How did you finally leave it with him?" Mom asks.

"I explained that if he didn't take immediate action to help my daughter I would."

"What does that mean?" I ask, already knowing what's coming.

"It means we're going to the school board," Dad says. "It's time the administration at Samuels learns they can't get by with this kind of favoritism anymore."

I wish Mom had let them turn me in to truancy instead.

As thoughts of Samuels tumble through my mind, I receive a panicked phone call from the principal at Kyle's school. She informs me that Kyle is in her office, threatening suicide. By now, every muscle in my body feels like barbed wire.

"Ms. Blanco, I'm so sorry to bother you, but Kyle is insisting that he'll only talk to you," she explains.

"Have you notified his parents?"

"They're on their way."

"Where's Kyle now?"

"He's with the counselor. He came into the office about an hour ago saying that he was going to kill himself."

"I don't understand. The last time we spoke, he said his classmates weren't picking on him as much as before."

"They weren't," the principal replies. "I had a long chat with the boys who were giving Kyle a hard time and they were making a real effort."

"Then what happened?"

"That's the strange part. Kyle seems to have been egging them on, as if he almost *wants* them to start up on him again."

"Let me talk to him."

I hear her calling Kyle and then handing him the phone.

"Sweetheart, it's Jodee. What's going on? Your principal tells me you want to kill yourself. Why?"

"Everybody hates me," he replies.

"But I thought things were starting to go better for you at school."

"I know, but now they're being mean again."

"OK, honey, we'll talk more when I get there. I'm on my way."

I peek my head into Mom's office to tell her what's going on.

"That poor little boy. Is there anything I can do to help?"

"Say a prayer I don't let him down again."

"Jodee, you did not let anyone down and I don't ever want to hear you talk like that!" Mom says. "You can't control everything that happens to these kids."

"I know you're right, but part of me still feels responsible."

"Honey, you gave Kyle your love and guidance, and you're still there for him. No one can expect any more of you."

Though what Mom says is true, it gives me little comfort. I've always been a perfectionist, and until now it's served me well. I'm starting to realize that as an activist it may prove to be my undoing. I understand that no one can save everyone, but when your whole life has been about aiming high and achieving it, anything less feels like failure.

"I better go, Mom. They're waiting for me at Kyle's school."

"It'll be OK," she says, giving me a reassuring hug. "I'll have chats."

When I was four years old, I asked my mom what the word "prayer" meant. She told me it was when you had a chat with God or somebody in heaven about whatever was on your mind. Ever since then, "I'll have chats" has been our secret phrase for saying a prayer. Whenever one of us uses it, the warmth and comfort of the mother-daughter bond wraps itself around us like a protective cloak, providing strength in the face of fear.

"Thanks, Mom," I respond, smiling.

Twenty minutes later, when I pull into the parking lot at Kyle's school, the principal is waiting for me. A pleasant woman in her mid-forties, she greets me with an apologetic smile. "I'm so sorry to drag you into this," she says. "But I know how much Kyle admires you, and he's in such distress."

"Please don't apologize. I'm glad you called. Have his parents gotten here yet?"

"A few minutes ago. They're with Kyle and the counselor now."

As soon as I open the door, I see that Kyle's mom has been crying: her eyes are red and swollen. His stepdad is nervously tapping his foot, glancing from Kyle to his wife, looking helpless. The counselor and Kyle are sitting across from them. Kyle is staring at the floor silently. The moment I walk in, he gets up and comes toward me, wrapping his arms around my midriff.

"Kyle, it's OK," I say, stroking his head.

"I want to die!" he sobs.

I take Kyle outside for a walk so we can talk privately. I tell him what the principal mentioned, that he seems to be instigating his own mistreatment. For a moment, he turns away and says nothing.

"Think hard, Kyle. Is it possible that you might be doing it without even knowing and that's why they're acting this way?"

"At least it's better than being ignored," he admits.

For a moment, I'm unable to speak. Specific images from my past assault me: answering questions in class using big words that I knew would invite ridicule when I could just as easily have responded with simpler language; convincing myself that I was doing the right thing defending students who asked me not to interfere and then agonizing over the teasing and rejection it created.

Oh, my God.

I went through the same thing Kyle is now experiencing and never saw the pattern until just this moment. I remember my parents fighting about it one night, Dad not wanting to believe I could be contributing to my own rejection but no longer able to deny the possibility, and Mom remaining adamant that it couldn't be true. We were at odds with one another over something that none of us understood. The more I think about it, the more clearly I see the cycle. It's a form of self-sabotage. When you're chronically taunted and shunned by your classmates, after a while a part of you grows so accustomed to their baleful attention that when they finally do leave you alone it's like a death, and you find yourself provoking them to bully you again, because if you're being ridiculed at least you know you still exist. It's as if circumstances drive you to make a choice between being a no one and being a target. Looking back now, there was a period when I became a *Rejection Junkie*, grateful for whatever fix I could get from my classmates, no matter how toxic to my self-esteem.

I bend down so that Kyle and I are eye level, and explain to him what I experienced and why I think the same thing may be happening to him. He looks at me and nods his head.

"Kyle, I don't want you to think you did something wrong or that you're going to get into trouble," I tell him.

"Isn't what's going on with me 'subconscious'?" he asks, struggling to pronounce the word.

"Yes," I reply, suppressing a smile. "Do you know what that means?"

"Yes, it means that my brain did it without my permission," he answers proudly.

"I never thought of it that way, but yes, that's right. Now how about we start walking back and see if we can't come up with some solutions to help you through this?"

"OK," he says, grabbing hold of my hand as we make our way to the counselor's office.

When we return, I describe my conversation with Kyle and my thoughts on why he's struggling with his classmates again. The principal is leaning forward in her seat, listening intently. "I exhibited the same behavior as Kyle," I explain. "I call it" . . . *and it just comes to me now* . . . "Rejection Junkie Syndrome," *a term I'll now incorporate into my formal presentation.*

The moment I say the phrase, it's as if the principal

heard the tumblers on a safe's lock clicking into place, and she begins furiously jotting down notes. *Wait! Don't write anything down yet. I should have this concept vetted by a psychiatrist or other mental-health professional first.* I don't know whether I'm overstepping my bounds giving names to what bullied children experience, or if I should be proud of myself because I'm helping to make sense of something important. Then I realize the knowledge I carry inside me, and that Kyle and every other bullied child carries inside them, is the stuff solutions are made of and I can't be ashamed or afraid to put what we know to the test. Doctors can help victims and survivors like us find the path to recovery, but without our memories and insights it's like writing a travel guide to a place you've never been. We're the access they need to ensure that their lay of the land is accurate.

"You may have helped a lot of kids today," I tell Kyle. "You're a very special young man, and this world would be a lesser place without you."

He smiles, and all I want to do is wrap my arms around him and will his school years to be over. I ask his parents if they enrolled Kyle in a park-district activity as we'd discussed a couple of months ago. "I made a similar recommendation at a high school recently, and I'm already receiving e-mails from students who are giving it a try and seeing beneficial results," I add.

"We planned to sign Kyle up for youth basketball at the park, but when things started to get better with his classmates he said he'd rather do an activity at school," his mom replies. "We had no idea he was having a problem again until today."

"Kyle, look at me," the principal says. "I'm going to ask you something, and I want you to be honest."

"All right," he replies.

"Remember when I had a talk with those boys who were making you feel bad and about a week later you stopped by my office and told me that it helped, that they weren't being as mean anymore?"

"I remember."

"What if I had another talk with them and explained things? Would you still be willing to join one of our extracurricular activities?"

"I want to, but I'm afraid nobody will want me on their side."

"I'm afraid of that sometimes, too," I interject. "Kyle, let's you and me make a pact that we'll both work on conquering that fear together. My first step was going to my reunion. This can be your first step." Kyle agrees to participate in the after-school basketball program. He also promises me that that if he ever has thoughts of suicide again he will tell his parents and ask for help.

Though I wish I could believe I was the hero who came in and saved the day, I know it's not that simple. Kyle has a long road ahead of him. His parents won't have it easy, either. While I can be there for them, I can't change the reality of what happens to all bullied children. Eventually, they are unable to escape the self-loathing that prompts others to perceive them in a diminished way no matter how they behave.

On my way out, Kyle comes running down the hall. He asks if I'd be willing to come back in a couple of weeks and give a talk to the entire school about bullying, which I tell him I'd be honored to do. When I get into my car and put the key in the ignition, I'm almost too exhausted to drive. It's then I realize the toll this crisis with Kyle has taken on me. It's one thing when helping bullied students like Kyle and their families reminds me of old wounds. It's another when it makes me feel like I'm looking at those wounds with a flashlight. I felt stronger in the dark.

As the day of my talk at Kyle's school approaches, a confluence of events erupts that unexpectedly puts me in the hot seat. The vice principal at Calvin Samuels and several of her staff finally read my book, and though Eileen assures me that they haven't said anything critical and are looking forward to my lecture, I can't help but feel on edge. Something keeps telling me that I should cancel my appearance, but the idea of letting that school get the better of me again is more than I can stomach. Whatever happens, I at least want to be able to tell myself I didn't bolt in the face of fear.

As I'm waking up on the morning of my talk, the phone rings. It's Eileen. There's been a hazing at a powder-puff football game involving the junior and senior girls at a high school on the North Side of Chicago. Apparently, it's an annual student ritual, but this year it got out of hand, with girls throwing garbage, debris, and even excrement at each other, and kids beating each other senseless. Some students landed in the hospital and a group of parents are suing. It's a media circus. The *Chicago Tribune* is planning a feature story and wants a quote from me as an expert.

"The reporter, Barbara Brotman, will contact you in a few minutes," Eileen says.

Seconds after Eileen and I hang up, Barbara calls. One of Chicago's most respected reporters, she finds stories where many of her colleagues wouldn't even think to look. Never one for small talk, she gets right to the point.

"This hazing must conjure up some pretty bad memories," Barbara observes. "According to Eileen, you endured similar abuse when you were in school. Tell me about what you went through."

I describe what my daily life was like during those years. I recount the story of how several members of the popular crowd in sixth grade took turns spitting on me at a party for refusing to play strip spin the bottle with them. I tell her about a physical deformity I had when I was younger that I was able to conceal until, one morning in the locker room after gym, some of the girls saw it while I was changing, and how they and their boy friends cornered me afterward in the hallway, chanting "Freak" over and over, laughing at me. As I relate the highlights of my adolescence, I can hear the clicking of Barbara's keyboard as she types what I'm saying into her computer.

"I can't imagine what it must have been like for you," she says, her tone softening. "Why do you think you were singled out?"

"The same reason all bullied students are," I respond. "For being different."

"Different how?"

As I consider her question, my mind drifts to Kyle,

Selena, and the other lonely, misunderstood children who've blessed me with unexpected enlightenment. The truth of why they struggle so hard to fit in at school and why I always did, too, defies conventional wisdom about bullying and flies in the face of what most experts espouse. *Stop worrying about what this reporter will think of your answers. All you can do is be honest with her. If you don't, you'll be letting yourself and these kids down.*

"The best way I can describe it, Barbara, is having to live with the paradox of being an *Ancient Child*," I reply. She asks me to repeat what I've just said, so she can be sure to get it down correctly in her notes. Buoyed by a sudden surge of confidence, I go on. "The bullied student is typically an old soul, a kid who's blessed or cursed, depending upon how you look at it, with a stronger conscience, and a more evolved sense of compassion and empathy than other kids their age. No matter how hard they try to hide it, in the end the sensitive, thoughtful adult inside them always wins out over the teen who just wants to belong."

"I never thought of it that way," Barbara remarks. "There were a few of those kids in my high school. I could see their faces as you were describing the Ancient Child."

"Were you friends with any of them?" I ask.

I think it may have disarmed her that I posed such a personal question. For a moment, there's silence on the other end of the line.

"No, I wasn't," she says. "I wish I had made more of an effort to reach out. I remember how some of the popular students used to make them the butt of their jokes. It was awful."

"Yeah, it used to happen to me all the time, too. And

what was worse was that the teachers and parents constantly turned a blind eye because these kids were, like, the perfect American teenagers. They were the *Elite Tormentors* of the school and no one saw them for what they really were except the people like me."

"Elite Tormentor, that's an interesting expression," Barbara remarks.

"I think the seniors responsible for turning that hazing into something ugly are perfect examples," I add. "And I understand why the juniors got caught up in it."

I tell Barbara what Noreen, Jacklyn, and Sharon did to me in the middle of the night at my slumber party, and how the image of my face caked in garish makeup, with mustard and ketchup dripping down my neck, still haunts my mom to this day. "Back then, no one used the term 'hazing' about middle or high school. It was merely kids being kids," I say.

"Why on earth didn't you stop them?" she asks.

"For the same reason none of those juniors stopped the seniors at that powder-puff game," I reply. "As much as I hated what they were doing to me, I'd rather be demeaned than excluded, so I convinced myself that it was all in good fun. When you're an adolescent, being accepted by your peer group means everything. No one really thinks about the consequences until it's too late, and then, most of the time, the adults get it wrong anyhow."

"In what way?" Barbara asks.

"What happened at that powder-puff game wasn't about the surge of violence in American culture, as some are suggesting. It was about the desperate need to fit in run amok. I'm not saying some of those seniors didn't enjoy being cruel, but I think many of them felt disgusted but chose to block it out rather than risk being perceived by their friends as wimpy or uncool. The juniors were afraid of the same thing."

"Did any of the girls who hazed you ever express remorse?" Barbara asks.

I describe Noreen's and my friendship today, and how both she and Jacklyn have apologized for what they did.

"A lot of people are concerned that some of the victims of this hazing could be permanently affected," Barbara comments.

"It's possible. But as horrible as this football game was, nobody was individually targeted; it was an entire class, and the abuse was a one-time experience. It's far worse when it's only one victim and she's being beaten down day after day. That person eventually will be consumed by self-loathing. I know firsthand."

As Barbara and I continue talking, I notice a vague sadness descending over me like a cloak. Though I'm grateful for the opportunity to be interviewed by such an influential paper, I resent it, too. Everyone is up in arms about this damn hazing, and, yes, it was terrible, but what about children like Kyle, who don't get the affirmation of news reports proclaiming that the kids who hurt him were wrong? The Kyles and Selenas of the world suffer in silence.

"Oh, my gosh, Barbara, I'm sorry, but we need to wrap this up," I say. "I've got to do an important favor for a little boy named Kyle and I lost track of time."

I can almost hear Barbara's wheels turning as she asks her next question. "Do you have a moment to fill me in?"

As I'm grabbing my purse and getting into the car, I

briefly tell her the story of how I met Kyle and bring her up to date on why I'm rushing to his school today.

"When did you say you were scheduled to begin your talk?"

"In forty minutes," I reply.

"What was the name of that school again?"

I give her the address and the phone number.

"I'm on my way, and I'll get a photographer to meet me there," she says.

Stunned, I call Eileen to let her know. "I'm not surprised," she replies, chuckling.

While I'm driving to Kyle's school, Clarke calls to wish me luck at Samuels the day after tomorrow.

"Are you nervous?" he asks.

"Yes, but it's not having to speak that has me worried. I'm afraid when I walk through the doors of that school the memories will come alive again and I won't be able to get rid of them."

"Do you want me to come with you? I could be your bodyguard."

"And protect me from what, ghosts? I love you for that, but I've got to face this one on my own." Though I don't know it now, I will regret not taking Clarke up on his offer. Memories and flashbacks will be the least of my problems when I get to Samuels.

"I've got to go. I just arrived at Kyle's school."

"Oh, right. You've giving a talk there today. Knock 'em dead, kid."

"Thanks. By the way, if I haven't told you lately, I'm so glad we're friends. It was worth waiting all these years for."

"Me, too. Give me a call after Samuels and let me know how it went, OK?"

"Sure."

I silently make a promise to myself that if and when I choose to move forward on a sequel, I will tell the truth no matter how implausible some of it might seem. All these experiences, from my unlikely friendships with my former classmates and my romance with Mitch to the surprising response from kids and the outpouring from adult survivors since I went public with my story, are all part of a plan. I feel it in my bones, and no matter how disheartened I may become on the days when the work is too overwhelming, I have to remember to hang on. I didn't choose to be an activist. Something larger than what I want chose for me. I have to learn to conquer these damnable flashbacks, master the ability to relive my past in front of audiences, and not be suffocated by the insecurity it conjures up. I am strong, capable, and determined. Now, if I can just get through the next hour.

The moment I walk inside the school, I see Kyle near the main office waiting for me. I ask him how he's feeling. He tells me that he's joined the basketball team like he promised, so it's not as bad as it was before. I tell him I'm proud of him for not giving up. He escorts me into the library, where I'll be speaking. All the tables and chairs have been moved to the back of the room and there are at least three hundred students from grades one through five sitting on the floor in a large circle. The principal and Kyle's counselor greet me warmly. This is the first time I've spoken to students this young, and part of me is concerned that I may not be able to hold their attention. I've also got the added pressure of knowing the biggest newspaper in Chicago will be reporting what happens.

Holding up a copy of my book, the principal introduces me. Kyle is sitting with his class toward the front. He's got this hopeful look on his face, and all I can think of is how much I don't want to disappoint him.

"Hello, everybody, my name is Jodee, and I want to talk to you about a very important subject: bullying. Who here has ever been bullied before?"

A large group of kids raise their hands.

"OK, you can put your hands down now."

As I get ready to relive my elementary school experience, I see Barbara and the photographer walk in. She whispers something to the principal and then takes a seat in the back. The photographer sets up near the front.

"When I was your age, I got bullied a lot. I cried myself to sleep every night because I felt so alone."

Several children stare at me in wide-eyed disbelief. "But you're so pretty," one little girl says. "Why would anybody pick on you?"

I explain that there are different reasons why kids bully, and that how you look doesn't have anything to do with it. Then I launch into the story of Marianne, a deaf student whom I befriended in second grade, and the agonizing choice my classmates forced me to make. "Every day at recess, I'd see Marianne standing by herself, watching the rest of us playing together," I recall. "One afternoon, I asked her if she'd like to go to the park with me."

"How did she understand what you were asking if she couldn't hear?" asks a curious first grader.

"That's an excellent question," I remark. "Does someone know the answer?"

"I know, I know," a girl with long, blond curls says excitedly. "Marianne could read lips!"

"Very good," I tell her. Pleased, she gives me a huge, toothless smile, as I continue my story.

"While Marianne and I were on the swing set, someone from school saw us and told my best friend, Joanne, and the next day at lunch — "

I then transform into the character of Joanne, reenacting the scene.

"If you want to be friends with that freak, then you can't be friends with me!"

The audience gasps.

"Marianne isn't a freak," I respond, switching characters again, this time portraying myself as a child. "She's really nice. Why won't you give her a chance?"

"She can't even talk normal," Joanne snaps.

"That's not Marianne's fault," I retort. "You can understand her if you try."

"Who cares? She's weird and if you keep playing with her, then you can't play with us."

"Joanne was the most popular girl at school," I recall, transforming back into the role of narrator. "Everyone in the cafeteria was taking her side and making fun of me for liking Marianne. They even threw food at me and called me stupid."

"That happened to me, too," cries a redheaded boy with large wire-rimmed glasses. "People can be so cruel!"

I glance over at the principal, who, having recognized an old soul, is staring at him in amazement, quietly chuckling to herself. I didn't think I'd be able to reach these kids as I did the high school students at Marron, but I'm starting to realize that as long as I'm honest and don't try to be the adult who thinks she knows everything I can get through to them. Each one of these little guys is watching me closely, listening to every word.

"Who was really my friend, Marianne or Joanne?" I ask the audience.

"Marianne!" everyone shouts.

"There's something I want to tell you, but I'm afraid once you hear it you won't like me anymore," I confess. "If I do, will you forgive me?"

Several students cast me blank stares. They're so unaccustomed to a grown-up asking for *their* forgiveness that they're unsure how to respond. Though I don't know it now, this moment is one of the most enlightening truths I will learn about reaching kids. Too often, adults won't admit to children that they made a mistake, because they're afraid it will diminish their credibility and make the child feel insecure. But they've got it all wrong. The more human you are — which means allowing yourself to be vulnerable once in a while — the more a child will trust you and open up.

"What did you do?" asks the little boy with the glasses.

"I wasn't as smart as any of you. I didn't understand that Joanne wasn't a true friend. Even though I cared about Marianne, I missed Joanne and my other classmates, and was sad that they weren't including me anymore. So one day at recess, right in front of Joanne, I went up to Marianne and told her she was nothing but a freak and I wouldn't be her friend anymore."

Disillusioned sighs ripple through the room.

"What did Marianne do?" asks one small girl.

"She hung her head and walked away."

Silence. Several children appear on the verge of tears. I can't help but wonder, how can they exude such empathy for Marianne yet still tease and make fun of their classmates, never realizing the pain they're causing?

"By the end of that day," I continue, "everyone had started playing with me again, and Joanne even invited me to a sleepover! You'd think I'd be happy because I got my old friends back. But I couldn't stop thinking about the look on Marianne's face, and how much I hurt her. The next afternoon, I saw her sitting alone at recess. She smiled at me but was afraid to come over. I wanted to run across the schoolyard and tell her I was sorry. But I just stood there, watching her, pretending not to care."

I pause for a moment to survey the library. One boy sitting near Kyle, whom I'd seen making wisecracks earlier, appears unnerved.

"After several days, I couldn't take it anymore," I recall. "I told Joanne and my other classmates that they didn't have the right to choose my friends, and then I apologized to Marianne for turning my back on her."

A group of students sound their approval.

"Did Marianne forgive you?" inquires the little girl with the blond curls.

"Yes," I reply. "Marianne was my *true* friend. How many of you are true friends?"

Dozens of hands eagerly go up in the air. "Now, I want all of you to say these words after me: If somebody makes me be mean to somebody else, they are *not* my true friend!"

They repeat the sentence. "Once more!" I say. They repeat it again, this time filling the library with their voices.

"Very good!" I check my watch and realize that I only have a few more minutes before the bell rings, and I need to find a way to inspire the bullies to acknowledge their behavior.

"OK, kids, let's quiet down," I say. As my mind is racing, trying to come up with a delicate approach to this challenge, out of the corner of my eye I notice a poster on the bulletin board of a policeman in a DARE uniform saving a student, and the answer comes. "Do we all know what a hero is?" I ask my audience.

They all nod their heads.

"But did you know that there are many ways a person can be a hero? You don't have to rescue someone from a burning building or fly like Superman. Being honest even when you're scared you'll get in trouble, or making amends for what you did wrong, can make you a hero. So I'm going to ask a question that some of you might be afraid to answer. But remember, heroes always tell the truth."

I take a deep breath and let my eyes sweep across the audience. "Who here thinks they may have been mean to another person or bullied them, like Joanne did to me or like I did to Marianne?"

A dozen students reluctantly raise their hands. A few more, emboldened by their classmates' forthrightness, follow suit.

"I know that was hard for each of you," I say, motioning for them to put their hands down. "But I'm proud of you for admitting you may have hurt someone. What do you think your next step should be?"

That boy sitting next to Kyle, whom I'd noticed before, appears as if he wants to say something. I watch him struggle, wishing I could help, but knowing that only he can do this for himself. Then he turns and faces Kyle. "We need to tell that person we're sorry and that we want to be friends again," he says.

Kyle, surprised by this unexpected admission, is looking around the room at his classmates, trying to gauge their reaction before responding. I know he's afraid that if he responds in a way his classmates don't think is cool, it could make things worse for him.

"It's OK," he finally replies. "I'm not mad anymore."

I see the principal watching this scene unfold, her expression a mix of joy and relief. At the other end of the library, Barbara is motioning animatedly to the photographer.

"What's your name?" I ask the boy.

"Jordan," he answers.

"Jordan, I think it was wonderful of you to say you're sorry. And, Kyle, you were very gracious to accept his apology, and I know he appreciates it a lot."

Jordan nods his head earnestly.

"You're both heroes today," I say. "Let's hear it for Kyle and Jordan!"

Everyone claps and cheers. I wait for them to settle down, and then continue. "Before I go, I'd like to give you all some advice and then I'll answer a few questions." For the next several minutes, I coach the kids on what to do if they're being bullied, beginning with the importance of eye contact, a fundamental principal of good communication that I'm discovering too many kids don't learn at home or at school.

"You guys are such good listeners," I tell them. "Has anyone been paying attention to where I look when I talk to you?" I walk up to a first grader, bend down, and stare directly at her knee for several seconds. "Have I been speaking to your knee?" I ask. She giggles. I go up to another student and focus my gaze on his nostrils, as if I'm searching for something. "Have I been looking you in the nose hairs?"

"No, that's silly!" he laughs.

"Where *do* I look when I talk to you?" I ask.

"You look us in the eye," Jordan declares.

"Exactly, and looking people in the eye when you speak to them is very important," I explain. "It's a magical power you have to help make others listen to you better. It even works on parents and teachers!" More giggles.

I then continue to explain that sometimes, when a person says or does something mean, they may not know they're hurting your feelings because they think they're just joking around. "That's why it's your responsibility to be honest, and what does being honest make us?"

"Heroes!" exclaim the students in the third grade section.

"Excellent," I reply. "So when someone makes us feel bad, step number one is to look that person —"

"In the eye!" volunteers another exuberant group.

I can feel the excitement of their enthusiasm surging through me.

"Step number two, say, 'Stop, you're hurting my feelings!'"

I raise my arms, gesturing for them to repeat it. Their

small voices, full of conviction, reverberate through the library as they recite the words.

"Step number three, tell an adult."

"But what if you tell an adult and everyone calls you a tattletale?" asks a student in the back row.

"There's a big difference between telling and tattling," I explain. "When a person is nasty or unkind to you, it's not because they hate you; it's because something else in their life is making them angry or sad and they're taking it out on you. When you *tell* an adult, they can help you by making that person stop, but they can also help that person with whatever is bothering them. *Tattling* is when you tell an adult just because you want to get that person into trouble, and that's very, very wrong. Always remember, tattling hurts, telling helps. Can you say that for me?"

"Tattling hurts, telling helps," they repeat, concentrating on each syllable.

"Now, what should you do if someone looks you in the eye and tells you that you've hurt their feelings?"

"Say you're sorry like Jordan did," someone shouts.

"And then you have to forgive them," Kyle reminds everyone.

"What if someone tries to force you to be mean to another person?"

"That person isn't your true friend, and you shouldn't do what they're telling you!" cries one of the fifth graders.

"Who can tell me the different ways someone can be mean?" I ask, suddenly aware that I haven't explained to these kids that bullying isn't only an act of cruelty but also the omission of compassion.

"Yes?" I prompt them, calling on one child after another.

"Making fun of someone!"

"Calling a person names."

"Hitting or pushing."

"Spitting is awful," a girl in the back row blurts out.

"Anything else?" No one answers. "What about ignoring somebody, letting them sit alone at lunch or never inviting them to play with you? Isn't that mean, too?" I see a handful of students begin to squirm. Satisfied that I've gotten my message across, I ask my audience to review each one of the steps they've just been taught, then I take questions, some of which are tough to endure.

A diminutive child with dark circles under her eyes, who has kept to herself during the entire presentation, beckons for me to call on her. "Yes, sweetheart, what would you like to know?"

"What do you do if the adult is the one being mean to you?" she asks.

I don't want to make her uncomfortable by asking her to divulge the details in front of her classmates, but I'm worried there may be abuse going on in her home. I look over at the principal, who is also concerned.

"You tell another adult you trust. If it's a teacher who's hurting your feelings you would tell your mommy or daddy, and if it was your mommy or daddy you would tell a teacher. Because remember, whatever that adult is doing to make you feel bad, it's not because they want to hurt you. Something else may be bothering them that you don't know about. By telling another adult, you help everyone."

"Would I be a hero?" she says hopefully.

"Yes, a very big hero," I answer, making a mental note to

be sure to follow up with her later on.

By now, dozens of kids are raising their hands, wanting to be heard. I notice the photographer snapping pictures, and Barbara jotting down notes. Part of me feels that they're violating these children's trust, another is happy for Kyle and his family and what this will mean to them.

The little girl with the blond curls has started hopping up and down, wanting me to call on her. "Yes, honey, what would you like to ask?"

"My mommy is in a special hospital for sad people, and I was wondering if you could tell me how to make her happy so she could come home."

I can't catch my breath to speak. What do I tell this child? She's asking me something there isn't any simple answer to. Practice what you preach, I tell myself. Just be honest.

"What's your name?"

"Kaitlin," she replies.

"Kaitlin, did you ever fall and get a bruise?" I ask.

"Yes, when I was at the playground I tripped by the sand-box and the next day there was this huge bruise on my leg."

"Was Mom or Dad able to make it go away?"

"No, Mom put ice on it to make it feel better but she said that it had to heal on its own."

"Your mom's sadness is like that bruise, except it's on the inside," I explain. "No one can make it go away. It has to heal on its own like yours did. But, like Mom made you feel better with the ice, you can make her feel better, too, by showing her how much you love her."

"What if I make her an extra-special card when I get

home from school today that Daddy can bring her when he visits?" she says.

"I think Mom would really like that," I tell her, wondering if the school was aware of her situation and how it might be able to help. I will find out later from the principal that Kaitlin's mother has been battling depression on and off for years, and that the school psychologist is concerned that Kaitlin may be exhibiting early signs of the disease. I will meet so many other children like Kaitlin, and my heart will ache for each and every one of them. That's why when I finally do burn out from this work, I'll feel so disillusioned.

The principal gives me a sign that it's time to wrap things up. "All right, kids, it's time for me to go. I want to thank you for being the best audience ever. I'd like you to give yourselves a gigantic round of applause." Everyone smiles and claps, and I'm moved by how wise yet vulnerable they all are. "Before I leave, I want you to know that I wouldn't have been here today if it wasn't for Kyle." A group of his classmates begin shouting, "Yay, Kyle!" I savor the look on his face as he digests this acceptance. Then they ask him if they can meet me. A beaming Kyle introduces us. Suddenly, dozens of kids are approaching us, asking for my autograph. "Can you sign my lunchbox?" a little girl asks. "Hey, what about my gym shoe, can you sign that?" a boy inquires.

The reporter makes her way toward us with the principal. "Kyle, may I speak with you?" she asks. Kyle looks at me expectantly. "Go on, Kyle," I encourage him. "This is *your* day."

For a moment, he hesitates. "Could it be Jordan's day, too?" he asks.

"Absolutely," Barbara replies.

The next morning, I receive a call from Barbara Brotman. She tells me that instead of a feature on the North Side hazing, the *Chicago Tribune* wants to run a story on Kyle, the courageous boy who took on the bullies and inspired a change of heart at his school, and the local author who made it possible. She also wants to mention several specific bullying incidents from my past.

"You're not going to do anything on the hazing incident?" I ask, surprised.

"I'll refer to it in the context that if there were more students like Kyle and Jordan hazings might stop."

As I'm feeling triumphant, she hits me with a bombshell. "By the way, I'll need the actual names of the schools you attended."

"Barbara, do you know what you're asking? There's a reason I changed all the names and dates in my book."

"I understand, but if you don't give them to us my editor will kill the story. You were a publicist. Surely you understand."

"When will it run?"

"The end of this week," she replies. "Jodee, I realize you're afraid of stirring up a hornet's nest, but —"

"Barbara, the day after tomorrow I'm giving a lecture at a teacher in-service day for my old high school!"

"You're kidding."

"No, and the school is already queasy about it. Can you imagine when they read this article? It'll look like I'm a hypocrite who came to their school pretending to be above it all just so I could turn around and slam them in a newspaper article two days later."

"I feel for you," Barbara says. "But do you really want to lose this piece? Think how disappointed the kids will be."

Knowing I have no alternative, I list each school by name.

"I'll be fair," Barbara says reassuringly.

"I know you will."

"Can I ask you something, though, off the record?"

"Sure," I reply.

"Why do you care what anyone thinks? The truth is that what happened to you could have been prevented if the adults in your school didn't have their heads up their butts. Why do you feel this need to protect them from the facts?"

"It's me I'm trying to protect. I still have to live in this community."

"It'll be OK," she says. "You're doing the right thing."

I sure hope she's right.

chapter eleven

A Soldier
Returns to the
Place of Battle

May - August 2003

I'm sitting in the parking lot of my old high school, nervous as hell. What if I have a flashback? What if I can't handle the rage it unleashes? Dear God, *why* did I agree to this stupid invitation? Then again, maybe Barbara Brotman has a point. Why should I worry about what anyone inside that building thinks? No one protected me from it when it was happening. Why should I care about protecting *them* from it now? No matter what, I refuse to let a bunch of teachers who turned their backs on me make me feel less than who I am. They're the ones who were in the wrong, not me.

Having mustered the necessary courage, I turn off the engine, get out of the car, and walk with purposeful steps toward the large glass doors that mark the front entrance of Calvin Samuels. The district has done tens of millions of dollars in additions and renovations, but the ghosts of my past still linger beneath the new architecture. Terrified but unwilling to retreat, I open the door and walk inside.

I am standing in the commons room. A handful of teachers are drinking coffee and chatting by a buffet area. It is strange being in this room as an adult. There are no voices shouting across tables mocking me, no classmates whispering to each other and snickering as I pass them, no smell of grilled-cheese sandwiches wafting from the kitchen, no school bell followed by the scraping of metal chairs across the floor and a rush of stomping feet as students scurry to class, no Styx or REO blaring out of the jukebox that used to sit near the vending machines, where A.J. and Sharon would hide and then plaster my hair with bubble gum, no cheerleaders preening in the lavatory, no trace of strawberry lip gloss. That was all a lifetime ago.

Then why does it still feel so immediate? Samuels may look bigger and brighter, wearing its tax dollars like a ballerina flouncing an expensive tutu, but underneath her twirling skirts are the same clumsy legs that were always there. And the population has almost doubled from the three thousand students when I was there. As I make my way toward the auditorium, the clicking of my heels echoing down the empty corridor, images are being sparked, electric jabs of pain from memories I wish would stay dormant, now awakened and unstoppable.

"Hey, ugly thing, got asked to the prom yet?"

"Oh, Jodee, want to hang out with us at the mall? Right, like THAT would ever happen."

"Loser!"

"Bitch!"

"Worthless, stupid, priss!"

No, please stop! I hate this school and everyone in it. You're sucking me dry. One day you will pay for what you've done to me. I will make you bleed. Do you all hear me? I will MAKE YOU BLEED!

I'm beginning to sweat through my blouse. I can't seem to get enough oxygen. Everything around here is too familiar. Despite how much this place has changed, it hasn't. The photos of star athletes decorating the hallways, the attendance charts on the classroom doors, the sign-in sheet hanging outside Dean Muldar's office, the trophy case by the gym.

"Mom, why can't I have the surgery this year?"I ask, tossing yet another bathing suit onto the growing pile of failures scattered across the dressing-room floor that I've been trying on for the past hour.

"Honey, you know what the plastic surgeon said. He can't do anything until you're more fully developed. He says that next year, when you're seventeen, he should be able to schedule the procedure."

"Look at me," I cry, the bikini top I've just put on hanging limply across my chest on one side. "I can't stand being this freak for another year! And I hate having to wear special bras. They only make me look more deformed."

"Jodee, if this is about gym class again, you know I can talk to the school and get you excused."

"What good will that do? Everyone will just use it as another reason to make fun of me."

"Honey, I promise, by the time you start college this will all be behind you. Soon your whole world will open up. Can't you at least try and be more positive in the meantime?"

"I can't even buy a bathing suit like a normal person! The kids at school are right. I should have been a miscarriage!"

My stomach is threatening to betray me. I close my eyes and imagine that I'm at Kamari Beach on the Greek island of Santorini, my toes immersed in the coarse black sand, the cool, clear waters of the Aegean licking at my ankles. When I was fifteen, my dad took my mom and me there for a family vacation. I fell in love with the people and the culture, and have been returning faithfully to the island ever since. I even learned the language. Sometimes, if I pretend I'm there, it helps me cope. "*Sigha, sigha,* easy, easy," I whisper to myself. "*Tha perasi,* this will pass." Within moments, I can feel the nausea subsiding. I slowly open my eyes.

A conservatively dressed woman is hurrying toward me carrying a clipboard, her smile forced.

"Ms. Blanco? We haven't met yet. I'm Vice Principal Collins."

"It's wonderful to finally meet you," I reply, shaking her hand. "Thank you for inviting me to speak today. I'll do my best to make my alma mater proud."

"Have you spoken to Eileen this morning?" she asks.

"My cell phone doesn't work well here. Why?"

"There's a formal protest against your giving the keynote speech today," she says.

"I assumed a few of the faculty might be a little uncomfortable, but an actual protest? Why?"

"There's concern that you're going to use this opportunity to teacher-bash."

"How hostile a protest are we talking about here?"

"If you decide not to proceed, I'll completely understand."

"You sound as if that's what you're *hoping* will happen!"

"Well, in all honesty — "

"Dr. Collins, this year at Samuels there were five student suicides. Can you tell me with absolute certainty that *none* of them were bullying-related?"

She looks away, unable to respond.

"What I have to say to you and your staff today could help prevent similar tragedies in the future. If anyone has a problem with that, let them call me on it."

"Oh dear, I hope I haven't given you the impression that the *entire* faculty is against your being here," she says.

"No, just the ones who used to be my teachers, right?"

Her silence is all the confirmation I need. "Please assure your staff that I have no intention of bashing anybody and unless someone plans on physically removing me from the premises before I take that stage, you'll all just have to trust me," I say.

For a moment, the vice principal appears to want to say something, but then thinking better of it, turns and walks away. I can't help but feel a sense of poetic justice. For four years, I spent every Monday through Friday from 8:00 to 3:00 in fear, wishing I could hide. When I'm handed the microphone this morning, that's how some of my former teachers will feel. Maybe now they'll finally be able to understand how hard it was for me back then, and it will be the impetus they need to help their current students.

"Is that Jodee Blanco?" calls out a familiar voice.

"Oh, my God, Ms. *Redson*?"

A gangly blonde with large green eyes and a quirky sense of humor, she was my favorite history teacher. Ms. Redson

188

always had a magical way with kids, especially those who were struggling to fit in. A product of the post-hippie movement of the seventies, she was the faculty outcast at Samuels, and often got snubbed by colleagues and administration for her progressive ideals. While the other teachers bristled when a student questioned one of their lessons, Ms. Redson encouraged us to challenge what we read in textbooks. She made me realize early on that standing up to authority with respect was my human right. When I started college, I was ahead of my classmates because of her influence.

"You look amazing," I exclaim, hugging her. "You haven't changed at all!"

"You're too kind," she replies, blushing. "By the way, congratuations on the book! You should be proud. I'm really looking forward to hearing you today."

"You may be the only one," I reply.

"Honey, don't let a bunch of old fogies get you down."

"Thanks," I reply, smiling.

"Samuels has never been easy," she says. "It's cliquish. The adults are worse than the kids."

"Why didn't you leave? Any other school would have been thrilled to get you."

"I always felt the students here needed me more because I'm one of the few teachers not afraid to defend the defenseless."

"I can't believe this school isn't kissing your butt!"

"Kicking it is more like it," she replies. "I'm retiring this year. I doubt many of my colleagues will be sorry to see me go."

"Your students will."

"Yes, and that's why I've put up with this place for as long as I have. But it's worn me out. You have no idea the bullying at the faculty level. It's no wonder students are getting away with it, too."

"It's gotten that treacherous for teachers?"

"Not all, just those of us irreverent educators who won't play politics."

"I like that, *Irreverent Educator.*"

"You can put it in your next book!" Ms. Redson says. Her voice taking on a more somber tone, she looks over at Dr. Collins, who's by the check-in table. "Jodee, please be careful. I don't trust these people. You're not the only person this school has failed. Anyone who's outspoken and honest around here pays a price." Then, grabbing my hand and squeezing it, she says, "You knock 'em dead up there, and don't you dare hold anything back."

As I watch her walk away, I'm filled with a sense of awe and regret. I should have stayed in touch. I can't imagine what she must have gone through, dealing with the narrow-mindedness that has always plagued this school district. I won't let her commitment to her students go unacknowledged.

Teachers are streaming into the theater. I decide to make a quick dash to the ladies' room. The faculty's is locked, so I'm forced to use the students'. As I stand in front of the same mirror where I first began to hate my reflection, rinsing my hands at the sink I used to sit on during lunch, wolfing down candy bars in exile, I can feel the present giving way to a pull inside me, dragging me backward in time.

Sharon is burning my wrist with a lit cigarette. Nadia and Jacklyn are giving each other high fives as they watch me crawling around on the floor near the toilets gathering the contents of my purse. Shelly and her friends are staring at me as I wash the ink off my skin from the broken pen that A.J. snuck into my coat pocket. . . .

I need to find a way to make these memories stop; I fumble in my bag for my checkbook. With trembling fingers, I open it up to the calendar page and locate today's date, focusing on the part where it says "2003," reading it over and over. Then, taking a deep breath, I drop the checkbook back into my bag and make my way to the theater.

The sound engineer approaches and hands me a cordless microphone. Vice Principal Collins steps up to the podium and briefly introduces me as the author of *Please Stop Laughing at Me . . .*, and a former graduate of Calvin Samuels. I walk out onto the stage. No one smiles or claps. Some teachers are grading papers on their laps and don't even look up. It's clear these teachers wish they were anywhere but here. I see many familiar faces. Their antagonism toward me is palpable. I'll always be the outcast at Samuels, but oddly, I now find comfort in that role. Being accepted here is no notable achievement. I ache for every student at this school who's different, and for the teachers who feel for them but are too intimidated by the faculty bullies to act.

Realizing that I'll never get anywhere with this audience until I deal with the pink elephant in the room, I decide to skip the pleasantries. "I know many of you gulped when you heard I'd be giving the keynote today," I say. "It's OK. I'm scared, too. Just being back in this place is terrifying for me, let alone having to address six hundred of you."

Nothing.

"I'm aware that there was a formal protest and that a large group of you petitioned to have this event canceled."

My language-arts teacher, who had been listening with smug detachment, suddenly bristles. A few rows down, the algebra instructor, who would put me on the spot at the chalkboard and then laugh with my classmates while I struggled, shrinks down into his seat. At the other end of the theater, several of the gym teachers are exchanging worried glances. Disquieted by her staff's growing uneasiness, Dr. Collins leans over and says something to the principal, who then gets up and stands directly in my line of vision, arms folded stiffly across his chest, eyes boring into me.

"Please try and understand how it must feel to be on this stage and know you're not welcome. Ladies and gentlemen, that says something about me, but it says even more about all of you. I respect each and every one of you enough to be here today despite how hard this is for me."

A few people nod their heads sympathetically, while others, still unconvinced, are maintaining their icy demeanors.

"I loved learning," I continue. "You have students who are just like I was. They adore you and want to learn, but hate school because they're always at the mercy of their classmates. Back when I was your student, there was no one to help you understand what the outcast goes through. None of us can fix the past, but together we can help your students today avoid what I had to endure."

As I say these words, I survey the theater, gauging the

audience's response. Dean Muldar is in the first row, chatting on his cell phone. Astounded by his rudeness, I stop speaking until he finally looks up and realizes that I'm staring at him. Smiling at me through clenched teeth, he puts his phone away and then focuses straight ahead. My freshman biology teacher, Ms. Raine, turns and stares at the chagrined dean and then, in an exaggerated gesture meant for everyone to see, gives me two thumbs-up. Suddenly, it's as if someone has thrown open a window in the theater and let out the stale air. Some of the teachers who had been exuding indifference are suddenly paying attention. Several of the old guard are glaring at the principal.

Come on, Jodee, just keep going.

Taking a deep breath, I get ready to enter the forbidden domain of our shared past, praying I can open hearts that have been so long closed, the hinges have rusted shut. As I'm contemplating how best to begin, I notice several of the athletic coaches dozing in their seats. One is actually snoring! Incensed, I walk across the stage to where they're sitting and look directly at them. "I hope you don't think this is rude," I say. "But it's not easy getting up here. It's hard just being in this building. I know many of you are tired and would rather be home. If that's the case, please leave. I won't be offended. But if you nap while I'm here trying to help you, it will offend everyone in this theater."

There's a small burst of applause. I will soon learn that little has changed since I was a student, and that the administration still panders to the athletic department, creating great dissonance among all the other staff.

"When I arrived today, I was assaulted by terrifying

images from when I was a student at Samuels, and it was all I could do not to run," I say. "I wonder how many of your current students would experience the same thing if they had to come back here twenty years from now. That's the effect that peer abuse can have on someone, even those students, like me, who go out and conquer the world afterward, because inside, that sixteen-year-old who's afraid of being rejected is lying dormant, one jeer away from awakening."

I pause and look out into the audience. "How many kids at this school are having their self-esteem bludgeoned every day while some of you refuse to intervene, convinced that it's all just a normal part of growing up?"

I see guilt flash across several faces.

"I'm here to tell you that it isn't. Bullying can damage a student for life, and it's often the most subtle forms that wreak the greatest havoc later on."

Realizing there's only one way to prove this point and silence the naysayers, I lay bare my own demons. I relate the disturbing episode in the bathroom before I went onstage and how I had to see printed evidence of today's date in order to pull myself out of the dark place my mind had gone. I describe the flashbacks I experienced in the commons and again when I passed the trophy case by the gym. I reveal that this wasn't the first time, recounting what happened when I visited Marron and how the memories evoked moments when I couldn't distinguish between the present and the past. I admit how I almost threw up when Vice Principal Collins warned me about the protest, and how, if it hadn't been for the encouraging words of one of their colleagues, I wouldn't have had the courage to go through with this lecture. There's a murmur of curiosity as everyone begins looking around, attempting to determine which faculty member I'm talking about.

"I know how much more difficult your jobs have become since the inception of the No Child Left Behind Act, and how overburdened you must often feel," I offer. "But don't let the harsh realities of our school system make you forget why you became teachers in the first place. As educators, each and every one of you has the ability to achieve immortality! Government policies come and go. School boards change. But the impact you have on a student is forever."

I walk out into the audience. "I don't remember how to do a quadratic equation," I say to the math teacher who helped me overcome my algebra phobia. "Nor do I remember the anatomy of a fern," I add, smiling at Ms. Raine. Then I turn for a moment and look at Ms. Redson. "But I do remember the life lessons my teachers taught me, like when to take a position against injustice and when to admit defeat with grace, how to find courage when you need it most, the difference between compassion that empowers and compassion that disables, how to push beyond your limits, how to rise to a challenge with confidence, and how to make your mark against the odds. You can change the world one child at a time, your influence passing from generation to generation."

I can feel a swell of enthusiasm, and I'm tempted to conclude the talk on this motivational note, but I realize I would be cheating all of us if I did that. Taking a deep breath, I begin to explore my experiences at Samuels, how I wish things had been handled then, and how they could be handled now. Some of my former teachers who ignored me when I first started speaking are now engrossed, a mix of regret and hope etched across their faces. Should I do it? I ask myself. Should I bring it up?

As images of the only classmates who ever meant anything to me at this school flood my memory, I delve into one of the most controversial episodes from my past. I recount how one afternoon my social studies teacher, a man who was badly deformed with spina bifida, casually referred to the students with Down's syndrome in the special-ed department as "rubber heads." I recall how I took this teacher to task, resulting in a districtwide scandal that forced him to make a formal apology to the school board. At the time, almost every faculty member in this theater turned their backs on me for going against one of their own. Though I wrote about it in *Please Stop Laughing at Me . . .* I never disclosed how truly brutal some of my teachers were afterward, how they would witness me getting bullied in their classrooms and, instead of intervening, actually encouraged the students who were assaulting me.

"I didn't revisit this painful event to make any of you feel bad," I say. "I addressed it because I don't want today's special-ed students to face the same prejudice those I defended did because of one thoughtless teacher who, more than anybody, should have known better. I hope that you will keep that in mind the next time you hear anyone make a disparaging remark about a group of students already facing adversity." As I hold my breath, wondering if I went too far by opening up an old wound, the head of the special-ed department stands and begins to clap. Others join in. Soon the applause is so loud I have to tap on the microphone to quiet the audience.

"Thank you for listening to me today. I know for some of you it wasn't easy. Before I leave, there's one specific teacher I wish to acknowledge, because without her I would not be where I am today. Ms. Redson, could you please rise and accept the public thank-you that you so deserve?" As the faculty loner for twenty-five years is finally shown the love and respect she has earned, some of her colleagues are beaming for her. Others are looking down, clearly self-conscious. It will not be the last time I make people uncomfortable in this district.

As I take a bow, I feel proud that I was able to overcome my fears and reach the most intimidating audience I've ever had. While I'm in the lobby, a few teachers approach me, wanting my advice. They confide that the athletic coaches have the administration in a stronghold, and that they're often coerced into decisions that aren't in the best interest of their students. One teacher confesses that last year the head football coach demanded she give a varsity player who was failing her class a passing grade so that he could play in the homecoming game. When she refused, the school put so much pressure on her, she was forced to acquiesce. I tell her that she was as wrong as the coach for not standing her ground. "Keep going up the chain of command until you find the support you need," I explain. "If you reach the school-board level and you're still not satisfied with the result, try the education writer at the local paper. You'd be amazed how quickly people reset their moral compass when a journalist is asking them questions."

"I never would have thought of that," she admits.

"By the way, if any of you ever find yourselves in a situation like that again, or need assistance with a bullied student, here's my cell phone number. I would be honored to help." As they're writing down my number, a young teacher taps me on the shoulder, requesting a moment alone with me.

"Ms. Blanco, I'm Penny Lawson. I'm the one who recommended you to Vice Principal Collins."

"I'm pleased to meet you," I reply.

"I wanted to thank you for coming today. Your speech made quite an impact. I know this audience was rough, but I hope you found this to be a rewarding experience."

"In more ways than you can imagine," I reply.

"I wanted to give you this," she says, handing me a flat box with a ribbon around it.

When I open it, I'm moved to tears. It's a copy of the 1982 yearbook.

"When I read in your book what Tyler did to yours, I started searching for it," she explains. "I know it can't make up for what happened that day, but maybe it can help."

"This is one of the most thoughtful gifts I've ever received," I respond, hugging her. I see in this young woman what I hope is the future of schools like Calvin Samuels, where the teachers who taught me are its past.

As I leave the building holding my yearbook, envisioning how much fun it will be getting my friends to sign it, I can't help but marvel at the unpredictability of life. Twenty years ago, I was running across this very same lot, clutching the very same yearbook, but instead of looking forward to having it signed, all I could think about was getting home so I could burn it. Sitting in the car, I trace the edges of the yearbook with my fingers, contemplating today's events. Toward the end of my talk, as I was gazing into the faces of my former teachers, I could feel rage rising in my throat. A part of me wonders if I let them off too easily this afternoon. Dismissing the notion, I drive to my office, not knowing that this community will be asking that question of themselves in the not distant future, and that a young girl's life will depend on the answer.

As the school year comes to a close and the demands on my time begin to lift, my relationship with Mitch and his daughters deepens and grows. I had dreamed of going to a rock concert and sitting on a blanket in the grass under a warm July sky, kissing a guy I was mad about. Mitch, knowing that was a part of high school I never got to experience, takes me to see the bands I listened to back then. I never imagined that my fantasy would come true all these years later on the arm of the boy I saw every time I closed my eyes. We take the children to carnivals and water parks, spend long, lazy afternoons at the beach building sand castles and talking about the future. It is an idyllic summer, full of giggles and intimate embraces, parties with friends and family barbecues. Despite how exciting New York and Hollywood were, they can't compare with the joy I discover finally being able to lead a life I hope will be defined by its normality.

chapter twelve

Our Maiden

Voyage

September – October 2003

The tranquillity of summer has become a distant memory as Eileen and I head out on our first national speaking tour. Having been on countless tours as a publicist, I thought I would be ready for whatever happened, but it's different being on this side of the enterprise. We're at the airport, about to catch our flight to Virginia. I'll be speaking to students at more than a dozen schools on the East Coast over the next week, plus media interviews. Next month we visit the mid-Atlantic, and then round out the tour before Thanksgiving back in the Midwest. Eileen and I both think we know what to expect. The truth is, neither of us has a clue what we're in for and we've begun to disagree, her wanting to do things her way . . . me insisting that since I'm the experienced one we should be doing them my way. On top of the personal tension, we're also dealing with the reality of how difficult the tour was to arrange. Eileen had encountered unanticipated resistance.

Many of the principals and counselors with whom she spoke said they couldn't find funding. Others adamantly denied that there was a bullying problem in their district, despite the fact that it was their own students and teachers who invited us to come. Many administrators didn't even bother to return Eileen's calls. Some were downright rude. I can tell that Eileen is still raw from the experience. By the end of July, she had talked directly with hundreds of decision-makers, many of whom strung her along until the last minute and then said no. Though in the end our schedule is a good beginning, she was counting on a packed schedule without any breaks and a waiting list of people eager to get me.

Eileen believes in me with such ferocity that I sometimes find myself getting so caught up in her enthusiasm it momentarily blinds me to the truth about this business — that it can take years to build a speaking career. In light of the apathy from the schools Eileen has to fight, I feel fortunate to have the engagements we've got. I'm hoping that, once this leg is over, word of mouth will have spread and the spring tour will start falling into place. The bills are piling up, and neither one of us has any other source of income.

As Eileen and I make our way onto the plane and settle into our seats, we're trying to be patient with each other. I know she probably thinks I've been coming on like a steamroller, but most of what she's been struggling to learn these past few months is second nature to me, and if I didn't scrutinize her progress, I'd be cheating us both. But getting Eileen to see it that way isn't easy, and as her friend I'm conscious of not wanting to bruise her ego.

"Please forgive me if I was inconsiderate this morning," I say. "I'm just so used to being the one in control on the road, and the adjustment is tough."

"I understand," she replies. "But I really am doing the best I can. Imagine how I feel knowing that whatever I do, no matter how hard I try, you could do it better and probably have."

"I'm sorry. I never thought of it that way. It's just that I'm worried if something does go wrong you'll want to protect me from it instead of taking advantage of my experience and letting me help."

"I promise I won't keep you in the dark about anything if you promise not to take over; otherwise, we'll never learn how to make this work."

"Deal," I reply, relieved.

As we clink our Styrofoam cups, toasting our agreement, part of me feels that I wouldn't want to take on the American school system alone and that I'm blessed to have this woman in my life. Another part wonders if I wouldn't be better off doing this on my own, without having to worry about anyone else other than the students. This will not be the first time I ask myself this question. What I don't know now is that Eileen will entertain similar doubts in the not distant future.

The rest of the flight, we review the profile of each school where I'll be speaking. Scattered throughout the week are several middle schools. This is the only grade level I haven't presented to yet, and I'm looking forward to it. I suspect that these are the kids who will benefit the most from our time together. For high school students, freedom is more imminent. Middle school children still have the prospect of high school looming in front of them, and when you're already lonely and miserable that can seem like a death sentence.

Eileen and I are met in baggage claim by Susan Peterson, the president of the local PTA. A petite redhead impeccably dressed in a cream-colored silk suit, she seems more like an executive on a mission than a mom working on behalf of a school. Eileen whispers in my ear that she was the one responsible for pushing the superintendent to approve the funding for us, and that she has enormous influence on the school board in this district.

Eileen had also explained to me about PTA moms, how some are dedicated parents who genuinely care about making a difference in their community, while others are looking to build their own social status through their children's popularity at school and care little or nothing about improving the quality of education for students. The moment Susan begins talking, I realize she is one of the latter. By the time we reach our hotel, I know more about her daughter's travails on the cheerleading squad than I do about the district itself, student needs I should be addressing, or problems I should be aware of. Though Eileen tries to steer her toward these questions, Susan keeps going back to her daughter and how the coach keeps passing her up when assigning the plum cheer routines. "My daughter is so popular, why doesn't she ask some of the other girls to back her up with the coach?" she complains. "She's letting everyone walk all over her, and I just don't understand it. Maybe you could talk to her."

"I'd be happy to speak with your daughter, but I wonder, is it possible that she just doesn't like cheerleading all that much?" I ask.

"I've been grooming her for this since she was little," Susan says. "It's what we've always wanted."

"Were you a cheerleader?"

"I never had Anna's talent," she says sighing. "There's no limit to how far that girl could go if she'd only apply herself."

"I'll talk to her but I'm going to tell her what I believe she needs to hear. If you're OK with that, set up a time."

As she's leaving a message on her daughter's cell phone, I shake my head. This woman is so self-involved, it hasn't occurred to her that I may not agree with her point of view. She's in for a surprise. I will meet many parents who are trying to relive their youth through their children. It's bad enough these teens have to navigate the difficulties of adolescence; it's unfair that they have the added burden of knowing their parents' sense of completeness is dependent upon them, too. I was lucky. My mom and dad were supportive, but they didn't smother me with the weight of *their* hopes and dreams; they let me have my own.

The next morning, on the way to my first speaking engagement, I notice that Eileen is distracted. I ask her what's wrong.

"I'm starting to have second thoughts about the schedule this week. You've never had this many back-to-back talks before. I wonder if I should have spread them out more."

"Why? It's more efficient this way, and besides, the schools wouldn't pay for any additional hotel nights."

"I know, but I'm concerned about the emotional toll it could take on you."

"It'll be OK," I say. "I'm starting to recognize the signs when I'm going into flashback and I'm getting much better at pulling myself out." I describe how at Samuels I used my checkbook register to force myself back to the present. Then, taking my wallet out of my purse, I flip to the calendar and show Eileen the page with today's date circled in red at the top. "I also have Clarke and Shelly's numbers in my speed dial, and I've warned them both that I may need to call them and to keep their cell phones on. I've already prepped them on what I'll need them to say to me when I call."

"All right, but if for any reason you become overwhelmed you've got to let me know. *Promise me,* Jodee."

"I swear."

I can tell she's not convinced.

"Wow, look at that," Eileen says, pointing ahead.

There's a huge sign at the front entrance to the school that reads: WELCOME AUTHOR JODEE BLANCO. Underneath is the title of my book and a list of my appearances in the district. Delighted, I curse myself for not bringing along a camera, when all of a sudden, Eileen whips one out of her purse and begins snapping pictures. I smile and shake my head. "Am I *ever* going to be one step ahead of you?" I ask.

"I hope not," she replies. "Then you'll really be impossible to live with!"

As we're getting out of the car, I see Susan coming toward us. Accompanying her is a beautiful, lanky blonde in a cheerleading uniform. "I'd like you to meet my daughter, Anna," Susan says. "She's a sophomore. Anna, this is Jodee, the woman I've been telling you about."

"It's good to meet you," I say, shaking Anna's hand. Her eyes dart nervously between her mother and me as if she's expecting to be embarrassed. "I hear you're quite the athlete."

"Don't believe everything my mom tells you," she says. "She makes too big a deal out of stuff."

"Anna!" Susan interjects.

"It's OK," I say. "Your daughter's humility is refreshing. I meet a lot of kids who are too full of themselves."

"See, Mom?" Anna says.

Susan, miffed, changes the subject and begins telling me about the school and what to expect from my first audience. She explains that I'll be speaking to sixth, seventh, and eighth graders, and that while these kids are generally well behaved, there's a group who can be difficult but that their teachers will keep them in line.

"Actually, I prefer if the teachers just enjoy the presentation and let me take care of any necessary discipline in the audience," I reply.

"You'd have to discuss that with the principal, and I'm afraid he's not here," she says.

"The principal won't be at the presentation?" Eileen asks.

"No, unfortunately, all the administrators and counselors in the district will be stuck in mandatory meetings most of the day," Susan explains.

"Then why wasn't my talk scheduled on a different day?" I ask, panicked, envisioning the chaos at Marron. "My presentation is intense, and many kids react very strongly. It's a mistake for the principal, and especially the counselors, not to be there."

"I know what happened at the high school in Pennsylvania, but we don't have those kinds of problems here."

"Then why have I received e-mails from students in this district telling me that you do?"

"Kids can be so dramatic," she says. "I'm sure the teachers can handle it, and most of the PTA will be there as well. Between all of us, I'm sure we can meet whatever needs arise.

"One more thing," Susan adds. "We'll need you to shorten your presentations to thirty-five minutes each."

"I can't — that's impossible," I reply.

"I'm sorry, but the faculty feels an hour is too long to keep the students' attention and it won't allow for any discussion time at the end of class."

"But I'll never be able to deliver my message in that short a time!"

"The decision's already been made," Susan snaps. "There's absolutely nothing I can do."

"What if you edit out a few of the stories?" Eileen suggests hopefully. I realize Eileen's been working hard on this appearance for months and she's nervous about losing it, plus she's worried about how it could affect my reputation as a speaker if a talk were canceled the first week I'm on tour. As much as I empathize with her position, I have to do what I know is right.

"Eileen, you more than anyone know I just don't get up there and speak. I pour out my *heart* to these kids, and it won't work if I have to rush through it!"

Acknowledging that she understands with a subtle nod of her head, she turns to Susan and says, "Either my author gets the hour promised by the school or we leave."

"*Excuse* me?"

"Susan, please," I interject. "If you'll let me have the full hour, I promise you'll be grateful you did."

"I really don't have the authority to make that decision," she hedges.

"Susan, clearly the people of this district have tremendous respect for you or they wouldn't have made you responsible for this event," Eileen points out. "I think you underestimate your influence."

At these words, Susan's demeanor visibly shifts. I have to give Eileen credit. She uses flattery like a jouster wielding a sword. I imagine all five feet of her in a suit of armor, brandishing her weapon, light refracting off the blade. "*En garde!*" comes her cry against the enemy bending them to her will.

"Well, I suppose I *could* explain to the teachers —" Susan acquiesces. While she excuses herself to call the faculty director, I walk over to Eileen, who's still fuming.

"Can you believe her?" she says.

"What would we have done if she hadn't given in?" I say. "There's nothing in our contract that says a school can't change the schedule."

"There will be from now on," Eileen says. "By the way, I'm sorry about back there, I —"

"It's OK," I respond. "I understand."

"I guess the learning curve this trip is going to be steeper for me than I thought."

"For both of us," I add.

"All settled," Susan says, returning.

As we enter the main building and make our way toward the gym, I brace myself for the first wave of memories. This time, I tell myself, I won't let them win. Though images from seventh and eighth grades begin flying through my head, they don't push me out of the present. My mind isn't succumbing to that dark place. Encouraged, I welcome my surroundings, appreciating the sights and sounds that a few months ago would have made me tremble. Then something unlocks itself inside me and pleasant memories begin tugging at the edges of my consciousness: the crisp smell of a brand-new textbook just out of the cellophane wrapper;

enjoying a Jolly Rancher candy in math class and dreaming about watermelon in summer; feeling my hands wrapped around the cool base of the trophy I won for taking first place in the national speech competition in eighth grade. For the first time, I'm inside a school and I'm not sick to my stomach. I look out across the empty gym and wonder, does this sense of peace I'm experiencing mean that I'm finally learning how to reconcile my past with my new vocation, or is it just a fluke, and when I least expect it, the terror will return? I'm immersed in my thoughts when I feel someone tapping on my shoulder. I turn and see Anna, who asks if she could have a private moment.

"I read your book," she says. "I could really relate to it. I'm going through a lot of the things you did."

"Does your mom know?" I ask.

"Are you kidding? She thinks I'm little Miss Popular. It would kill her if she knew the opposite was true."

"What do you mean?"

"I've *never* fit in and, no matter how hard I try, nothing works. Not even cheerleading has helped."

"Are you being bullied?"

"Yes," she says. "I get teased and harassed all the time, and it's not just during the day anymore. Some of my classmates have been sending threatening text messages at night and hassling me over the Internet. Last week I had to cancel my Web page on MySpace because some girls were posting such horrible things on it."

"I know how mean kids can get on those blogs," I comment.

"I don't understand why the government just doesn't

shut that stupid site down," she declares.

Anna is not the first student who's told me she's being cyber-bullied. Many adults assume peer abuse is worse now than it was when we were kids. They're wrong. The abuse has always been the same. The only difference today is that the methods have become more sophisticated. When I was in school, if someone passed a nasty note around class it would only reach the students in that particular class and by the end of the period be discarded. Today, that same nasty note could be sent via e-mail blast or posted on a blog like MySpace and reach hundreds, even thousands, of kids, not just a measly class-roomful. It could also be saved on a computer file, and sent again and again, each recipient adding her own nasty comments before passing it on to the next reader. The Internet has made possible a chain of cruelty. No wonder kids like Anna wish the government would regulate it.

"Why do you think you're getting picked on so much?" I ask her. I'm surprised that a cheerleader is getting picked on. It seems a contradiction, but what it describes is the dimension of the problem. No one is immune.

"Because I'm an Ancient Child," she says.

For a moment, I'm almost too stunned to speak. Now I know how the contestant on *American Idol* must feel the first time she walks into a store or a restaurant and hears one of the tracks from her own CD playing. Though she knows she made the recording and it's been released, it doesn't feel real until that moment when she hears it in public and people are paying attention. It builds and humbles the spirit all at once.

"I heard you on the radio talking about it once," Anna continues. "And I knew right then you were describing *me*."

"So you're always defending the underdog, huh? And I bet you wouldn't step on a bug, either."

She nods her head sadly.

"I know how heavy a burden it can be seeing the world from a different perspective than other kids," I tell her. "But it's also something to be very proud of."

"I wish the kids at school could see it that way."

"What about the other cheerleaders?"

"I never wanted it. The only reason I'm on the squad is to please Mom."

"You're not friends with any of them?" I ask.

"They leave me alone, for the most part, and I pretty much keep to myself outside practice, but I tell Mom we hang out all the time. She thinks I'm going to a party at one of their houses this weekend."

"Keeping up this front must be hard on you," I observe.

Anna is silent.

"What will you do this weekend when your mom thinks you're at this party?"

"Pretend to be all excited when I'm walking out the door and then go to the movies until curfew."

I worry for this girl. And I will meet many other teens just like her, who would rather live a lie than disappoint a parent. Cupping her chin, I gently raise her face so that I'm looking directly into her eyes. "Honey, I realize this is the last thing you want to hear, but you shouldn't be going through this alone and you need to be honest with your mom so she can help."

"I can't," she replies, her lower lip quivering.

"Anna, I know your mom is overbearing, but she does love you, and you can't keep living a lie. Maybe she'll surprise you."

"I'm scared she'll think less of me."

"You at least have to give her a chance."

"I've wanted to say something, but every time I find the courage Mom starts on about how proud she is of me and I can't go through with it."

By now, Anna is in tears. Why can't her mother see what she's doing to her? I glance over at Susan, who's at the other end of the gym with Eileen. I can hear her bragging about how Anna will probably be crowned homecoming queen next month. God, I want to throttle this woman.

"Do you really think it'll be OK—I mean, if I tell her the truth?" Anna says.

"Yes, I do," I answer.

Dear God, please don't let me be wrong.

As I watch Anna walk away, I hear my name being called for the sound check. Clipping the microphone onto my shirt, I begin counting from one to ten. While the engineer adjusts the volume, I see the gym beginning to swell with students. There are rows and rows of bleachers on all four sides of the space, extending from the floor almost to the ceiling. I'll be addressing over fifteen hundred kids. As the stragglers settle into their seats, Susan brings over the eighth grader who'll be introducing me. Then she steps out into the center of the gym, speaks for a few moments about the ills of bullying, and hands over the microphone.

"Hello, everyone. I'm Calvin Brightman, president of the Student Council. I want to introduce Judy Blinko, author of *Don't Stop Laughing at Me . . .*, a novel for school bullies."

You've got to be kidding!

I make a mental note to remind Eileen to add into our

contract that schools *must* use an introduction we provide. Then I close my eyes and take a deep breath, preparing once again to travel back in time.

As I begin the talk, I'm aware of a powerful difference in how I feel compared with what it was like in that gym at Marron. Then, it was as if I was groping my way in the dark, wary of every step. This time it feels like I have a flashlight, and I'm more confident because I can see where I'm going and I'm less afraid of the demons from my past hiding in the underbrush. Though it's still difficult to relive those memories, at least today, I have control of my emotions.

It's also easier knowing what to expect from the audience. I don't gulp at the disruptive outbursts or the occasional snicker from the back row. I know how to handle it now. Even better, I'm discovering that a lot of what happens to me as an activist I can share during these talks and it intensifies the bond between the audience and me. I describe what it was like when all those students came up to me in tears at the end of my presentation at Marron. I relate the story about what I went through with Kyle last spring, asking students if they know anyone like that here and what they'd be willing to do to help them. I describe what it's like hanging out with the former bullies from school, and how sometimes I get flashbacks that make it difficult to breathe. The more I open up, the more they respond.

By the time I get to the reunion, I can see that Eileen and I will be doing one-on-ones the rest of the morning and well into the afternoon. Unlike Marron, where there were dozens of students in tears, there are hundreds of kids visibly upset today. There is an intensity to their hurt, a desperate quality to their cry for help, that is even more profound than the pain I witnessed among the high school students. I look over at Susan, who is surveying the room, her face ashen. Her fellow PTA members appear equally rattled. Eileen is standing off to the side, shaking her head. We're both thinking the same thing: Why couldn't you have *listened* to us?

"Remember, kids," I conclude. "It's not just joking around!" The applause is deafening. I wait for a few moments until the students calm down, then open up the floor to questions.

A sweet, doe-eyed girl sitting in the special-ed section is the first to raise her hand. I'd noticed her earlier, when I was describing how some of my classmates treated Roger. She was listening to every word as if she didn't realize the story I was telling happened in the past and she wanted to leap out of the bleachers to rescue him.

"Yes, honey?" I say.

"Can you talk to the teachers?" she asks. "They're mean, too."

There's a ripple of laughter from the teachers, and it's all I can do not to scream. I walk over to her and gently ask her to elaborate.

"How are they mean?" I ask.

"When you say that someone is bullying you, they don't do anything, and tell you to stop being such a baby."

"Any teacher who does that is very, very wrong," I say. "And I'm glad you said something, sweetheart, because you've helped me realize how essential it is to include teachers in my program."

Several of the faculty squirm.

"Yes?" I say, pointing to a boy wearing a football jersey.

"Will you be talking to parents while you're here?" he inquires.

When I explain that, unfortunately, I'll only be addressing students, his frustration is palpable. "That really stinks," he says. "Because some of the parents in this town need to hear your message more than their kids do."

"Yeah!" another student volunteers. "I keep trying to tell my dad that ignoring bullies doesn't work, but he never listens."

Others begin shouting their agreement in unison. A tall plain girl with slumped shoulders stands up and says she's being tormented by kids at school — that they spit at her and call her "whore" and "pig," and that all her mom ever says to her is that one day she'll look back on this and laugh. "I hate my mom for always saying that to me. Please, can you make her understand?" By now, she's crying, and the two girls sitting on either side are trying to comfort her.

Now I'm convinced that reaching out to the kids may not be enough, that if I want to have a lasting impact in their lives, I have to sensitize their parents and teachers, too. No matter how successful I am at inspiring the bullies to be more compassionate and the victims to defend their dignity, if their classroom environment condones a different ethos and at home they're living according to the misguided standard that "kids will be kids," it'll only be a matter of time before any good I've achieved is undone.

Scores of students are trying to get my attention, wanting to speak. And there are just as many teachers with their hands up now as students. The atmosphere has become electric with conviction. It reminds me of those town hall meetings during election season where the audience starts out marginally engaged and by the end of the hour people are leaping out of their seats, demanding answers of their candidate. Knowing I've got to get the room under control again, I tap on the microphone to quiet the crowd.

"I'm sorry there won't be time for me to do a parent or teacher talk," I say. "But the main office has the list of student presentations for the rest of today and tomorrow, and you're more than welcome to invite your parents to sit in. Also, I'm going to be here all day, and if any of you would like some one-on-one time with me or are in crisis and wish to consult your counselor, please talk to Susan Peterson at the PTA table. She's kindly volunteered to handle all post-presentation follow-up." Upon hearing these words, Susan looks as though she might faint.

"One last thing. Eileen, could you please wave your arms so everyone can see you?" Eileen does as she's asked. "Everyone, this is my manager, the Little General." Several kids giggle. "I know some of you are struggling getting your parents to understand what you're going through. I can't make any promises, but if you think it would help if I talked with them, please see the Little General and she'll try and arrange something while I'm here."

As I'm unclipping the microphone, Susan comes running up to me harried, holding a clipboard. "There are over a hundred students who want to sit down with you," she exclaims. "How on earth are we going to fit all of them in?"

"I've got names of fifteen parents that I need to call," Eileen adds, walking up.

"My God, what are we going to do?" Susan says.

"It's OK," Eileen replies. "Give me your list and a conference room. Jodee and I will handle the rest."

"Shouldn't there be a counselor in there with you?"

"There should at least be a representative from the school available if I need one," I say.

"I feel like such a fool giving you a hard time earlier. I had no idea—"

"It's all right," I say. "You'll need to make sure the principal, or at least one of the counselors, will be available by phone this evening in the event I encounter a suicidal student or possible abuse in the home."

"Absolutely," she responds, scribbling down the instructions.

For the next three hours, I do back-to-back one-on-ones with kids in crisis. It's a breathless montage of faces, some of which will haunt me long after I leave this town. One boy, an eighth grader, confesses that his biological father has been molesting him since he was in fourth grade. Stunned, I ask him if his mother knows. He says that she's been sick for a long time and that he doesn't want to put her under any more stress. "Besides," he adds, "she'd never believe me." I ask him if he has a good relationship with his school counselor and if he would be willing to talk to him. He says that he likes his counselor and has wanted to confide in him but is terrified that the police will put his father in jail, and then who would support his family? Knowing I have to report this abuse, but not wanting to betray this boy's trust, I ask him if he would give me his blessing to talk with his counselor on his behalf. I explain that there are people who work for the government whose job is to help families get through difficult times like this. He finally agrees. Later, when I speak with the boy's counselor, he promises to contact social services immediately and assures me that he will do everything he can for this child.

The hardest part of all this for me will be when I have to pack my suitcase and move on to the next town. Even though I know I'm helping these children, I feel like I'm abandoning them, too and it sucks.

A seventh grade girl wearing all black, a nose ring, and dark, dramatic makeup comes to see me. Though her look is extreme, there's a sense of style about the way she's put herself together. Her outfit is punk, but the lines are flattering to her figure and the design youthful and fun. She says that everybody thinks she dresses this way because she's a freak. "But that's not true," she cries. "I like being creative, and this is one of the ways I express it." She tells me that she hopes to be a fashion designer one day and that she makes all her own outfits. "You're kidding!" I reply. "You made what you've got on now?"

"Oh, yes," she says. Then she pulls a sketch pad out of her book bag and shows me some of her designs.

"You're very talented," I remark. I will come to realize that exceptional adults, as this girl will surely become, have almost always been bullied.

"Yeah, but what good is it if everybody hates me? Why can't they like me for who I am? What difference does it make how I dress?"

I tell her that she has a style all her own and that she should be proud. I encourage her to get involved designing costumes for the school play or a park-district community-theater program. "The more you use your talents, the more doors you open for making friends," I say. By the end of our chat, she's full of enthusiasm, eager to get started on what we've discussed. It's amazing how just a little common sense can help these kids, and I wonder why the adults in their lives aren't providing it.

One after another, they keep coming: the quarterback of the football team who says he's always been a jerk to anyone who's not popular and wants to know how to change; a sixth-grade girl whose friends turned on her because they found out her father was serving ten years in prison for selling drugs; a boy, apparently with Asperger's, who describes how everybody always laughs at him; an obese student in foster care who begs me to adopt her. Then there are the kids who seem to be calling out for attention that I worry may be hiding something far more significant and are just too afraid to confront it; the girl who's mad at her best friend because they both have a crush on the same boy; the seventh grader who's got tons of friends now but wants to talk about how once, in first grade, this one kid made fun of his lunchbox; the captain of the girls' volleyball team, who's angry because her friend Tanya started a rumor about her friend Jenna, who won't go to the movies now with her this Friday. At one point, unsure I can take any more, I get up and peek through the doorway to see how many more students are waiting to see me. The line is still extended to the end of the hall-way. Concerned, I motion for Eileen to come over.

"You need lunch," she says. "You haven't eaten anything since early this morning."

"Can you bring me some nuts from the car?"

"Jodee, you need to take a break. It's nearly two in the afternoon, and you've been going nonstop since six."

"I know, but the kids have to be the priority."

"I've got an idea," Eileen proposes. "Let me ask these kids who are still waiting if any of them would be willing to see you in groups. That'll at least give us enough time for you to sit in the car for a little while and rest."

Most of them agree, with a few still requesting to see me alone. As I'm sitting in the car, I'm starting to realize that the ones who are dealing with the most severe problems deplete so much of my emotional energy that it's hard for me to be patient with those coping with more superficial issues. What I have to remember is that it may not seem superficial to them. It's important that I give each child my undivided attention during our time together and not pass judgment on the legitimacy of their pain. But I'm discovering that when I'm tired, hungry, and irritable, it's easier said than done.

The rest of the day goes smoothly. By the time I'm done with the last of the one-on-ones after the second presentation, and meeting with parents who wanted to talk with me, it's late in the evening and most of the restaurants have closed. Eileen and I are so exhausted, we just buy sandwiches from a local Subway and eat them in our rooms. As I'm sitting in bed, my throat raw from talking all day, I think again about Anna, and wonder if she'll ever be able to confront her mother with the truth about what she's going through at school.

I'm about to drift off when the phone rings. It's Mitch, wanting to tell me good night. As I tell him about the events of the day, I curl into the covers, letting the sound of his voice wrap itself around me, soothing the sore place inside me that is always there after having so many kids pour out their hearts to me.

The next morning, Eileen comes bouncing in full of energy. Holding a cup of coffee for me in one hand and the local paper in the other, she looks as if she's about to burst.

"What's got you so perky?" I ask.

"Feast your eyes on this!" she says, spreading out the paper.

I'm staring at a huge photo, that was taken yesterday, of me surrounded by dozens of visibly emotional kids. The story itself, which takes up half the front page, also mentions that I'll be giving two more presentations today at the high school. Though I'm humbled by the coverage and understand that it's great for our cause, I also worry that it may be too much too soon. As the day unfolds, my concerns will prove well founded.

When Eileen and I go downstairs, Susan is waiting for us in the lobby, her attitude much warmer than it was yesterday. She's quoted in the article, and says her friends have been calling her all morning to congratulate her. The drive to the high school is pleasant and uneventful. I've got one talk scheduled this morning, addressing the freshmen and sophomores, and a later one in the afternoon for the juniors and seniors.

As we're making our way to the gym, Eileen realizes that she's got several voice mails and tells Susan and me to go ahead and that she'll catch up with us shortly. About fifteen minutes later, after I've completed the sound check, by which time the bleachers are packed with wall-to-wall students and the senior-class president is getting ready to introduce me, I look out into the audience and realize Eileen isn't here yet. Soon I'm a half hour into my talk, then an hour, and, before I know it, I'm in the middle of the Q&A, and there's still no sign of her. Suddenly, she comes running in, gesturing for me to wrap it up. Thank God I only see a handful of students in tears. The requests for one-on-ones shouldn't be as numerous as yesterday, I tell myself hopefully. Though part of me is relieved, another part is insecure and wonders why I didn't elicit more of a response with this group. I quickly finish the last question, thank the audience, and then start heading toward Eileen, when, to my surprise, I'm swarmed with students trying to push one another out of the way to get to me.

"I loved your talk," says a pretty Latina girl with deep-set eyes. "I was wondering if there was someplace we could talk."

"Could I talk to you, too?" asks a boy, standing next to her.

One after another, they keep coming. Hearing their stories, I begin to understand that some schools have a more overtly emotional culture than others, but that the misery is the same, the need just as great.

"Kids, mind if I grab her for a moment?" asks the Little General, pulling me aside. "Jodee, I need to talk to you."

I find out that all hell is breaking loose because of the article in this morning's paper. We're being hounded with phone calls from parents frantic to meet with me. Our Web site is getting deluged too with e-mails from lonely, alienated kids, many of whom want to know what hotel I'm staying at. The superintendent's office is being inundated with messages from overwrought teachers in other districts, begging me to stop by and talk to their students. To make matters worse, Susan was just contacted by the president of the school board, who's insisting that I squeeze in a third talk today because the district's alternative high school was inadvertently overlooked due to a bureaucratic mix-up and it would be unfair to deny the students.

"There's no way you can do another presentation today plus deal with everything else that's going on," Eileen says.

"But what if there's a child in trouble at one of those schools who really needs help?"

As if on cue, several kids approach Eileen and me, saying that they only have passes to meet with me during this period and that the bell is going to ring soon. "Please, we'll get in trouble if we're not in our next class," one of them says.

"Go ahead," Eileen says. "I'll find Susan and ask her to see if we can do the alternative school next."

Twenty minutes later, we're on our way. The drive over is a microcosm of the day. Susan is on her cell talking to the counselor at the alternative school, trying to obtain as much information as she can so that I'm not going in there blind. Eileen has her day planner spread open across her lap and is trying to make a dent in the growing list of urgent messages. "I'm sorry your daughter's going through so much," I hear Eileen telling whoever is on the other end of the line. "I wish Jodee could sit down with you, too, but unfortunately we're leaving this evening and her schedule is jam-packed. I can set up a time for the two of you to chat by phone if you like. What? That's very gracious of you but — yes, I understand — I'm sorry, can you hold a minute? Hello, this is Eileen — "

As they're working their cell phones, I'm reviewing a stack of e-mails that just came in from students in this district who heard me speak. To my dismay, a few of them are nasty. One goes as far as to suggest that I'm lying about the morning I discovered my favorite shoes floating in the toilet because "everyone knows that the night janitor would have seen them when he cleaned the bathroom and would have taken them out."

"I don't know what to say to some of these parents," Eileen says, as we pull into the school, jolting me out of my concern. "One mother volunteered to *drive* us to Baltimore, saying she'd bring her daughter along so you could talk to her on the way."

The moment we step inside the building, I shudder. The walls are dingy and gray, and, unlike most schools, where you find student artwork hanging in the halls, here there's nothing but the occasional burst of graffiti, some of which is old and faded. There are two armed cops standing guard outside the door to the principal's office. The reception window is made of bulletproof glass, and there are security cameras conspicuously present throughout the building. How can they expect anyone to learn under these conditions, especially kids who already have to cope with family circumstances most of us couldn't comprehend?

The bell just rang, yet the scene that unfolds here isn't anything like what you'd see in a mainstream school. These students, some of whom look more like rap stars than high school kids, aren't rushing to class. Instead, they move slowly, deliberately, a weariness about them. Some are scarred from having been stabbed or shot and wear their wounds with defiance, as if they were expensive tattoos. There's a group of girls standing by the lockers. Their eyes are dull and tired, and contain a hopelessness that makes me concerned for their futures. One of them looks pregnant.

Susan introduces Eileen and me to the counselor. An African-American woman with a voice that resonates with

conviction and passion, she is a stark contrast to the oppressive pall in the corridor. She explains that she chose to work
here because, like most of her students, she, too, was raised
in the projects and spent most of her youth in foster care. "A
lot of our kids see anyone who's part of the system as the
enemy," she explains. "Nearly half of our student population
has been involved in gang-related violence, and many of
them have served time in juvenile facilities."

She takes us to meet the principal, who isn't at all what
I expect. Affable and rotund, with a ruddy complexion and a
gentle wit, he reminds me of John Candy in *Uncle Buck*. It's
hard to imagine he has anything in common with these kids,
but it's obvious that many of them adore him. While we're
standing there, a few come up and start joking with him with
an easy familiarity that doesn't diminish his authority.

"It's amazing how these kids respond to you," I remark.

"I've had my share of challenges, too," he says soberly.

He then explains that I'll be speaking to a small group of
young men and women who are active gang members. "With
all due respect," I say, "you want me to convince kids who
have probably been shot at that *bullying* can damage you for
life?"

Before he can answer, the counselor is escorting in a
group of fifteen students: ten boys and five girls. Some of the
boys scare me, they're so physically large and menacing in
appearance. They eye me suspiciously as they take their
seats and then sit with their arms folded tightly across their
chests, their faces expressionless.

"Eileen, where are you going?" I gulp, noticing her trying
to sneak out.

"To the bathroom, but I guess I can hold it," she says, sighing.

Though this audience is intimidating at first, by the time I get to the part of the talk where I describe how Nadia and her friends were throwing dirt into Roger's eyes, there's an audible gasp in the room. As I continue, the lingering resistance on both sides dissipates, and all I can feel is this incredible sense of connectedness between us where our empathy for each other eclipses the differences in our backgrounds. Even though our exchange is at times nonverbal, I come to understand that, no matter how harrowing my experiences were, they pale in comparison to the harm done to these young men and women. When I'm done speaking, this time, I'm the one who's in tears. Even though these students are not members of cliques—the social structure that defines bullying in schools such as Anna's—and their gang membership is their attempt to replace the nuclear family, the result of my engaging them is equally cathartic. I will later learn from school psychologists that my program has many of the same healing benefits on active gang members as it does on mainstream students.

The afternoon proves to be as demanding as the morning. After we leave the alternative school, we have to race back to the high school, where I'm scheduled to give my second talk, this time addressing the juniors and seniors. At the end of the presentation, I'm again deluged with requests for one-on-ones. While I'm dealing with that, Eileen is in the main office trying to respond to the e-mails that keep coming in from parents, as well as the telephone calls from teachers in other districts, which the superintendent's secretary has now referred to Eileen's cell phone because she can't keep up with them, either.

"What's going on with the e-mails?" I ask Eileen.

"It's reaching the crisis point, I tell you!"

I don't know why — maybe it's how she says it, or perhaps it's the harried look on her face — but all of a sudden the whole thing strikes me as comical and I'm unable to hold back. I burst out laughing. For a second, I worry that I may have offended her, when suddenly, she explodes into laughter too. Soon we're both doubled over, tears streaming down our cheeks.

"For a second there I was worried I might wet my pants," Eileen says, dabbing her eyes.

"Sometimes you have to find the humor in things or you'll go nuts," I reply.

When Susan finally drives us back to the hotel, Anna is waiting in the lobby. She looks apprehensive.

"Anna, what are you doing here?" Susan asks. "You're supposed to be at practice."

"I know, Mom, but I need to talk to you."

"Honey, what is it, what's wrong?" Susan says.

"I'll tell you when we get home," Anna replies. "I'll be waiting in the car."

As she's walking out, I grab her hand. "It'll be OK," I reassure her. "Just tell your mom what's in your heart. And if you need anything from me, just call."

"Thanks, I will."

After Anna leaves, Eileen and I thank Susan for her help these past two days.

"We could never have done it without you," Eileen says.

"Promise you'll stay in touch, and let me know how things work out with Anna," I say, hugging her goodbye. As I watch her walk away, I say a quiet prayer for both mother and daughter, knowing they may have a bumpy road ahead of them.

"We've got an hour before we have to leave for the airport," Eileen says.

In the middle of packing, the stress of the past two days tumbles in on me. I've been surviving on adrenaline, and now that the rush is over my mind, body, and spirit need rest. I thought the flashbacks were going to end up being the hardest part about touring. I'm finding out that everything is the hardest part.

Every time I tell myself this work is too much, something always happens that reminds me why I started doing it in the first place, and why I can't walk away. By the time Eileen and I are settled in our Baltimore hotel, I'm cranky and tired and just want to go home. I begin to have doubts that I'm as strong and unselfish as I thought, and that maybe I'm like the bride who elopes, then discovers that she was never cut out to be a wife. The problem with being an activist is that people expect courage and selflessness from you all the time, and when you need some privacy, not only do they often think less of you but you think less of yourself, too. Then one day you wake up with a chip on your shoulder the size of a cue ball. I don't want to become that whiny author-activist I often had to work with during my publicist days, who resents how much she's had to sacrifice. The night before my first talk in Baltimore, I come crashing into this realization, only to have the angelic hands of hope wrap around my throat and choke the fear out of me. Will I get to the point where I'm more afraid of hope than of doubt, because hope is guaranteed never to let me out of this relentless race?

I learn this in Baltimore.

Though a few students request one-on-ones with me after my first talk, I can't help thinking that I blew it, that this audience didn't respond the way previous ones have. A large group of kids were whispering to each other and passing notes throughout the entire presentation and didn't appear to be paying attention. Despite my repeated attempts to engage their interest, I couldn't get them to come around. As I'm beating myself up, wondering where I went wrong, a student approaches me and introduces herself as one of the "preps," the most popular clique at school. She says her name is Brittany and asks if she and her friends can talk with me privately. Surprised, I tell her that I'll be in the all-purpose room which the principal, who's really on the ball in this district, arranged for me to use in anticipation of one-on-ones. Moments later, Brittany walks in, accompanied by at least thirty other students, the same ones who I could have sworn weren't hearing a word I was saying. Impeccably dressed, they look like they just jumped off the pages of a J. Crew catalog. "Your speech really hit home," one of them says.

"For me, too," several others respond in unison.

"I didn't think you guys were listening," I remark, stunned.

"You had us totally freaked."

"Why?" I ask.

"You know how you said you're damaged because of what happened to you?" Brittany says.

I nod my head.

"There's this kid, Eric, and we've been treating him the way you were treated in school, and we feel bad about it," she says. Then, glancing around the room at her friends, for support, she adds, "We want him to know how sorry we are."

I call Eileen, who's in the main office returning e-mails, and ask her to find Eric. Moments later, I'm standing with him in the hallway outside the all-purpose room. Tall and gangly, with a hint of facial hair, he is painfully self-conscious, as if the body he inhabits doesn't fit right. I've never met anyone like him before. He exudes sadness and sweetness, and I ache to protect him, but there's also a dissonance that makes being around him like listening to beautiful music being played on a piano that's out of tune. When I explain to Eric that some of his classmates want to apologize for bullying him, he looks at me with the guarded reserve of a precocious child and then starts listing what they've done to him since fifth grade. Each sentence rolls into the other, punctuated by an occasional flurry of tics, that he tries to control, but they seem to have a will of their own.

When we enter the room, we're greeted by a flutter of uneasy smiles. Eric swallows hard and looks back toward the door, as if he's calculating how long it will take him to reach it should he need to escape.

"Can I say something first?" he whispers.

"Go ahead," I encourage him.

He turns and faces his classmates. "I would give anything for you to like me, but I don't blame you for thinking I'm weird," he says. "I have a disorder called Asperger's syndrome and sometimes I can't help the way it makes me act. But it's not the only reason I'll never be normal." He bites down hard on his lower lip to prevent himself from crying.

Brittany and her friends are glancing at each other guiltily, their remorse palpable.

"I used to get on my dad's nerves a lot because of my Asperger's, and he and my mom would fight about it all the time. One day, while she was out shopping, he came into my room with this look on his face that I'd never seen before and said he just couldn't take me anymore. Then my dad went downstairs and killed himself."

There's a collective gasp, and then I hear a choir of voices murmuring, "Oh, my God," in hushed tones. No one seems to know what to say to Eric, who is equally uncomfortable. Suddenly, Brittany walks over to him. She gently wraps her arms around him, telling him how sorry she is for what he's had to go through, and how terrible she and everyone else feels that they made things worse by being so cruel to him all these years. Then she and her friends ask for his forgiveness and his friendship. I'll never forget the look on Eric's face in that moment. It was as if someone turned a light on inside him. He will become one of the kids who continue to stay in touch with me through letters and e-mails. His progress will inspire me on days when I need it most.

Eileen and I return home convinced that there's no way around it, I have to start adding both a teacher workshop and a parent/family seminar at every school if I'm serious about making life better for these kids. I wonder how many more Erics are out there with parents who need to know they're not alone. What about the students who keep asking me why I'm not addressing the adults in their lives? So, instead of just offering two student presentations on bullying prevention, we start positioning *It's NOT Just Joking Around!*™ as a comprehensive day-long program. By the time we embark on the second leg of the fall tour, Eileen's already persuaded several of the school districts that have booked me to incorporate the additional talks into the schedule.

Most professional speakers, especially those who deal with deeply personal subjects, are savvy enough to know that if you don't erect stringent boundaries delineating how much of yourself you're willing to give, this work will eventually suck you dry. Typically, you're supposed to go into a venue, do a ninety-minute talk, a brief Q&A, and then leave. If your presentation evokes an emotional response, you may end up chatting with a few audience members afterward, but rarely does any speaker encounter the magnitude of raw desperation that Eileen and I continue to come up against with these kids. We've entered uncharted territory. We're navigating our way forward through a thicket of unknown variables and, no matter how much we may *think* we know what to expect, something always happens that proves we're still babes in the woods. One of the unexpected things I've learned is the degree to which schools mimic principals. If the principal is warm and loving, the students are more open and less defensive. If the principal is intolerant and rigid, the teachers are more likely to be unforgiving and bureaucratic.

chapter thirteen

Everything

Old Is New

Again

November – December 2003

I'm exhausted and exhilarated at the same time. I just returned home from the final leg of the fall tour, and I'm reconciling myself to the fact that my life is actually newer than my shoes. New boyfriend, new home, new career, new friends — new everything. And the irony is that it's all sprung from my childhood roots, which I believed, if unearthed, would cause disaster. I'm making my way back full circle. But, like traveling any circle fast, it's dizzying. It's late morning the day before Thanksgiving, and I've stopped by Shelly's for a visit. We haven't had a chance to talk since I was in Baltimore, and I've been filling her in on how the rest of the tour went. Her fourteen-year-old daughter, Leah, who was recently diagnosed with bipolar disorder, is with us in the kitchen making decorations for tomorrow.

"You're *kidding*!" Shelly says, handing me a peeler and a small bag of potatoes.

"No, some teachers actually got up and walked out," I reply.

"A lot of people will only listen to what they want to hear."

"Yes, but what about what they *need* to hear! That's the reason I wanted to do these teacher workshops to begin with."

"It was your first," she points out. "Maybe you came on too strong."

"I'll admit I didn't hold anything back, but if I was a teacher in that audience that's exactly what I would have wanted. If I had students who were bring brutalized by their classmates and there was someone who'd been through it, too, and was willing to help me help my students, I would have been all ears!"

"Jodee, that's *you*. Not everyone is as comfortable with honesty as you are, especially when the truth may be unpleasant."

"Are you saying I might be better off toning it down next time?" I ask, tossing a skinned potato into the large bowl she's put on the table.

"No, because that would be the same as a lie for you. But I do think it wouldn't hurt to be as honest with yourself as you are with everyone else."

"What do you mean?"

"I think when you spoke at Samuels it resurrected a lot of old anger, and it may be that some of it is seeping into your teacher workshops."

Though I don't want to believe she's right, there were moments during the workshop when I did feel a sense of satisfaction watching those teachers struggle with their guilt as they realized that, despite their good intentions, they were making a lot of the same mistakes my teachers made. But I couldn't help it. I spoke with hundreds of their students, many of whom said the bullying problem at the school is off the charts. I heard one horror story after another about how kids are being publicly humiliated by faculty, who insist that they need to stop whining and learn to fight their own battles. Yet, at the same time, the school has instituted zero-tolerance policies, defining any act of self-defense, be it verbal or physical, as a punishable, and in some cases even expellable offense. These poor kids are caught between a rock and a hard place, and as I was addressing the faculty, trying to explain the problem, I'm sure my voice did become shrill at times, or my tone indignant, and I understand it was wrong, perhaps even offensive to some. But when I go into a school, I have one day, *one day* to try and make a difference. These teachers were lucky I didn't throw my bottle of water at them when they started walking out that door. The problem is I can't let my empathy for the students become so great that it affects my ability to appreciate those teachers who genuinely care, even if they don't always make the best decisions. Not every teacher that afternoon abandoned my workshop. Some stayed, nodding their heads in earnest agreement with what I was saying and jotting down notes like crazy. Somehow, I've got to find a balance that lets me be honest without alienating the people students need to protect them. This will prove easier said than done.

"Did the principal give detentions to the teachers who left in the middle?" Leah asks, squirting a fresh dollop of glue onto what appears to be a turkey's wattle.

"I don't think so, sweetheart," I reply, touched. "The principal wasn't even there."

"No wonder that place is having problems," Shelly comments. "It's the principal who's supposed to set the tone, and this one obviously could care less."

"You know what this administrator's excuse was for not

being able to make it?"

"What?"

"She had a hair appointment and couldn't reschedule."

"Unbelievable!" Shelly says.

"Truthfully, I'm glad she sent her assistant instead. I might not have had the confidence to remain onstage if it weren't for him. He kept encouraging me throughout the entire workshop. At the end of my talk, he stood up and applauded."

"What else happened on your tour?" Leah asks, holding up a beautiful paper turkey for Shelly and me to see.

"That's really good, honey," her mom says. "Why don't you see if your brother would like to make something?"

"I want to hear more about the tour first!" she says.

"It's OK," I tell Shelly, who's smiling apologetically.

"I bet you met a lot of mean popular kids talking at all those schools."

"Leah, not all popular kids are mean," I respond.

"Yes, they are," she says bitterly.

Shelly, who's just put the last of the peeled potatoes into a large pot of water, glances up from the stove at her daughter and sighs, a sound so hopeless that it makes me think of my own mom when I was Leah's age. For the first time, I realize that the effervescent cheerleader I see whenever I look at Shelly is an illusion kept alive by the sixteen-year-old outcast inside me who always ached for her friendship and is still excited to have finally won it. The real woman is tired and weathered, with a soulfulness born of rare heartache, and though I may not have noticed her before, I'm glad I can see her now.

"No, honey," I explain to Leah. "I met many popular kids on the road who moved me to tears, they were so kind."

"Like who?" she challenges.

I share with Leah the remarkable scene between Eric and his classmates.

"But Brittany and her friends were mean in the beginning," she argues.

"Yes, that's true, and no matter what they do they can never erase the damage they caused," I explain. "But when they apologized and offered their friendship it helped Eric feel better."

"I would give anything if that would happen to me."

Eileen and I have approached Leah's school many times, asking if they'd let me speak. I even offered to give my talk pro bono but we've yet to receive a response. I give Leah a reassuring hug. She snuggles into me. This is an affecting child, her ability to love almost volatile in its intensity. She and I share a profound bond, both of us having learned at an early age what darkness feels like when it lodges inside you and won't let go. There are times, when I'm with her, that I feel like I should be protecting her from her own heart, as if it might swallow her whole, like the whale did Jonah.

"Tell me another story from the road!" Leah begs.

"Honey, why don't we give Jodee a break?" Shelly says.

"Just one more?"

"OK," Shelly agrees.

Just then my cell phone rings. It's Eileen and she sounds rattled.

"What's wrong?" I ask.

"Do you remember that mom from Oregon who had a

sixteen-year-old daughter named Crystal?"

"Yes, Crystal was the girl everyone said was overly sensi-tive. Her mom asked me to talk to her. I still hear from Crystal every once in a while."

"When was the last time you checked your personal e-mail?"

"Yesterday, why?"

"Crystal sent you dozens of e-mails over the past twenty-four hours. She's been hounding me, too. I left a message for her mother, but I haven't heard back yet. Jodee, I'm worried. There's this ominous tone to them."

"What do you mean, exactly?"

"I think this girl is dangerous. Do me a favor. Where are you right now?"

"I'm at Shelly's."

"Jump on her computer and go through them and then call me back."

"What's going on?" Leah asks, full of curiosity.

"There's this girl who may be in trouble, and I need to see if she sent me an e-mail," I say.

Shelly, sensing a need to act, sends Leah to check on her younger brother and then sets me up at her computer. When I open my e-mail and begin going through my in-box, I shiver. There are thirty messages from Crystal, each one more irra-tional than the next. In the first few, she's demanding I call her. Then, in the next several, she's pleading with me to fly to Oregon for Thanksgiving dinner with her family. With the next couple of e-mails, she's asking why I haven't responded to her yet and threatening to start cutting herself if I don't do what she wants. Then the e-mails become apologetic, imploring me to forgive her for "bugging me" but that she doesn't have anyone else to turn to. It's the last three e-mails that frighten me the most. In each one, the line "I thought you were my best friend" is repeated over and over in creepy gothic-looking font, single spaced, the typeface growing larger as I scroll down, until the last sentence is cut off because of the size of the letters. I see the progression of her disillusionment and anger there on the screen.

"Jodee, are you OK?" Shelly asks.

"Take a look at this."

As Shelly reads Crystal's e-mails, the color drains from her face.

"What will you do?"

"I'm going to call Crystal's mom for starters and tell this woman she needs to get her daughter help," I answer.

"Just be prepared," Shelly advises. "It may not be easy to get through to her. Some parents go into denial at the mere suggestion that their child may be struggling with emotional illness. It took me a long time myself."

I call Eileen back, briefing her on Shelly's insights and asking if she's heard from Crystal's mother yet. She says she just got off the phone with the mom, and that while she expressed concern about her daughter's disturbing behavior, she didn't feel it was a cause for alarm.

"The way she explains it, Crystal was simply having 'another one of her episodes,'" Eileen says. "She compares them to thunderstorms, intense and unrelenting when they hit but gone quickly."

"Is this woman out of her mind? Crystal should be seeing a psychiatrist!"

"I suggested that," Eileen replies.

"And?"

"She said she agrees but I fear Shelly may be right. I could hear the denial in this woman's voice, and I think by next week, she'll have convinced herself that she overreacted when she spoke with me."

"We should call Crystal's school and at least give her counselor and the social worker a heads up."

"Already done," Eileen says. "There was no one there because of the holiday, but I left an urgent message."

"I'm tempted to report this to the Department of Child and Family Services," I announce. "I mean, isn't ignoring this kind of desperation in a child a form of neglect?"

"You need to really think about that one," Shelly interjects. "Just because Crystal's mother is having trouble accepting that her daughter may be ill doesn't mean she's an unfit parent. If you and Eileen contact DCFS, you can't imagine what that family will have to go through. I'm not saying it won't be necessary later on. If things don't improve with Crystal, you might not have any choice, but right now I think you should give her parents and the school counselor a chance to intervene before bringing social services into the picture."

Though I know what Shelly says makes sense, what if Crystal hurts herself or someone else and Eileen and I could have prevented it by contacting DCFS?

"What's your take?" I ask Eileen, sharing Shelly's thoughts with her.

"Let's give it a couple of weeks," Eileen proposes. "I'll stay in touch with Crystal's mom and we'll see how things progress."

After Eileen and I hang up, I send Crystal an e-mail letting her know that I care very much about her and that though I appreciate how much she wishes I could be there for Thanksgiving, I'm going to be home with my family. Then I say a prayer for this poor girl, hoping the adults in her life will get her the help she needs. This will not be my last contact with her.

"Is your life always this dramatic?" Shelly asks.

"Leah, cut it out!" I hear Shelly's middle daughter, Terry, yelling from upstairs. "Mom, Leah's borrowing my sweater without asking!"

"Go ahead," I say, smiling. "I better check the stove or those potatoes will turn to mush."

While I'm tending to matters in the kitchen, still haunted by the unsettling incident with Crystal, Clarke calls, immediately brightening my spirits. "Hey, I was wondering, Shelly's fortieth birthday is next month. Would you be up to throwing a surprise party with me? We'll invite the whole gang."

For a moment, I'm too thrilled to speak. I've never been invited to such a party with the cool crowd before, let alone asked to *co-host* it. It occurs to me that though I may have convinced myself that I'm no longer affected by flashbacks, it isn't true, and I'm learning that they exist in different forms. It's one thing to be pleased that a friend thinks of you first when planning a special occasion. It's another to be practically hopping around the room, you're so excited. It isn't only being included in the party that's making me react this way, though. It's how Clarke referred to "the whole gang," as if it were the most natural thing in the world that I was always part of it.

I hate that simply *not* being excluded still evokes this ridiculous involuntary giddiness in me. It's embarrassing for everyone involved, but it feels wonderful and that's what worries me. Though I try to hide my overreaction from friends, because I'm ashamed that I still haven't gotten past worshipping being accepted, when it does slip out everyone seems to understand. But what happens when they grow tired of my not being able to move on? Will they start to think I'm weird again like when we were in school and reject me? The tour has taken more of a toll on me than I thought. During the summer, I barely had any insecure moments at all.

"Jodee, are you there? Jodee?"

"I'm sorry, Clarke, I got distracted. Of course, I'd love to do it!"

"Great, why don't we get together over the weekend and make the plans?"

"Terrific, talk to you then."

Just as I'm hanging up with Clarke, Shelly walks into the room. She's tapping her foot on the floor, and giving me a look of consternation. "I know you were talking to Clarke. What are you guys up to?" she asks, her eyes narrowing.

"Nothing, why?"

"You're grinning like an idiot, and I haven't trusted Clarke since freshman year, when he told me his name was *Harold*."

"You're being paranoid."

"If he happened to mention anything about my birthday, honestly, I do not want a party, OK?"

"What makes you think we're planning one?" I ask.

"Promise me, Jodee."

"OK, OK," I reply, hoping she can't see me crossing my fingers.

Satisfied that she's gotten her point across, Shelly changes the subject. "Is Mitch spending Thanksgiving with you and your mom?" she asks.

"Yes, we're all going to my cousin Jeanine's. It's the first Thanksgiving I've ever had a date."

"You're kidding," she says.

"No, when I lived in New York the guy I dated always had too many family obligations to get away and come home with me to Chicago."

"You mean excuses," Shelly says.

"Yeah, I'm starting to realize that now."

"I'm happy for you and Mitch," she says. "And don't forget to remind him that if he hurts you again I'm coming after him with my son's baseball bat."

"I will," I reply, grinning.

Thanksgiving is a delight. Gone are the frustrated tears of years past, sitting with my family for Thanksgiving dinner and pretending to be happy for their sake and then, as soon as the plates were cleared and I could hear the hum of the dishwasher, sneaking up to my room and letting out the pain into my pillow. Last year, as I was eating a meal I couldn't taste, knowing Mitch was spending the holiday with Kathy, I remember trembling while trying to convince my mom I was OK. This Thanksgiving, I didn't have to pretend I could taste the food, which always looked delicious but I was too dead inside to enjoy. Loneliness took away everything for me during the holidays, and Mitch being with me this year gave it all back. I only wish my dad and my grandparents could have shared in my happiness. I know Mitch missed his mom, too. Somehow, I believe they were there with us in their own way, as full of contentment as we were of delightful food.

As December rolls in, between planning Shelly's surprise party with Clarke, spending quality time with Mitch and his daughters, getting ready for the holidays, responding to a surge in pleas for help from adult survivors and kids in crisis, and working with Eileen to prepare for the spring tour, I've been moving at breakneck speed to stay on top of it all. There isn't much opportunity to reflect, and perhaps that's a blessing, because, despite the joy of finally being able to experience what a full, well-rounded life feels like, I'm also quietly battling the pall of what Eileen has begun referring to as "bully head," and thinking about it only makes it worse. It's a paranoia-infused insecurity that behaves like a cancer that goes in and out of remission. What's more worrisome is that *anything* can trigger it: unexpectedly seeing a former classmate at the grocery store, thinking I hear something off in Clarke's or Shelly's tone when they talk to me and then taking it personally and panicking that they don't like me anymore. And it's starting to bleed into other aspects of my life, too.

The other day, I left a voice mail for an old friend in the movie industry whom I've worked with on many successful projects. When he didn't return my call by the next morning, I went into a tailspin, scared I'd said something to offend him. I worked myself up into such a state that I wrote him a long e-mail asking him to forgive me, not even knowing what I was sorry for! Thank God part of me was still rational enough to hold back sending it. Less than forty-eight hours later, his assistant called, apologizing for not getting back to me sooner but that she just received my message, and that my friend was in Europe but would contact me as soon as he returned this weekend. Prior to my new career — and social life, my reaction would never have been so out of proportion. This time, I was able to override the impulse to make a fool of myself. What happens if, next time, I can't?

While all this is going on, my friend Kaye calls to ask if Clarke and I need any help with Shelly's party. She and I reconnected briefly at the reunion and have had dinner together several times since. Kaye was one of the bystanders in school and associated with a group of girls who, though they were accepted, were never really *included*. I tell her that I'd be grateful for the extra hand, and we make plans to meet for breakfast Saturday and spend the day together preparing for the surprise party that evening.

The week passes quickly, and by Friday morning I'm so excited about Shelly's party, I think I might burst. I spend two hours at the mall searching for the perfect outfit, something that makes me feel both sexy *and* elegant. I try on dozens of possibilities, finally settling on a tight pair of jeans, a light blue Abercrombie shirt, and funky seventies-style heels. My cell phone keeps ringing with people calling to confirm their attendance. Some of the girls want to know what I'm wearing or if Mitch is coming. All of a sudden, it's as if I'm in high school again and I'm the giddy, bubbly teenager I fantasized about being but never had the chance to become. Toward the end of the day, when I see Mitch's number flashing on my cell phone window, and my stomach fills with butterflies, I realize that I'm in full flashback, but this time, instead of it being a dark, dismal experience, it's an addictive high. If a psychiatrist ever told me I should try and fight it, I'd seethe with resentment at the suggestion.

Then, as quickly as the bubble-gum popping, lip-gloss loving, bouncy teenybopper rears her head, the insecure outcast reaches out and grabs her by the hair, pulling her down and kicking at her until she can no longer remember what she had been excited about. "No, please stop!" she cries, desperately trying to fend off her nemesis, only to be pounded at over and over again. Finally, bloody and defeated, with no fight left inside her, she curls her body into a ball, crouches in the corner, and retreats.

"And Clarke told me the name, but I can't remember," I hear Mitch's voice still talking on the other end of the line.

"I'm sorry, what were you saying?"

"The birthday banner—Clarke called and asked if I could pick it up and drop it off at his house later, but I forget what store he said it's at."

I give Mitch the name and location of the party store. I feel bad not being candid with him about my "freak-out" a moment ago, but our relationship is going well and I don't want him or anyone else from school thinking there's something wrong with me. If I lost their acceptance now, it would hurt even worse than never having it when we were kids, because you miss something more once you've had it, and once your heart has come to rely on it.

After I leave the mall, I stop by my family parish and go into the tiny prayer vestibule at the back of the church.

Kneeling down, I repeat the familiar ritual. Confident that He heard me, I switch gears and ask "Hail Mary" to please get me through Shelly's party tomorrow so that my friend has the most memorable birthday ever and my fears don't ruin it. When I was little, my mom and I used to say the Hail Mary every night before she tucked me in. Kids are literal. I thought Hail Mary was a name, like Beth Ann or John Paul, and that Hail was the first part and Mary was the second. So that's what I always called her when I prayed to her: "Hail Mary." By the time I became old enough to understand Hail was a salutation, I was accustomed to calling her that, and still young enough to be worried that she wouldn't know it was me when I prayed if I called her anything else. I remember one afternoon asking Father McGinnity, the kindly old priest who ran the parish, what I should do. He smiled and told me that this was obviously something special she and I shared together and it would probably hurt her feelings if I called her anything else.

When I get home, there's a message on my voice mail from Noreen. She and her husband have a wedding, so they won't be able to attend Shelly's party. I dial her number. As I'm waiting for her to pick up, I begin flipping through the 1982 Samuels yearbook I was recently given, which I keep on the coffee table. I tell myself, as I'm looking at the pictures of my classmates, that we're all adults now and everything will be fine Saturday night.

When Noreen answers, she immediately senses that I'm uneasy and dispenses with the chitchat. "OK," she says. "I want to know what's wrong."

"I feel like an idiot even saying it," I reply.

"Just tell me," she demands.

"What if I start having flashbacks at the party?"

"I thought you said they haven't been as bad lately."

"They haven't, but something happened today that spooked me," I reply.

"Tell me."

I share with her what happened at the mall earlier this afternoon, and how it was pleasant at first and then became terrifying. "I'm starting to think there's really something wrong with me."

"Jodee, think of all the changes in your life this year. *Anyone* would be going crazy. But I do think talking with someone might help."

"I could call Dr. Winter," I say. "I went to him when I was a teenager, and he helped a lot. My mom stays in touch with him."

"I think you'd feel better, if for no other reason than to hear a doctor tell you that you're no nuttier than the rest of us. You're just dealing with a few extra curveballs right now."

"I'll call him, I will," I promise.

"Good, I'm glad," Noreen says. "By the way, I'm bummed that I won't be able to be there tomorrow. Please tell Shelly happy birthday for me."

"Will do. And, Noreen?"

"Yes, hon?"

"Thanks."

After Noreen and I say goodbye, I beep Dr. Winter, who gets back to me right away. I've always adored Dr. Winter. Whimsical and wizened with a hearty giggle that can make even the most sullen of teenagers smile, he reminds me of one of those lovable gnomes in fairy tales who lead princes and damsels out of dark forests, except he wears a suit and tie and has an MD. When my parents started taking me to him, I had reached a point where I no longer trusted psychiatrists, having seen too many who thought the solution for my loneliness was to numb me with meds and wait for me to "grow out of it." Dr. Winter helped me survive the blackest days of my life by insisting that the opposite was true — that I wouldn't ever grow out of who I was, but that others would grow into *me*, and that numbing the pain also meant diminishing who I was and that who I was should be celebrated, not extinguished.

The moment I hear his voice, I feel calmer and more in control. I bring him up to speed on my life — my romance with Mitch and my blossoming new friendships with my former classmates, stopping short of my battle with flashbacks and "bully head." Up until now, I could tell myself that it was just a consequence of writing about my past and then reliving it on tour, and that eventually these vexing symptoms would magically go away. But by telling Dr. Winter about them it's as if I'm elevating their importance and won't be able to go back to deluding myself that they're no big deal. For a moment, I decide not to say anything, but then realize I'm only hurting myself by withholding information from the one person who has always been able to help me. Taking a deep breath, I launch into the details of what I've been going through, culminating in the episode at the mall today, and my concerns about this weekend. I explain to Dr. Winter how Shelly's party is at my condo. I tell him that, at least at the reunion and the book signing, I knew that if my mind started playing tricks on me I could escape. But how can I escape my own home?

"The one thing that's giving me hope is that Mitch will be there," I say. "Imagine me, the former outcast, hosting a party for the cool crowd, with the class heartthrob at my side!"

"I'm with your mother," Dr. Winter says. "We both told you the worm would turn."

"And part of me is delighted to finally have my fantasy come to life. But another part of me is angry."

"Why?" he asks, his tone more somber.

"Why couldn't this have happened twenty years earlier? And is it sick to be so stuck in the past? But what do you do when your past *is* your present?"

"Exactly what you're doing," Dr. Winter states. "You keep moving forward, take the challenges as they come, and lean on your friends for support. Quite frankly, I think you're doing remarkably well, considering the circumstances."

"Really?" I reply, relieved.

"Yes, *really*, but I would like you to start coming in so we can work on helping you control these flashbacks and stop you from going into — what did you call it — 'bully head.'"

After setting up an appointment, he asks me to beep him Saturday night if I need him. Feeling better, having spoken with him, when I go to bed I sleep comfortably all night. In the morning, I wake up full of optimism, looking forward to hosting my first party in my new home.

"Aren't you in a good mood?" Kaye observes, blowing on her coffee to cool it off. We've just sat down at Starbucks and are reviewing last-minute details for the party. "So, what's our plan for today? . . ." she asks.

The day passes quickly, and by the time Kaye and I are in the car on our way to my condo, it's nearly time for the party. While we're making our way to the elevator, our arms loaded with groceries, Clarke calls to tell me his friend Jeff Hoffman, who RSVP'd he couldn't come, will be attending after all. "That's terrific," I tell Clarke.

"What's terrific?" Kaye says.

"That was Clarke," I say. "It looks like Jeff Hoffman's business trip got canceled and he'll make it tonight after all."

"You never told me Jeff was invited!" Kaye says.

"I didn't even realize you knew each other that well."

"We know each other all right," she says, grinning mischievously. "He's the only guy I ever came close to cheating with."

"You almost cheated on your husband with *Jeff Hoffman*?"

"No, on my boyfriend," she says. "It was just one date, but wow was it intense!"

I look at her, utterly speechless.

"Not now, my boyfriend sophomore year."

"In *high school*? Kaye, that was almost twenty-five years ago!"

Is that how I sometimes come across to my former classmates, too, I wonder. Do they often have to resist the impulse to roll their eyes and shake their heads at how sad it is that I can't get past high school, the same way I'm biting my tongue with Kaye right now? And am I the worst hypocrite on the planet to even be asking myself these questions? But I can't deny that Kaye does sound pathetic, fretting over one date she had with a boy who probably doesn't even remember it anymore. On top of that, all she talked about while we were running errands this afternoon was how tired she is of the popular kids ignoring her, and that she'll be damned if she's going to give them the satisfaction of being the one to initiate all the conversation tonight. "They can come to *me* this time," she said, more than once today. I feel sorry for Kaye that she's still taking all this high school stuff so seriously. Then again, I was just on the phone with a *shrink* about how seriously it's affecting *me!* It's strange, seeing it from the other side with Kaye. On the one hand, it's not pleasant having it in your face what you know you must be like sometimes. On the other, it makes me have new respect for Clarke and Shelly, and how patient they are with me when almost anyone else would probably write me off as a flake. Feeling bad because Kaye is obviously genuinely upset about the possibility of bumping into Jeff at the party, I try to reason with her.

"Kaye, I can understand why you're uncomfortable, but honestly, I really do think it will be OK," I encourage her. "In fact, you and he might even get a good chuckle out of the whole thing."

"I don't know."

"Besides, I need you there tonight, Kaye. It wouldn't be the same without you."

"You promise you *won't* let Jeff get me alone!"

"I promise," I reply, wincing inside, because Kaye reminds me so much of me.

"Ooh, I better get going," she says, noticing the clock. "Call me if you need me to pick anything up on the way back."

I tell her that I will, and reassure her that everything will be all right this evening. With an hour yet to kill, I decide to take a bath. As I soak in the soothing water, I contemplate the plight of every Adult Survivor of Peer Abuse. Some of us end up an annoying caricature of our former adolescent self and others a puppet of those dreams and disappointments. I don't want to be either one, but I realize, especially after spending the day with Kaye, that I'm both.

The party is a success. When Shelly walks in the door and everyone jumps out at her and yells, "Surprise!" she bursts into happy tears. It makes me feel buoyant seeing her so animated and pleased. She sparkles all evening, like the old Shelly from school, who could make you fall down laughing with her quick wit. It is a festive evening, with friends toasting each other and reminiscing about old times, their shared history set against the soundtrack of clinking champagne glasses and the rhythmic pulse of classic rock. Though there are moments when I find myself growing wistful, I'm able to successfully push those feelings away and have a good time with my friends. The most remarkable part of the night for me is Mitch. Despite my heart sinking every time I check the clock and see how late it's getting, I keep looking out the window, hoping to see his car pulling up. When I still haven't heard from him by nine o'clock, I call him on his cell. He apologizes, saying he just doesn't feel up to coming to the party. Then he walks in the door! I swear, my heart leaps out of my chest.

"Got you!" he says.

"Oh, my God, I can't believe I fell for that!"

"Did you honestly think I wouldn't show up tonight?" he asks, smiling. Another dream come true. Everyone can see how in love we are, and it's magical. While the rest of the guests are immersed in enjoying the party, Mitch and I slip out to the terrace for some privacy.

"I want to kiss you so badly," he whispers, gently tracing the edges of my mouth with his finger. He kisses me hungrily, enveloping me in his arms. We giggle and neck like teenagers. Then, pulling away, he cups my face in his hands and tells me he loves me.

"I love you, too," I say.

It's the next morning, and I'm still on cloud nine. I'm at Mom's having coffee with her and Jeanine, relaying the events of the evening. They're both enjoying my happiness even more than me. Suddenly, my cell phone rings. It's Kaye and she's not in a good mood.

"You certainly made yourself scarce last night," she sniffs.

"Excuse me?"

"You spent half the night on the terrace smooching with your boyfriend and completely *ignored* your guests!"

"I apologize if that's how you felt, but don't you think you're exaggerating just a bit?"

"No, I was very offended and, believe me, I wasn't the only one," she complains.

My mouth suddenly goes dry. "What are you talking about?"

"It's probably best I don't repeat it," she says.

Though I'm trying to keep my insecurity at bay, it's as if Kaye is deliberately pushing my buttons. Mitch and I were on the terrace for only a brief period, and I made certain the party was well under way before I stole those precious few moments alone with him. I'm sure Kaye didn't approve of my style of entertaining, either. At the time I dismissed the thought, but now I realize that she *was* giving me a dirty look when she saw several people making themselves a drink. I also noticed that Nadia seemed aggravated, but I couldn't imagine why. I never want company to feel like company, but more like family. I told each of my guests the moment they walked in the door to make themselves at home, and I made sure the bar was well stocked and the buffet table continually replenished. Though I've always liked Kaye, it's dawning on me that she has a mean streak, and when you hear that whiny, snide tone in her voice it's time to duck and take cover; otherwise, you'll be pummeled.

"Kaye, you obviously didn't have a very good time last night, and if I contributed to it in any way I'm genuinely sorry," I offer.

Silence.

"Speaking as your friend, next time you invite people over, you might want to consider having it catered."

The moment I get off the phone with Kaye, Mom asks me what's wrong. When I relay the conversation, she dismisses my concern with a perfunctory wave of her hand. "She was probably jealous, watching you and Mitch together."

Though I sense Mom is right, it still doesn't ease that needling fear in the back of my mind. Wanting further reassurance, I call and talk to Shelly.

"My God, what's *with* that woman!" Shelly says.

"So nobody thought I was a terrible hostess?"

"No, you did an amazing job last night! It was the most memorable birthday I've ever had."

"Kaye sure didn't make it sound that way."

"My phone's been ringing off the hook all morning with people calling to tell me what a blast they had," she replies.

"Really?"

"Yes. Kaye has a chip on her shoulder and you can't let her get to you," Shelly insists. "I also think she was miffed because Jeff Hoffman never made it."

"I would have thought she'd be relieved. She made such a fuss when she heard he'd been invited."

"Don't kid yourself," Shelly says. "She was itching to be the center of what she imagined would be all that drama."

"She means well," I say. "I feel bad for her."

"I know, I do, too, sometimes," Shelly remarks. "But not when she pulls stuff like that phone call she just made to you."

Shelly is fiercely loyal. I always used to think when I was in school that if you were a bystander, that automatically meant it was because you were weak or indifferent. Now I'm realizing it's not that simple. I'm sure that, those times when Shelly saw me getting picked on by her friends and didn't intervene, it wasn't because she didn't care or was afraid but because in her mind it would constitute an act of betrayal to embarrass or shame her friends in front of others. If she had to make a choice between embarrassing or shaming her friends or allowing them to do so to me, she would err on the side of loyalty. It's not unlike the person who witnesses a loved one commit a crime, knows it's wrong, and experiences great sympathy for the victim, but still refuses to testify against that loved one even if it means facing the possibility of going to jail.

"Hey, Jodee?" Shelly says. "I didn't say this last night, because things got so busy, but thank you for being such an extraordinary friend. I'm blessed to have you in my life."

"Right back at you, my dear."

The days leading up to Christmas are punctuated by unexpected highs and lows. Eileen and I find ourselves in an escalating battle with Crystal's mother, who, despite the frightening warning signs her daughter continues to exhibit, refuses to admit the possibility of mental illness. She insists that Crystal's doing well, and as Eileen so aptly predicted, claims she overreacted at Thanksgiving and doesn't feel her daughter needs professional help. I wake up in the middle of the night, the rage I saw in Crystal's e-mails burning in my brain, and I have to turn on the lights and watch sitcoms before I can fall back to sleep.

I hear from Anna, who says that since she came clean with her mom about not wanting to be in cheerleading anymore, Susan is surprising her every day with her love and support. Though their relationship still needs a lot of work, she's daring to be hopeful about the future.

I find out that a town in California has censored my book. A group of ultra-right parents have denounced one of the chapters as objectionable because it addresses the issue of adolescent sex. The irony is that the whole point of this chapter was to show kids that they shouldn't give in to peer pressure. I tell the story of how when I was in sixth grade, the most popular girl at school invited me to my first boy-girl party. Her mother was chaperoning, and I figured there wasn't much trouble a bunch of eleven-years-olds could get into with a parent in the house. At the party, we start to play spin the bottle. Soon, bored with "kissing," my classmates decided they wanted to elevate the stakes to strip spin the bottle. By the time one of the girls had gotten down to her underwear, several other kids had divided into couples and snuck off into the attic. When I looked through the slats and saw what they were trying to do, I called my mom to pick me up. Of course, everyone turned on me after that because they all got into trouble with their parents. I became the outcast once more, and was forced to transfer yet again to another school the following fall. This group of parents in California have become so fixated on the five sentences where I describe what my classmates were doing in the attic that they missed the larger lesson I'm trying to convey, which is don't give in to the crowd.

The censorship issue ends up polarizing the town and making front-page headlines. I write a long letter to the editor addressing the concerns of these parents and explaining why I chose to put this episode from my youth in the book. After documenting my position, I conclude the letter by saying, "I believe as responsible parents it is our job to prepare our children for reality and not just to protect them from it. Adolescent curiosity about sex is one of those realities, and I wanted my young readers to know that if I was able to maintain my self-respect in the face of peer pressure, so can they. Example is the purest form of inspiration."

I wonder how many of those parents who attacked me, their hostility fueled by willful misinterpretation, were bullied when they were young, and how many of them were the bullies. Or perhaps they were the bystanders and still can't tolerate anyone who takes a stand that's contrary even if the awareness it provokes could prevent one of their own children from making a serious mistake.

Though I try to shrug off the censorship incident, it changes me. If some people thought I came on too strong before, just wait.

chapter fourteen

An Unexpected
Epiphany

December 2003

Mom's house smells like vanilla candles and fresh pine. The tree is twinkling with ornaments, some of which are family heirlooms, including the ones I made in nursery school—Mom calls her favorite treasures. Judy Garland's "Have Yourself a Merry Little Christmas" is playing on the stereo in the living room, and Jeanine and her husband, Tom, are in the kitchen chatting with Mom. I'm still upstairs getting ready. It's Mom's annual Christmas Eve party, and we're expecting a houseful of guests.

I've been waiting for this night all my life.

Most women fantasize about their wedding day, but for me it was always about Christmas. I remember in school the last day before Christmas break, year after year, standing by the lockers, hearing everyone talk about the parties they'd been invited to and the plans they were making with one another. For kids who have friends in school, life is more fun during holiday vacation, because they hang out with one another and get lost in their own world. For the student out-cast, vacation breaks cut two ways. On the one hand, they promise relief from the constant bullying. On the other, all that time by yourself wishing the phone would ring reminds you that much more how alone you truly are.

As I grew older, I thought the longing I experienced every Christmas during those teen years would eventually subside. But I discovered that, even surrounded by family and friends, there was a part of me that wished some of the kids from school would walk through the door and that I had a boyfriend whom I could kiss under the mistletoe. I never got to be a teenager even when I was a teenager. The hunger to experience Christmas through the eyes of an adolescent with a crush on a boy who makes her skin tingle whenever she hears his voice never left me. Tonight, I'm finally able to be that teen with Mitch. And though I know this shameless regression makes me pathetic, better that than the empty, angry woman I found myself becoming every Christmas because that hole inside me couldn't be filled.

As I'm putting on the last of my makeup, I hear the tinkling of bells. Curious, I tiptoe across the hall, look down the stairs, and see Mom's mischievous fur balls, Kitty and Baby, opting for a game of cat tag under the tree. For as along as I can remember, my mom always adopted dogs, but when these two orphaned felines found their way to her home they became immediate members of the family. Everyone in my family has always rescued abandoned and injured critters, from baby robins and floppy-eared bunnies to scruffy mutts, aging hamsters, and even a stray turtle big enough for a toddler to ride that wandered into our garden one afternoon.

My parents, grandparents, aunts, and uncles always taught me that if something is helpless and needs your love you never, *ever* consider turning it away. I won't kill *any* living creature, because who am I to take the life of something that can also give life? I remember *Charlotte's Web*, and *Horton*

Hears A Who!, and I learned my lesson after reading those books: just because something is small doesn't mean it's insignificant. I feel like Horton a lot these days, trying to get the world to listen to me about school bullying, and praying that I can keep everyone in Who-ville safe until they do.

Though I realize a lot of people would consider me and my family eccentric, it's our willingness to go to extremes to save innocent creatures others might overlook that I'm most proud of. I know becoming an activist is no accident and that it was in me even as a child. I just didn't realize it at the time, and assumed that, compared to my classmates and their families, my parents and I were just weird. I wonder how many other activists thought themselves odd when they were young. Perhaps activism is hereditary, I tell myself, as I'm signing a check to Tender Loving Care, a local animal shelter that my parents and I have been involved with since its inception. Every Christmas I make a large donation to the shelter in my family's name. Now that Dad's gone, it means even more.

"Jodee," Jeanine calls from downstairs. "Shelly and Clarke are here!"

"Coming," I reply, tucking the check into a Christmas card to put under the tree.

I chuckle as I make my way downstairs. All along the staircase, playfully peeking out from in between the banister posts are dozens of whimsical stuffed Christmas toys that Mom arranges every year to look as if they're winking at you. Each of these cherished yuletide ornaments represents a tiny piece of history; a Scooby-Doo with reindeer antlers that my grandmother found discarded on a grocery-store shelf that looked so alone she had to give it a "good home"; "Frantic Santa," whose hair is an explosion of bright white fuzz as if he had accidentally stuck his hand in an electric socket, which my grandfather said reminded him of my dad who on a crazy whim had gotten a perm that holiday; a Daffy Duck dressed as a holiday elf that my Aunt Eve handed my mom the year two mallards decided to nest atop our pool cover for the winter, which we fed and cared for until they flew away in spring.

"Where's Mitch?" Shelly asks, taking off her coat.

"Yeah, don't tell me I'll be the only guy again in our group," Clarke teases.

"He's on his way," I say, smiling.

"Hi, kids," Mom says, coming in from the kitchen. She hugs my friends warmly, telling them how delighted she is they came. Watching Mom interact with my friends, I realize this is as much her night as it is mine. We've both waited for this moment and seeing Mom beam is the best Christmas gift I could receive. As I'm getting Clarke and Shelly their drinks, the doorbell rings.

"Oh, Clarke — please can you hang this in the hallway?" I plead, handing him some mistletoe along with his beer. Smiling, he does as he's asked. Meanwhile, I race to answer the door and find Mitch standing there with a beautiful bouquet of flowers and a bottle of wine. He's dressed in a black cashmere jacket, black silk pants, and a festive red tie. I'm practically melting looking at him. Suddenly, I hear Clarke.

"Don't tell me I just hung this stuff for nothing!" he says.

Mitch walks me under the mistletoe, takes me in his arms, and kisses me. Then, breaking away, he searches my eyes. For a moment, the whole world goes away and all I can feel is the love in his gaze filling that hole inside me.

"Don't they make the cutest couple!" gushes my eighty-seven-year-old Aunt Judy, who's just arrived. Legendary for her outspokenness, Aunt Judy could make a stone blush. "You sure are a doll," she says, coming over and hugging Mitch. "Time for you and my niece to take this show to the altar."

"Aunt Judy!" Mom says.

"Oh, that's OK," Mitch says, grinning at me. "Now I know where Jodee gets it from."

"Very funny," I reply, poking his ribs.

There's a line from one of my favorite movies, *Broadcast News*, that asks, "What do you do when your life exceeds your dreams?" That's exactly how I feel tonight. I soak in every giggle and smile, every gesture of affection and sparkling bit of conversation with my loved ones, basking in the warmth and comfort of this festive gathering. The next day, Mom and I join Mitch and the kids at his parents' house for their yearly Christmas bash. A lavish event full of sumptuous food, engaging company, and colorful characters, it is one of the most memorable Christmases of our lives. Mitch's family is gracious and fun, and by the time the afternoon is over I can almost taste the future, and it's all I can do not to squeak with glee on the ride home.

The week between Christmas and New Year's proves prophetic. Clarke invites Mitch and me to attend an impromptu get-together with a group of our former classmates to celebrate the season. Though Mitch is working that evening and can't make it, he encourages me to go. Shelly and I decide to drive together. The local pub Clarke chose is known for its lively ambience and good food, and, like Skinny Jim's, it's popular among Samuels graduates.

"So, who's coming tonight?" I ask Shelly as we're pulling into the driveway.

"Mark, Nadia, and I think just us," she replies. "Oh, and I called and invited Kaye."

"I did, too," I respond. "I know she can be difficult but—"

"I agree," Shelly says. "Did you talk to Noreen?"

"She's in Wisconsin this week," I reply. "She said she'll get together with us after the holidays." I hesitate before asking the next question. "You're sure Nadia's cool with me?"

"Yes, fine," Shelly answers. "In fact, I talked to her earlier and she said she was looking forward to seeing you tonight."

"That's good."

"You don't sound convinced."

"Maybe it's my imagination, but she seemed to be acting kind of cold toward me at your party," I reply.

"Maybe she was just in a bad mood that day," Shelly reasons. "Honestly, Jodee, I think you're worrying for nothing."

"You're probably right," I say, secretly wishing I didn't have to face Nadia tonight. I don't know why, but I'm uneasy. My concerns will be well founded but they won't have anything to do with Nadia, who greets me warmly the moment Shelly and I walk in to the restaurant.

"I'm sorry if I seemed a little off at Shelly's birthday," she says. "Mark and I were fighting."

Shelly stares at me triumphantly.

"Oh, I'm *so* glad," I reply. "I mean, I'm not glad you guys were fighting, but — "

"It's OK, I understand," Nadia says, smiling.

Just then, Kaye arrives. She begins chatting animatedly with Mark and Nadia, a little *too* animatedly, as if she knows she doesn't belong but if she can keep the conversation lively, no one else will suspect it. Standing here observing Kaye, I wonder, do I sometimes want to avoid her because I'm starting not to like her and can't admit it, or because we're kindred spirits and whenever I'm around her it forces me to take a long, hard look at myself? And am I a big enough person to endure Kaye's emotional idiosyncrasies because of it, the same way Clarke, Shelly, and the rest of my friends put up with mine, or will I end up doing to Kaye what I'm always secretly afraid they'll do to me — turn my back on her?

"Has anyone gotten us a table yet?" Shelly asks, looking for the hostess.

"Over here," Clarke calls out, emerging from the rear of the dining room.

After we've settled in and ordered our drinks, Mark and Nadia begin talking about their son and how relieved they are he's into sports because he'll be entering Samuels soon and it's still such a jock school. I share some of what I observed when I spoke there last spring, and how, hopefully as the new generation of teachers grows in numbers and influence, they'll be able to phase out many of the unfair practices condoned by their predecessors.

"Aren't most high schools jock schools?" Mark asks. "It can't just be Samuels."

"They are," I reply. "There's no denying that if you're into sports it can give you an advantage."

"There's nothing wrong with that," Nadia interjects.

"No, but sometimes the imbalance is so large it's detrimental to everyone including the athletes," I respond.

"What do you mean?" Mark asks.

I relate how when I was on tour a few months ago, I encountered a school whose principal scheduled the big annual football rally and bonfire for the same night I was giving an antiviolence seminar. At this rally, the coaches and parents were providing a car painted in the colors of the opposing team and a dozen baseball bats.

"For one dollar which would go into the athletic department coffers, anyone could bash the car in with the bat of their choice," I explain.

Everyone is looking dumbfounded.

"The irony of doing a seminar on antiviolence while, a few hundred feet away, students would be destroying a car with the principal and coaches cheering them on wasn't lost on the community," I continue. "It sparked a debate that was picked up by the local paper."

"Did the school reschedule the rally?" Clarke asks.

I shake my head.

"You're joking!" Shelly says.

"No, and they wouldn't eliminate the violence either, insisting that everyone knew it was just in good fun."

"What finally happened?" Kaye asks.

I recount how, the night of the seminar, the gym was nearly empty because everyone was next door, dollars in hand, waiting in line for their baseball bats. "As I clipped on the microphone," I continue, "I could hear glass shattering, the heavy thump of wood on metal, and the roar of the crowd from the football field."

"I can't imagine how that must have felt," Nadia sympathizes.

"The kicker to the story is I was approached by the most unlikely group of students. Later, when I was on my way out, a group of cheerleaders came up to me in tears, saying their coaches forced them to stay at the bonfire and wouldn't let them come back to hear me even though they pleaded with her. Can you believe that? One kept asking over and over, 'What's wrong with the adults in this town?'"

"You must get that question a lot," Kaye observes.

"You have no idea."

Though everyone at this table thinks what that school did was horrible, if the same thing had happened at Samuels when we were students, I doubt any of us would have forsaken the bonfire for a seminar either. But if I asked anybody sitting here right now, they would deny it, wanting to believe they would have been bigger than that. When are schools going to realize that fostering a healthy competitiveness is one thing, and pandering to the basest of human instinct, even if it might help win a game or two, is another? And if the adults in a school are ignorant enough to set that kind of tone, what does that say about the future of those students who admire them?

"No idea about what?" asks a familiar voice.

I turn around and see Clarke's oldest friend, Tom, standing behind me. He played varsity football with Clarke, and was one of our class's biggest jokesters. "I just got your message," he tells Clarke, joining us.

Though I like Tom now, it wasn't always that way. When

we were in school, he bullied me relentlessly, often to the point that I would crumble the moment he walked away. Ironically, Tom's mom, who was a teacher at our middle school, was forever chastising students for being mean-spirited, but never seemed to get around to recognizing those impulses in her own child. At the reunion, Tom apologized for how he treated me all those years, and while I don't see him often, when we do bump into each other at the gym or in the neighborhood, the rapport between us is easy and comfortable.

"My mom read your book," Tom says.

"What did she think?"

"She remembers you as being old for your age, but she wasn't aware of the rest."

"Please let her know how pleased I am that she read it."

"I sure will," Tom responds. "By the way, guess who I ran into?"

"Who?" Shelly asks.

"Jerry," he says. "He lives in Minnesota now, but I saw him when he was home for Christmas."

"I haven't seen that guy in years," Clarke remarks. "What's he up to?"

"He's the national sales director of a big pharmaceutical company," Tom replies.

"I can see why he'd be good in sales," Mark comments. "He was always such a character in school."

"Yeah, but a lot of people don't know what that kid went through," Tom says.

"What do you mean?" I ask.

"You know that crazy snowball fight we had in eighth

grade?" Tom says.

"Yes," I answer, swallowing hard.

He doesn't remember me gagging as he and his friends kept stuffing fistfuls of snow into my mouth, or how I begged them to stop only to have Jerry egg everyone on, shouting I should be punished for defending Roger "the retard." When Tom looks back, he sees only a group of kids having fun in the snow.

"Afterward, a bunch of us went back to my house for spaghetti," he recalls. "When no one was looking, Jerry practically inhaled the food off everyone's plate. That kid was always famished. He had six brothers and sisters and his old man didn't have a job. And to think we called him a pig and teased him about it."

Oh, my God.

Jerry was given a ten-day suspension for that attack on me. His first day back to school, he snuck up behind me at the bus stop and pushed me into moving traffic. All these years, I thought Jerry was nothing but a bully who tried to be cool by acting mean to students like Roger, and that he hated me because in his eyes, I was "weird." I felt vindicated when he was punished, and wondered why he got off as easy as he did. Listening to Tom, it occurs to me how wrong I was. It wasn't a misguided attempt to be cool that made Jerry torment Roger or lash out at me. Jerry didn't hate me. He simply hated being *hungry*. Wanting Jerry to be punished was redundant. Life was already punishing him. At least in school his friends could sneak him food. By the time he finished serving his suspension, he had lost ten pounds. No wonder he was angry.

"Jodee, are you all right?" Kaye asks. "You became so pale all of a sudden."

"I'm OK," I reply. "I just never knew all that stuff about Jerry."

I guess my former classmates aren't the only ones who sometimes see the past through distorted lenses, interpreting it the way they want instead of how it was. One thing's for sure. When I go back on the road, I'll have an additional message to share with teachers, administrators, and parents. It isn't only the victims of bullying who are bleeding. *The bullies are bleeding, too.* Though I don't know it now, tonight will mark the beginning of a determined push to inspire America's schools to abolish traditional punishment in favor of a new discipline that I will develop in honor of Jerry and the thousands of kids like him who are woefully misunderstood. Jerry was one of the fortunate ones. He overcame the poverty of his youth. What about all the kids who don't?

It comes to me why bullying flourishes in so many schools. It's the system itself that perpetuates it with its archaic approach to influencing student behavior. All we're doing with traditional punishment methods like detention and suspension is making angry kids angrier. And where are they going to release that rage? Not in the direction of the popular students or their friends, because that would be too much of a social risk. Instead, they direct it toward the most socially expendable kid at school, the outcast. And then, when the outcast finally snaps because he's tired of being the scapegoat, everybody is scratching their heads wondering what happened. Our faulty system is what happened. If these schools thought I came on strong before, if some of these parents were taken aback by the honesty in my book, if certain principals and superintendents were wary of my unconventional ideas *before*, watch out America, because I'm just getting started!

For the rest of the evening, my mind is swirling with a million ideas. After Shelly drops me off at home, I get on the computer and begin typing reams of notes about this unexpected epiphany. God gave me the most wonderful Christmas gift of all in that restaurant tonight — enlightenment. No matter what, I must honor that gift by doing everything I can to make these schools understand what needs to be done.

New Year's Eve Mitch and I host a slumber party for his daughters and a dozen of their friends. One of the characteristics of a suburban community is that everyone knows everyone, generation to generation. It hits me when the parents are dropping off their kids for the party. I open the door and standing there, holding her daughter's hand is Sharon — the same Sharon who with Noreen and Jacklyn humiliated me that night at my slumber party, who threatened and taunted me in the halls every day, who made me the butt of every sick joke, and whose face I still sometimes see in my nightmares. She didn't attend the reunion. The last time I saw her was on graduation day. I suck in my breath and smile, not wanting to make either one of us uncomfortable by bringing up something she probably barely remembers, if at all. I will come to discover as the evening progresses that her daughter has the same mean streak. Though I don't know it now, the unexpected encounter with Sharon will be the first of several such experiences in my hometown, and an omen of things to come.

Despite the shaky start, the evening is magical. We play charades with the kids, help them build a fort in the living room out of old blankets and sheets, make popcorn, and watch funny movies. Shadow, Mitch's black Lab, is the prince of the party, prancing around with a paper hat that the kids place on his head, and that miraculously stays put long enough for us to shoot some of the most adorable photos I've ever taken. At midnight, while the kids are toasting the New Year with sparkling apple cider, Mitch grabs my hand, pulls me into the other room by the fireplace, and kisses me. It is the most memorable New Year's I've ever had.

By the time the holidays are over, I'm refreshed and ready to take on the world.

chapter fifteen

The Toughest
Audience
of All

January 2004

Eileen and I are on a plane headed for Houston. We're touring for two weeks in the Southwest. I haven't worked out all the kinks in my teacher workshop yet, but I've got a much better idea of where I need to go with it. I don't want teachers to think I'm blaming them for the ills in our school system, because I'm not, but I do hold every teacher responsible for the ills in their own classrooms. And when the system makes it more difficult than it should be, then it's up to every teacher who's sick and tired of being frustrated to take a position and say enough is enough. Schools are stuck in a rut. Teachers can get us out. I want to help them do it. But first I've got to make them understand that just because some of my ideas are unconventional doesn't mean they won't be effective. I have a fresh perspective that's practical and could save lives, and I've got to get educators to believe in me as much as their students do.

As we taxi down the runway, I put on my headphones and try to rest, but my mind is racing with thoughts of our previous tour—what worked, what didn't, what I need to remember, what I hope I can forget, the grateful tears, the icy stares, the disbelief on some faces, the recognition on others, the looks that said you changed my life and those that said we don't care, a thousand images, each one superimposed over the next, snapshots of success and failure, of stalemate and hope, all coming at me, making my head pound. I feel like I'm on one of those carnival rides that spin you around and around until everything becomes a blur. Being on tour is similar. Even after you get off, you're still dizzy and as much as you may have enjoyed the ride, you swallow hard before going on the next time.

The building is austere and pristine and reminds me more of an English country manor than a private academy. As I wind my way through the ornate garden leading to the main entrance, I see a small group of female students chatting on the steps. They're clad in the school uniform: plaid pleated skirt, knee-high socks, and leather loafers. Though their individual expression may be restricted by the dress code, they have compensated richly with their hair, makeup, and accessories. One of them is carrying a Fendi bag. Her two friends look as if they just breezed out of the beauty salon. These girls are haughty and self-entitled. They are a cliché not unlike some of the kids at the alternative school, substituting their personas for their true selves because they think it's the only way to survive their environment. I admire the student who doesn't surrender to that strategy, but I shudder for her, too.

I remember when my parents sent me to a place like this.

"But, Mr. Warren, Steve hit me," I say, my cheek stinging.

"Perhaps you deserved it," he says.

I stare at my teacher, too enraged to speak.

283

"Enlighten me, Ms. Blanco. Why weren't there ever any problems like this in my class before you arrived?"

"That's not true! Dave's always been picked on, too. Sometimes even worse than me."

"He's another one," Mr. Warren sniffs.

I see images of Dave trying not to cry as half a dozen of his classmates pelt him with dirt and gravel by the bus stop; the hurt on his face as he watches Kelly place an invitation to her birthday party on everyone's desk except his; the sight of him wincing as his finger's getting twisted because he didn't help someone cheat in math class.

This isn't happening, I tell myself. Of all the speaking engagements the Little General couldn't attend, why did it have to be this one? I should have realized I'd get flashbacks here. What if the teachers at this school are like Mr. Warren?

I'm jolted from my thoughts by a tapping on the shoulder. "Jodee, do you want anything?" Eileen asks, as the flight attendant hands her a cup of coffee.

"No, thanks."

"Hey, are you OK?"

"I was thinking about that academy I spoke at right before Thanksgiving."

"I know how frustrated you were," Eileen says.

I describe how the superintendent tried to threaten me into silence because I was more interested in helping her students than in playing the role of celebrity author to their parents.

"You never said anything about a threat," Eileen says,

her hackles rising.

"I didn't want to upset you over the holidays."

"I'm more upset you didn't tell me," she replies.

"I'm sorry."

"What happened?"

"During the one-on-ones, a bunch of students said they were being harassed by classmates and when they went to the superintendent she made a big fuss but never did anything. When I asked her about it, she laughed and said they were being overly dramatic."

"Do you think they were?"

"Eileen, there's no way any kid could fake the pain I saw."

"Did you tell her that?"

"Yes, and I also told her I saw some of it myself during my student presentation. So did half the faculty."

"What did she say?"

"That I'd better not discuss it with anyone if I care about my reputation."

Eileen shakes her head.

"I wouldn't expect an invitation to speak from another private school anytime soon," I remark. "I'm sure I'm on that superintendent's blackball list." I notice a grin spreading across Eileen's face. "What are you smiling at?"

"This is why you need to tell me these things," she gloats.

"What are you talking about?"

"I just received a letter from one of the teachers at that academy who was at the parent seminar when you spoke on behalf of those bullied kids. You inspired a lot of people that night. She said the superintendent has been getting inundated with phone calls from parents and academy alumnae congratulating her on addressing this problem instead of sweeping it under the carpet like so many other academies would."

"And I thought I'd blown the chance of ever speaking at a private school again. That's why I didn't say anything to you. I was scared you'd be furious with me after all the work you've done."

"Let's get something straight, Blanco," the Little General says. "What makes you think I didn't know what was going on? We're in this together."

The remainder of the flight, Eileen and I discuss the details of the schedule for this week. I tell her about the epiphany I had because of my encounter with Tom, and we discuss how I might incorporate it into the teacher workshop. We also talk about an unusual phone call she received on her way to the airport this morning. She tells me that a principal from a middle school in suburban Chicago wanted to know if I could come to his school as soon as we're back from tour because he has a delicate issue he needs to address with his eighth graders and he's concerned that he'll be too embarrassed to be effective. When I ask Eileen what it is, she says it has to do with the new fad at many of the nation's middle schools called jelly braceleting.

Several kids have told me about it. The bracelets are gel-filled bangles that are sold at tween specialty boutiques. These bracelets come in about a dozen different colors, and each color represents a different sexual act. If a girl at school is wearing one and a boy pulls it off, she's expected to perform the act represented by the color. When I first heard about this practice, I was shocked. The students who confided that they'd experimented with it admitted not having gone farther than a kiss. The handful who did confess to doing things they shouldn't have, I referred to their school counselors. I also told them the story that got my book censored in that small town in California. Many of these students sent me e-mails afterward telling me how much that story helped them. I should send those e-mails to the parents in California who are still giving the library a hard time because they've stocked my book again.

"The principal found two eighth graders having oral sex under the stairs by the gym," Eileen continues.

"Are you serious?"

"Their friends were betting on whether or not they'd get caught," she adds.

Who are their parents?

"What, exactly, is the principal requesting?"

"That you talk with his eighth graders."

"Can't he do it himself?"

"He will if he has to, but most of the kids read your book in English class and he thinks you'd get through to them better."

"I don't guarantee I'll even be lucid after two weeks of touring, but I'll give it a try," I reply.

"I already told him you would."

"Hey, can I ask you something?"

"Sure, what?"

"Is it just me, or are kids more screwed up today than when we were young?"

"They're exposed to more, that's for sure," Eileen says. "But we were just as screwed up."

"I was definitely a mess, but I thought I was the exception."

"Look at the adult survivors who contact us," she points out. "How many e-mails have you gotten in the last month from people terrified to attend their high school reunions? And what about that guy who called in when you were doing that radio show and said he was on his way to kill himself until he heard some of the other people you spoke with that night?"

"I could never forget that."

"Jodee, families kept stuff hidden when we were young. Parents were ashamed if they had a child who was getting bullied and the schools rarely did anything."

"What if I can't do it?"

"Do what?" Eileen asks.

"Make America take this whole bullying thing more seriously, not just when someone gets killed."

"You already are," she says. "Don't underestimate the power of enlisting one person at a time. Look how far the gay community has come in the past twenty years, and that's how they did it."

"It's how the animal-rights activists made a difference as well."

"That's right," she says. "And so will we."

When we land, Eileen finds a quiet corner to check her voice mails while I head to the baggage claim. Just as I'm retrieving our suitcases, I see her running toward me waving her hands. "What is it?" I ask, not sure whether I should be happy or scared.

"You'll never guess who I just heard from!" she says.

"Who, for goodness' sake?"

"The Department of the Interior," she answers.

"OK, I'm impressed," I confess. "What did they want?"

"The largest Navaho reservation in the country heard what you've been doing in schools and asked for approval to bring you there. Apparently, bullying is a serious problem in Native American communities."

"That's major, isn't it?"

"I'd say so," she replies, grinning.

"There's more. The FCCLA called, too."

"You mean that huge organization in every school in the country?"

"Right, it's the Family, Career and Community Leaders of America. It used to be called the Future Homemakers of America when we were kids."

"What did they want?"

"They would like to know if you'd give the keynote address at their annual convention next year."

"All this happened while I was getting the bags?"

"And you thought we weren't reaching people," she chides.

Maybe Eileen is right. I have to stop measuring our progress based on my old New York publicist standards that if you're not on *Oprah* or *Good Morning America*, headlining in *USA Today* or in the pages of *People* magazine, you're small time. Looking back on it now, I'm ashamed that I could have gotten so caught up in the hype publicists buy and sell. I'm not saying I wouldn't love all the magazine and television coverage. Anyone in my position would welcome the help communicating their message. But, as I'm standing here contemplating the events of this past year, I wonder if the fact that I'm not big yet is what's giving me my credibility in the trenches with people like those on that reservation or the FCCLA members. I'm getting through to individuals on a rare personal level right now, and if I become highly publicized will something be lost at the expense of what might be gained?

"I'm so busy working, I can't get any work done," Eileen announces, flustered, as she dials her home office to check messages. The moment she says it, we both burst out laughing.

"But seriously, I'm going to need help, at least someone to stay on top of the e-mails when we're on tour," she says.

"Do you know anyone? We won't be able to pay much."

"My friend Terri has extra time. I'll ask her."

"Sounds good," I respond as we walk toward our rental car. Another lesson Eileen and I have learned is that it's better to have our own car than to rely on someone from the school district to escort us. It's less pressure for them, and gives us more control. It also helps us avoid uncomfortable situations, such as being asked to attend someone's child's soccer game, or their daughter's Girl Scout meeting, or join their family dinner, when all Eileen and I want to do is go to our hotel rooms, eat something, and watch TV. Though we're grateful for their kindness, it's hard for anyone to understand how exhausted I am after speaking ten hours straight, being surrounded by hundreds of people all day, and how demanding Eileen's role is, having to manage it all. I need that time alone. And Eileen and I need time away from each other, too. Though many nights, when we get back to our hotel, as I'm dragging myself up to my room, I'll see Eileen sneak into the business center. When I go to sleep, she'll still be returning e-mails and reviewing the next day's schedule.

The drive to our hotel is pleasant. Eileen and I joke about the obvious lack of decent places to eat in this part of town. We're starting to discover that humor is the only way to survive on tour. The last town we visited this fall was so far in the boondocks, that there wasn't anything but fast-food joints and strip clubs, so we lived on trail mix and dried fruit for two days. The nearest hotel was fifty miles away, so we stayed in a motel with paper-thin walls and the sound of trucks whooshing past the window all night. Once, a school district put Eileen and me in a motel that reeked of urine and sported a pimp prowling the parking lot.

It feels good to laugh about it now, because none of that stuff matters in the end. It's not the bed bugs (yes, we endured those once, too) or the cold coffee or lumpy beds that we remember once we're back home. It's the faces of those kids who allow us to enter their lives, the teachers who are grateful we came, the parents who tell us we've given them hope that make it worthwhile. That's not to say we're not thrilled to check into a hotel where the sheets are cool and crisp and there's a decent restaurant nearby.

We eat at a local diner where the food is surprisingly good. The grilled cheese is gooey and delicious, and the French fries fresh-cut and crispy. Then, we check into our hotel— nothing fancy, but it's clean. When morning comes, we're alert and ready to start another day!

Eileen and I are having breakfast at the same roadside diner we discovered last night, reviewing details for today. It looks like this will be our primary spot to eat while we're here. The local population is less than two thousand and apart from a few fast-food joints, there isn't much here. This town is a popular truck stop and a large number of its residents either work in one of the businesses that cater to the truckers or on family-owned farms. According to our contact, beneath the community's affable demeanor is a deep social divide, and the school has become a microcosm of the problem. Bullying-related suspensions have been on the rise, and one teacher decided to step up and do something about it.

"So it wasn't a principal or counselor who brought us in?" I ask.

"The English teacher at the middle school," Eileen says. "Her name is Mary Munson. She did the fund-raising herself."

"How did she hear about me?"

"An old friend of hers is a teacher at Marron," she replies. "When you meet Mary, please make a fuss. She worked day and night to make this happen."

Listening to Eileen makes me wonder about a pattern we've seen emerging that I'll never understand. The small municipalities, which have little or no money, find a way to bring us in or will die trying. But the larger, more affluent communities often all but ignore the issue of bullying. Ironically, those are usually the schools that need us the most. Though Marron is in one of the most prosperous school districts in that state, I wonder if they would still have told my publisher yes if I hadn't been willing to speak pro bono. Eileen was telling me about this one wealthy district that strung her along for nearly a year and then pulled the plug at the last minute because the school board decided to use the funds they'd allocated for my appearance toward resurfacing the parking lot instead. Meanwhile, we've been receiving e-mails from students in the district imploring us to come anyway because the bullying problem is so bad.

It frustrates me when the kids reach out to us but our hands are tied because the adults won't cooperate. Even though Eileen and I barely survive, I hate charging schools. I wish some great benefactor in the sky would sponsor us so we wouldn't have to watch those administrators who make the issue a priority scrounge for the money. I also wish the government would do for school bullying what they did for academics with the No Child Left Behind Act. While I realize this act has its flaws, at least it attempts to establish a sustainable standard. There isn't one consistent definition for school bullying in this country, let alone a cohesive, federally funded initiative to prevent it. My fantasy is to help lead a government task force specifically designated for this purpose. Mom says if Eileen and I keep pounding on doors, eventually, the right ones will open. But you'd think with so many thousands of students and their parents calling out for our help, we'd see it happening more quickly.

After breakfast, we leave for the school. Eileen, who would make punctuality the eleventh commandment if she could, always insists that we head out as early as possible in the mornings. Though I like to be prompt, I think she's being overly cautious and explain that I don't see why we have to allow an hour to get somewhere that's only fifteen minutes away.

"Never take chances," states the Little General. "Better early than late."

It turns out that the directions we have from the district are muddled. We get lost on one of the back roads, make half a dozen wrong turns, and end up in the middle of a dairy farm before we finally find our way to the school nearly an hour later.

"Go ahead, say it," I tell her as we're pulling into the school parking lot with time to spare.

"OK! I *told* you so."

When we get out of the car, we pause for a moment to appreciate the simple beauty around us. It's as if we're standing in a page from a photography book on America's heartland. In the distance, I hear the steady hum of a tractor and the hiss of irrigation sprinklers. I inhale deeply, letting my lungs fill with the optimistic smell of turned earth. Directly in front of us is the school. A quaint red brick building overlooking an infinite expanse of cornfields, it doesn't seem possible there could be so much unrest in so idyllic a setting. Mary Munson is waiting for us in the main office when we arrive. Dressed conservatively in a white button-down blouse and gray pleated pants, this woman radiates strength and resolve. It's in the firmness of her handshake when she introduces herself and the unwavering determination in her eyes when she speaks.

"I guess Eileen's told you some of the problems we've been having here," Mary says.

"She said a lot's being fueled by economic and social prejudice."

"Some racial, too," she adds.

"I'll address that with the kids. Is there anything else you think I should know before we go to the gym?"

She hesitates. "Some of the teachers here are very old school."

"If you're referring to the part in my talk where I reveal what Tyler wrote in my yearbook, I always ask the principal how he would like me to handle it," I reassure her. "I can give an abridged version or tell the kids the truth straight out which is what I prefer."

"Oh, a single swear word is not a problem," she says. "In fact, we have a very progressive principal and I'm sure he'll want you to go for the full, dramatic impact."

"Then what is it?"

"A few of the faculty said they heard that you tell students you sympathize with the Columbine shooters."

"Mary, I never use the word 'sympathize.' They're taking what I say about Columbine completely out of context."

"I know," she says. "My friend at Marron sent me a tape of your presentation. It's what convinced me that we had to get you here."

"Then what's your suggestion?"

"The principal and I support you completely and don't want you to change a thing, but I thought I should warn you if you get a dirty look or two not to let it bother you."

"Thanks, I really appreciate that," I say, relieved.

"Dealing with those teachers must be difficult for the principal," Eileen observes.

"I honestly don't know how he does it," Mary replies. "He came here from Houston last year and they've been giving him a hard time since day one."

"Why?" I ask.

"They're a small, tight-knit group who have been here a long time and don't like change," she explains. "It's a shame, because he's the best principal we've ever had, but if this keeps up I doubt he'll stay."

"Has anyone talked to the school board on his behalf?" Eileen inquires.

"Several of my colleagues and I have approached them, but they're hesitant to step in. It's ironic that our principal can't get the support to make the changes he was hired for because of a handful of teachers who would benefit in the end, anyway."

As I'm listening to Mary, I realize I never really thought about how tough certain principals have it. The way most districts work, the principal has the authority to hire faculty, but not fire them. The most he can do is make a recommendation to the superintendent and the school board, but they have to approve the dismissal, which can be an elaborate process. I wonder how many teachers have gotten tenure that don't even belong in a classroom because a principal who feels helpless and has convinced himself there's nothing he can do looks the other way. Districts that don't empower their principals lose in the long run because a tired, discouraged leader is no good to anyone.

I don't care what the unions say. Nobody who works for a school, from the superintendent to the cook in the cafeteria, should be exempt from getting the boot if he's not doing his job, and while the process should be fair, it also needs to be efficient. I've been to many districts that are getting it right. When I encounter one that isn't, the activist in me wants to bring the issue out into the open. Though it gets me in trouble occasionally, it's worth it when I read the e-mails, some from students, others from parents or teachers and even school board members themselves that thank me for speaking out because things are starting to change in their district.

As we make our way to the gym, the hallway is bustling with students rushing to first period. This middle school is smaller than most we visit and only has seventh and eighth graders. The district has a separate school for the fifth and sixth graders, which I'm scheduled to speak at tomorrow. We're greeted by the principal. Young and athletic with warm, blue eyes and freckled cheeks, if it wasn't for his bald spot, he'd almost look as if he could be a student himself.

"I'm so delighted to meet you," he says, shaking my hand. "And you must be the Little General," he adds, grasping Eileen's. "Welcome to Noonan Middle School."

We chat for a few moments. He confirms what Mary said earlier, that he wants me to speak frankly to his students and sugarcoat nothing. "I don't have a problem with you repeating exactly what Tyler wrote, as long as you do it in the context of how badly words hurt," he says.

I assure the principal that we're on the same page and thank him for trusting me and not trying to place restrictions on the presentation. "You'd be surprised how many educators do," I tell him.

"I promise, you won't get that from me. If I didn't have faith in what you could achieve, you wouldn't be here."

I can see why Mary has such great respect for this man. He has a strength and confidence far beyond his years, yet he's also approachable, the kind of principal a troubled student would want to turn to. "I bet the kids really respond to you," I comment.

"I demand a lot from my students, but they know they can trust me."

"You should be proud of that."

"It's what keeps me going," he replies.

The student presentation goes well, and the audience is open and responsive. I take several moments to explore the issues that Mary mentioned. Many of the kids express visible remorse upon learning how much they've been hurting each other, while others seem like miniature versions of Archie Bunker, as if they were pickled in prejudice as infants and the scent has never left them. The social dynamic at this school won't shift overnight, but judging by some of the students' reactions today, I believe change is possible. Now, if I can just get the teachers on board.

This principal is requiring his staff to attend my faculty workshop, which I soon discover will be the exception and not the norm at most schools. There will be mornings when I'll be giving my student presentation and I'll watch the pained expressions on teachers' faces as they witness students breaking down, and I'll be thinking, I'll see them later at the workshop. Then, to my surprise, only a handful show up. Why do some teachers encourage their students to do extra credit, but when they get the opportunity themselves, choose not to? And unfortunately, many administrators won't force the issue because they don't want to risk complaints from the teachers' union. I understand the unions are only trying to protect their members by not allowing school districts to make more demands upon teachers' time than they already do. Everyone, the districts, the teachers' unions, all have the best of intentions. The problem is the more I witness, the more I think my grandmother was right about the road to hell being paved with good intentions.

Then there are compassionate warriors, such as Mary Munson, who stand up for what's right no matter who they have to take on, the district administration, the school board, or even the union itself. Teachers who make sacrifices for their students like Mary and Ms. Redson far outnumber those who don't in the American education system, but it will be a while before I come to realize this. I'll meet a lot of tired, burnt-out teachers, who may be the minority but sometimes feel like the majority, especially on those days when I have to deliver my workshop to a room full of empty chairs after having just listened to distraught students who tell me their teachers don't know how to help them.

I'm beginning to realize that there isn't much gray in education. The people who are dedicated live and breathe it, and those who for whatever reason have lost that spark end up becoming a drain on everyone, including themselves. Despite the disheartening moments when all I can think about are the ones who don't care enough, it's like Eileen said, I'm making a difference one person at a time, not one gym or one auditorium at a time, but one human being at a time, and for now, that'll have to be enough.

As we're walking into the library for the faculty workshop, a teacher pulls me aside. "I was amazed this morning," she says. "I've never seen my students sit still that long."

"Thank you," I reply.

"But don't you think you would be better off not glorify-ing popularity so much?" she scoffs.

"Excuse me?"

"You focus too much on how badly you wanted to fit in when what you *should* be telling these kids is that it isn't important."

This teacher only heard what she wanted to hear. Though I want to be politic in how I handle her remarks, it's difficult to refrain from losing my cool. "Thank you for shar-ing that with me," I respond. "I respect a person who's not afraid to voice an honest opinion."

"Well, I—"

"But I am sorry that's all you got out of my story," I add.

For a moment, she doesn't quite know what to say, when one of her colleagues approaches us.

"I don't mean to be critical, dear, but are you sure it's wise to advise students to take on the bully?" she says.

No, not take on! Stand up to, nonviolently!

"Perhaps you're unfamiliar with zero-tolerance policies?"

"Not to mention it's always more dignified to walk away."

OK, that's it!

"Ladies, why not open all this up for discussion in your classrooms?" I say. "You may be surprised by what you hear."

Eileen, who's been in the library chatting with the prin-cipal, must sense the need for a rescue, because all of a sud-den, she bursts out the door and as loudly as possible announces that it's time to begin, and any more questions or comments will have to be directed to me during the Q&A at the conclusion of the workshop.

As the principal escorts me to the podium, I look at the teachers seated around the tables. Some seem genuinely curious what I have to share, while others appear to be annoyed at this intrusion on their day.

Dear God, please let me get it right this time.

chapter sixteen

If They
Would Have
Known Then

January - February 2004

The murmur of conversation has stilled in the library, and as I look into the expectant faces of these teachers I realize that no matter what happens in the next hour, whether I'm jeered at or lauded, I'm giving everyone here the benefit of something I wish my teachers had had: the truth. I ask the audience to turn off their cell phones and pagers. Then, noticing that several people are already "resting their eyes," I put to use my experience with the sleepy athletic coaches at my Samuels talk.

"I know you've all had a long day and how tired some of you must be," I say. "If any of you don't feel up to this, please don't stay to be polite. There's nothing more disheartening for a speaker than to see somebody nod off during their presentation." I pause and let my gaze sweep from one table to the next. "Those who wish to leave, please do so now. No one will be offended." I look over at the principal, who's seated next to Mary. Both of them are grinning.

"Think of me as the voice of your bullied students," I begin. "If only my teachers had known what I'm about to tell you." Recalling my conversation with Shelly before Thanksgiving, I remind myself to let the strength of my resolve and not old anger guide me during this workshop.

"How many of you saw one of my student presentations

today?" I inquire. They all raise their hands. Though I don't know it now, this will be a crucial element in effectively reaching teachers. Eileen and I will soon find out that those teachers who aren't exposed to my student presentation and who don't witness the reaction themselves will often be less open and sometimes even hostile toward my ideas. We'll come to learn it's the kids who inspire my credibility with the adults, and that's why when we go into a school and I address students first, then faculty, and parents at night, we get the best results. Schools that demand we adjust our format to accommodate their schedule and think we're inflexible because we resist don't realize that what they're asking us to do will cheat everyone in the end.

"These are the things my teachers and other adults used to say that drove me nuts when I was being bullied," I say. Several teachers open up their notebooks and grab their pens.

"Ignore the bully and walk away."

The two faculty members who approached me outside the entranceway earlier glance at each other and roll their eyes. Undaunted, I continue: "It's the worst possible advice you can offer. First of all, you're imposing adult logic on a teen circumstance. In the adult world, if you ignore someone who's purposely annoying you, chances are they'll probably stop. But in adolescent land, when you ignore the bullies, it only makes them try that much harder. They'll start saying things like 'What are you, too stuck up to talk to us?' And what began as teasing can escalate into more severe forms of cruelty. All you're doing with that well-meaning suggestion is guaranteeing it."

I can feel the adrenaline surging through my system. No matter how many times I give this talk, it's always exciting.

"What is it that we preach to students everywhere?" I ask. "We say, 'Don't be a bystander, if you see someone being picked on, stand up and defend that person.' Why is it we'll tell a child to defend someone else who is being bullied, but if you're the one being picked on, just ignore it? That's a dreadful mixed message."

A group of teachers grimace. Several others are writing frantically.

"Kids are literal," I point out. "They don't understand nuance and context like we do." I describe how one hot August afternoon when I was little, my aunt, who saw me drinking a cola on the patio, warned me not to spill any because it would draw bees. "As soon as she was out of sight," I continue, "I ran into the kitchen, grabbed the six-pack out of the refrigerator, and then proceeded to dump one can at a time onto the ground, watching intensely for the sticky brown liquid to form in the shape of a bumble bee." Everyone chuckles.

"That's how a kid's mind works," I say. "Teenagers are equally literal except the situations are more complex. How often have you offered a student advice in a specific circumstance, and then weeks later, you'll reprimand him for something he's done only to be informed that's what you *told* me to do! 'Yes,' you'll cry, 'but I didn't mean in *this* situation!'

"That's why when you tell a student to ignore the bully, the message you may inadvertently be sending is that it's OK to ignore a problem." I pause to allow the other teachers who've now started taking notes to catch up. "And the biggest reason you should never counsel a student to ignore the bully is because to them what you're actually saying is not only do I think it's so unimportant that your dignity is being diminished and your spirit broken that I'm going to ignore it, but I think you should ignore it, too. And then we wonder why twenty years from now that same child will end up marrying someone who takes advantage of him, will work for a boss who promotes everyone else except him, will raise kids who one day walk all over him, and will turn into the kind of citizen who never stands up for anything. It's because when he was being maligned by his classmates, we kept telling him to ignore it. And so that's exactly what he does for the rest of his life."

A male teacher with pockmarked skin winces.

"And how many of you have said this phrase to a bullied student when referring to their assailants?" I ask, leaning forward. "'They're just jealous. You threaten them so they put you down to build themselves up.'"

Bitter sighs of recognition fill the library.

"The girls who treated me the meanest were beautiful and popular, got invited to every party, and dated the hottest guys at school," I say, an image of Nadia flickering at the edge of my consciousness. "I was skinny and sickly-looking with stringy hair and never talked to anyone. I knew they weren't jealous of me. And all I could think of whenever one of my teachers would say that to me was, why are the people who are supposed to be nurturing my intelligence insulting it instead? I'd also wonder, why is it grown-ups always assume that if we the bullied students understand the motivation of our tormentors, it'll help ease our suffering? And why does everyone constantly rely on *us* to understand the mean kids? Why don't they ever make the *mean kids* try and understand *us*?"

I can feel the room swelling with discomfort. Though I realize how hard this is for some of the faculty, I can't let their anger at themselves intimidate me into downplaying what I know they need to hear.

"The reason is that most adults fall victim to a powerful illusion," I say. I then go on to describe the Ancient Child, how this is the typical profile of the bullied student, and that because these children tend to be socially and intellectually evolved for their age, everyone surmises they're emotionally mature, too. "Their outward sophistication fools even the most sensitive of parents and teachers," I explain. "But no child, not even these gifted ones, can be more emotionally mature than their biological years will permit, and adults who expect them to be are a bullied student's greatest burden."

As I watch the light bulbs going on and see the excited expressions on peoples' faces, I think of Kyle, and how if it wasn't for his principal reaching out for my help that day, I might never have spoken these thoughts out loud. It's amazing how every experience seems part of a divine dynamic, like a karmic connect-the-dots game, except instead of it being a page in a coloring book, it's my life.

"Ever say something to a student like 'twenty years from now you'll be famous and successful and the kids who are picking on you will be scrubbing floors for a living, in jail, or worse'?" A few teachers smile feebly and nod their heads. "Grown-ups told me that all the time, only they added the word 'writer' after famous. And they weren't too far off!" Everyone chortles.

"But you know what used to go through my head every time I heard it?" I say. "Who cares about what happens in twenty years! It won't make me friends today. I need this loneliness to go away *now*!

"Kids are immediate," I explain. "We're the ones who need Deepak Chopra to remind us to live in the moment. Kids do it automatically. To a kid, the future is after school, and the distant future is whether or not they have someone to hang out with at the mall on Saturday. The moment you begin any sentence with 'When you're older' or 'Years from now,' you've lost their attention and the opportunity to comfort them."

A wave of knowing looks filters through the library.

"When was the last time a student came rushing up to you in the throes of a severe panic attack, concerned about their 401(k)?" A handful of teachers laugh. Returning to a more somber tone, I continue. "I remember feeling like I was getting trampled whenever a grown-up tried to shove the future at me," I say. "I was on my knees begging them to recognize the pain I was in at that moment, and they were too busy pointing into the distance to see me shivering from loneliness." Some teachers have shut their eyes as if remembering. I forge ahead, their reaction fueling my conviction. "Then there's always the adult who says, 'I know how you feel.' I can't even begin to recall how many times a teacher said that to me, and while I know they genuinely meant well, it never helped."

More guilty stares.

"Ladies, imagine that it's your worst episode of PMS ever," I say. "You're bloated, achy and irritable, and have been craving Doritos all day." Everyone cracks up.

"How would you react if your husband came breezing in the door after work, took one look at what a mess you were, and said, 'Honey, I know how you feel'?"

"I'd want to throttle him!" blurts out a voice from the back of the room.

"Exactly! And kids are the same way," I explain. "The first thing that goes through a child's mind when an adult says 'I know how you feel' is '*great*, here you go making the conversation about *you* again.' Then they say to themselves, 'My teacher's already decided what I'm going to say, so what's the point?'

"When a child confides in you, it's like they're offering you a gift. When you pre-empt what they're about to say by telling them you already know, it's as if you're yanking that gift and opening it before they even have the pleasure of being able to give it to you."

I must have struck a nerve with that one.

"Last but not least," I say, "I couldn't stand being told, 'be patient.' None of you would ever dream of commanding a child to sprout chest hair or will themselves to menstruate," I observe. "Can you imagine saying to one of your students — grow three inches right this minute, young man, or it's detention for you!" More laughter. "But when you tell a child to be patient, isn't that exactly what you're doing?"

When I first started posing these rhetorical questions, I could feel the audience becoming defensive, but now the response I'm getting reminds me of the awareness exchanged by a group of people sharing a private joke. While these teachers aren't pleased to discover much of what they've been doing has been more harmful than good, instead of resenting me, there's a graceful acceptance blossoming in their expressions, and I'm no longer insecure about my decision to be brutally honest.

"Patience is a biological reality that develops over time as a child grows and matures and it can't be demanded anymore than the onset of puberty can. Consider this, when I find myself wanting to tell a child to be patient, it's usually not because *he's* being impatient, it's because *I'm* the one growing impatient with *him*."

Murmurs of reluctant agreement. Satisfied, I press on.

"I've told you what you shouldn't say to a bullied student, now what *should* you say and do?"

I notice those same two teachers who approached me by the entrance whispering. One of them raises her hand. "Yes?" I say.

"Before you go any further, there's something I need to get off my chest." She gets out of her chair and stands up.

I gulp.

"It's no secret some of us resented having to be here today," she states. "We were wrong." Then she quietly sits back down. "One last thing, could you go a little bit slower so I don't miss anything in my notes?"

"Absolutely," I reply, stunned. As I delve into the next section of the workshop, I notice a handful of teachers smiling approvingly at the principal, who is soaking it in like sunlight.

It's the next day and I'm giving another workshop in another school, this time to a much larger group of faculty and administrators. I'm standing on a stage in an auditorium. This is a good crowd. They're lively and engaged and their energy is contagious. When I gave my student presentations earlier, the kids were unusually open in front of their teachers, a good sign that the rapport between the student body and faculty is strong.

I'm about to review how to intervene with a bullied student one-on-one when an image of Ms. Redson suddenly pops into my head. I keep hearing her words Irreverent Educator and as the ideas flow, I realize that giving a speech wasn't the only reason God intended for me to be at Samuels that morning.

"There are two different types of educators, and it's important you're honest with yourselves about which one you are, especially for step one of the intervention process," I explain. "The Irreverent Educator is the teacher with the instinct of an activist. She isn't afraid to stand up to authority or challenge the status quo and will break the rules when necessary."

It's as if there's a voice inside me, guiding my words.

"The *Reverent Educator* respects the rules and prefers established policies and procedures to get things done. Both types are equally vital to the system. One is the catalyst for change, and the other the facilitator, and it's the blending of the two that makes a school run efficiently."

Everyone is writing excitedly.

This is amazing.

"One more thing before we get into the intervention steps," I say as I hear the crackling of notebook pages being turned. "It's important to understand the difference between authority and *Emotional Credibility*." I explain that authority comes with the job, it's something you're given, whereas Emotional Credibility must be earned. "How many of you are parents?" I ask.

Three-quarters of the audience raise their hands. I then act out a conversation between a child and a parent. The child, who's concerned about what to wear to the big school dance, is asking the parent if she would take her shopping on Saturday. When the mom agrees, the child bombards her with questions, like: what time can we go; what car will we be taking; what store should we try first? On and on the questions continue until the flustered mother finally says, "Today is only Monday, could we perhaps discuss this on *Friday*?" The parents in the audience smile at the familiar scenario.

"Did you ever wonder why that child is so eager for all those specifics?" I ask. Several people start shouting out possibilities. "The kid's obviously spoiled," announces one. "A demand for attention?" proposes another.

"Fear," I answer. "Imagine you're at the doctor's office and he's just told you something might be seriously wrong and you'll have to go in for tests. You'd want to inundate him with questions: How sick am I? Should I be worried? What are you looking for exactly? Are these tests painful? How would you feel if he lost his patience with you and hissed, 'For God's sake, the lab won't even be able to squeeze you in for another two weeks, couldn't we discuss this *next* Thursday?'"

The school counselor who's been gradually slumping further into her seat since the workshop started opens a bottle of aspirin and pops two into her mouth.

"Even though getting your questions answered won't change reality," I continue, "the information can make you feel less helpless and more in control, correct?" Everyone nods. "That's one of the tenets of Emotional Credibility." Citing some of my own experiences, I explain how kids *always* feel like everyone else has control over their lives except them and it's even worse for bullied children because on top of the power their parents and teachers wield, they're controlled by the bullies, too. "Taking the time to be specific, even when you're not in the mood to answer a million questions can help balance those scales," I point out. "And remember, just because we may think a child's concerns are trivial doesn't mean he sees them that way. That girl who's bugging her mom about going to the mall isn't trying to be unreasonable. She's scared to death about the dance, and the opportunity to search for the right outfit is her only available means of feeling any sense of control." To me, so much of this is common sense, but judging by the looks on some of these faces, you'd think I'd just discovered the genome.

It's getting to the point I don't even know what city I'm in anymore. When I go to sleep at night, I have to look at the notepad by the phone to remember the name of where I'm at. It's midafternoon, and I'm in a different town in a different state addressing a small group of faculty at the high school. This is another one that wasn't mandatory, and though the staff exceeds two hundred, there are only twelve people here. In fact, the workshop was supposed to be in the district's new theater, but the showing was so poor, they switched the venue at the last minute to the small conference room. Though Eileen keeps telling me I shouldn't be discouraged, it's still tough whenever I'm reminded how little some teachers care. The sad part is that I know most of them didn't start out that way. I wish I had the magic formula for helping them to reconnect with the part of themselves that made them want to teach in the first place. As I look into their eyes today, I see both hope and exhaustion, and I wonder if it's not me that's feeling those things, and I'm transferring it onto them.

This entire leg of the tour has been like a roller coaster. There have been days when the faculty workshops and parent/family seminars had standing room only crowds. Then it'll be like this district. The ups and downs are extreme. Add to that, I've been getting flashbacks again. They weren't too bad the first couple of weeks, but after a month on the road, I realize that it's not good for me to be gone this long without a break. I'm homesick and miss Mitch and the kids, not to mention Shadow, whose furry tummy I would give just about anything right now to bury my nose in.

Though I'm frustrated by the measly attendance here, and ache for the students who have to endure this apathy on a daily basis, I'm giving my best to this audience, because those who did come deserve whatever heart and soul I have to offer.

"Step one, you say to the student, 'I *don't* know how you feel, I *can't* imagine what you're going through, it must be awful.' Then you sit back and listen." I return to the example of the woman with PMS. "If your husband came home, looked you in the eye, and offered those honest, sympathetic words instead of volunteering false empathy, I bet you'd open up like never before, right?" Everyone smiles.

"But before you let any student confide in you," I advise, "close your eyes and visualize that you're switching hats from that of teacher to friend, and promise yourself that no matter what you hear you'll approach it from the helpful perspective of an ally, and not the rigid stance of an authority figure."

I take a slow breath to relax, then continue.

"Step two, say to your student, 'Let's talk about an action that we can take together today to help solve the bullying problem you're facing.'" I review each portion of the sentence so they understand the importance of repeating it to the student exactly as stated. "Have you ever told a bullied student in distress, 'Let's think about some things we can do' and then, after discussing ideas and making every effort to follow up, the student still complains you barely did anything?"

Members of the audience lean forward.

"You know what went through my head every time a teacher said that to me?" Assuming the tone and body language of a frustrated kid, I shout, "I don't want to *think* anymore! That's all grown-ups ever do and it never solves anything!" Then, switching back into the role of lecturer, I explain that ambiguous language like "some things" leaves too much room for interpretation and sets everyone up for potential disappointment.

"'Let's *talk*' encourages *concrete* communication. 'About *an* act' indicates one act, a *tangible* promise that when delivered can be measured. 'That we can take together' reinforces the friendship hat. 'Today,' the most important word in the sentence, validates the child's need for *now*. 'To help solve the bullying problem you're facing' makes your student feel that you're tackling this together, versus 'your problem *with* the bullies,' which makes the student feel as if he *is* the problem." I stress that semantics count with kids, and that when you pay attention to what you say, it can go a long way toward establishing your Emotional Credibility.

The Little General just walked in. She immediately senses the electric atmosphere in the room and grins. I know the moment I'm done with this workshop, I'll probably hear an "I told you so!"

"You've gotten your student to open up and have laid a foundation of trust by being *specific* in your communication," I state. "But now how do you fulfill the expectation of hope you've created?" Some of the teachers are looking at me wide-eyed, eager for the answer. One, however, appears to be teetering on emotional overload.

"Imagine that you're a paramedic on the scene of an accident," I say, looking right at her. "Your patient is lying on the ground bleeding at the jugular." Then, feigning a thick New York accent, I become the paramedic. "Oh, my Gawd," I exclaim, bending over my imaginary patient and gesturing wildly. "There are two phone numbers in your wallet! Which person do you want me to call to bring you some fresh clothes?" Everybody cracks up. She does, too. Relieved, I continue. "Though that's a concern you may have to deal with later, the first thing you'd do would be to stop the bleeding because if your patient dies, what good is a clean shirt?"

I explain that the bullied student is bleeding, too, just like that accident victim, but it's in the form of loneliness, and that if you want him to survive long enough for you to deal with the larger issues, you need to help the kid make some friends as soon as possible. Then I remind them the advice I gave their students about seeking an alternative social outlet through the park district, public library, chamber of commerce, or community center one town over.

"Step three," I say. "Sit down with your student and contact these organizations either by phone or via the Internet, and request a list of their youth programs," I say. "Help him identify what activities would interest him the most." I underscore the importance of going outside the district so the student is guaranteed a fresh start with new faces. Several members of the audience are nodding vigorously, and I can't help but wonder what the big deal is. To me, this is so obvious.

"Now that you've gotten your student to open up, made him a specific promise that you then fulfilled in a way that gave him *hope*, it's time for step four, talking to the parents." I then ask the audience if they've ever hit a brick wall when informing a parent of a bullying-related issue. Everyone in the room raises their hand. I suggest that instead of starting out the conversation on a note that could make the parent defensive or fearful, such as "your son is getting bullied," or "your daughter is having problems," position it from a perspective that takes advantage of every parent's natural sense of pride in their child.

"For example, you might want to try something like, 'you have a remarkable daughter and it's an honor having her in my class. I'm not sure if she's mentioned anything to you, but she's been encountering a few challenges recently, and together we've come up with wonderful solutions which I want to discuss with you.'" A faculty member in the back asks me to stop for a moment so she can finish writing this down. Smiling, I do as she asks, adding that this also works well when dealing with the parents of bullies. A couple of rows in front of her, the teacher who I was worried might lose it before the workshop was over seems calmer and more comfortable, as if she's reconciled her regrets and is ready to try some of my ideas. I couldn't ask for anything more.

It's midmorning and I'm in a gymnasium deep into another teacher workshop. The district brought Eileen and me in because there were two bullying-related attempted suicides at this school last year, and it's determined to prevent anything like that from ever happening again. The entire faculty, administration, and school board are here and you can feel the tension. This audience's responses are all over the place. Some teachers are nodding their heads in agreement as I share my ideas. A few even applauded when I was reviewing the things you should never say to a bullied child. Then, there are others who have been glowering since I arrived. The principal, though privately supportive, is someone who likes to keep the peace, and rather than trying to encourage his more closed-minded teachers to give me a chance remains hidden in the background.

"Now, let's talk about how to intervene in a bullying situation in the classroom or when there's a group," I continue. "Let me tell you about two of my old teachers, Mr. Stein and Ms. Swenson." I describe how one afternoon while I was in Mr. Stein's class, several girls started chanting "ugly bitch," under their breath at me. He overheard what they were saying and chastised them in front of the entire class, then sent them to the principal, who doled out detentions. "The next day in the school parking lot, those girls grabbed handfuls of rocks and began whipping them at my face."

I then explain how if you publicly reprimand the bully, all you're doing is elevating his social status among his peers, not to mention guaranteeing retaliation against the victim. "I didn't ask those girls to taunt me," I recall bitterly. "I didn't ask Mr. Stein to send them to the principal's office, nor did I ask the principal to punish them, and yet I was victimized twice.

"Let me tell you about Ms. Swenson," I say. I describe how she understood what I was going through because she had been teased all her life. Since childhood she had been struggling with obesity and had to use a walker, her knees had become so bad. "One morning in the hallway just before class," I continue, "a couple of girls started singing over and over under their breath that I should have died during childbirth. Ms. Swenson, pretending to need my help to retrieve something from the supply closet, asked me to accompany her. When we were around the corner, she asked my thoughts on how I thought these girls should be handled.

"We all know if Ms. Swenson didn't like my answer, she'd do whatever she wanted." The audience chuckles. "But by asking for my opinion, she avoided making me feel invisible in my own life." I recount how I pleaded with her to leave it alone because I didn't want a rerun of what happened when Mr. Stein intervened. "'Jodee, I can't just let this go,' Ms. Swenson countered. 'But this is what I want to do and I'd like your blessing.' How *brilliant*," I observe. I remind the audience about Emotional Credibility, and that by Ms. Swenson's choice of the word "blessing" instead of "permission," and her willingness to welcome my input on a decision that affected me directly, she fortified her Emotional Credibility without once ever jeopardizing her authority.

I then describe how she and a colleague approached these girls discreetly after school. They told them they'd noticed they'd been acting mean spirited toward some of their fellow students, and that they cared about them and wanted to know why they were behaving this way. I explain that Ms. Swenson included the other teacher and kept the conversation general so the girls couldn't attribute what was being discussed to any one incident, safeguarding me from potential retaliation.

"One of the girls broke down," I continue. "She admitted that two months earlier while the two of them were watching TV, her father went on a drunken rampage, threatening her mom with a revolver and that they'd been too afraid to tell anyone."

"Those poor things!" someone says. "How awful," comments another.

"Ms. Swenson helped get both families into counseling and then a few weeks later, sat down with these girls again and explained that though they suffered a horrible ordeal, it still wasn't an excuse for hurting someone else. But instead of giving them a suspension, she chose a more enlightened approach." I describe how she demanded each girl perform an unexpected act of kindness for a different person every day for two weeks. Each night before they went to bed, they had to record in their journals the kind act, the recipients' response, and how the response made them feel. Ms. Swenson required them to obtain signatures and phone numbers from the recipients so she could verify compliance. "Those girls ended up becoming two of the nicest students at school, due to Ms. Swenson.

"Traditional punishment doesn't work!" I exclaim. "It only makes an angry kid angrier." I'm vibrating with creative energy and I can feel everyone else getting caught up in it, too. Even the teachers who were resistant earlier are paying attention now. Bursting with confidence, I move in closer to the audience. "Bullies suffer from something I've labeled *Empathy Deficit Disorder.*" *Where did that come from? It's like a dam broke inside my brain and I can't stop the surge of ideas.*

"Think of empathy as a muscle. With Empathy Deficit Disorder that muscle is weak and underdeveloped and needs to be exercised and strengthened." I explain how traditional punishment disables a child from being able to use this muscle, and that eventually, it will atrophy. As I watch my ideas being considered by people who have been working with kids their whole lives, I can't help but feel sad that it took someone else to make them see the light. I haven't said anything today they aren't exposed to in one form or another every time they interact with a bullied child. "The bully and the victim are flip sides of the same coin," I go on. "Both are bleeding, both need love and compassion." To illustrate the point, I relate the story of what happened to Jerry and what I figured out that night I bumped into Tom (they were always teased).

"Rather than suspend Jerry for ten days, what should that principal have done?" I say. By now, many audience members are wiping their eyes, the image of a hungry, misunderstood boy too much for them to bear. I explain that the principal should have called Jerry into his office, told him he knew what a good kid he was, and that he was concerned about him. Then he should have looked him in the eye and just like Ms. Swenson did with those girls, asked him what was wrong. "If Jerry wouldn't admit he wasn't getting enough to eat at home," I reason, "that principal could have talked to the wrestling coach or one of Jerry's siblings. If he was curious enough, he would have discovered the truth."

I'm pleased by the indignant anger that rises from the audience. I comment that next, that principal should have found a welfare service to help feed Jerry's family, and when Jerry was no longer suffering from hunger, he should have sat him down and told him that while he sympathized with how hard it was at home, it didn't excuse what he did to me. Then, because the whole thing started over my defending Roger, the principal should have required Jerry to give up his free study hour for two weeks to volunteer in the special-ed department and work with the Down's syndrome students so he could see for himself why I loved them. "But what did this principal do instead?" I ask. "He takes a kid that life is already punishing and punishes him some more in the name of *administrative policy*."

I glance over at the section where the administrators are sitting. A couple of them don't look too good.

"The solution is *Compassionate Discipline Driven by Curiosity*," I continue. I offer some additional examples of what I mean, such as requiring the girl who teases an overweight classmate to volunteer as a candy striper in the pediatric eating disorders unit of a local hospital. "She'll learn firsthand what picking on someone about their weight can lead to in this society." I offer another example: if you're struggling with materialistic students who continually taunt their less fortunate classmates, organize a meal for the homeless and require these students to assist. "The possibilities are infinite." I explain that the key is to impose tasks that help a student reconnect with the human being he is instead of feeding the angry teen he's become, and that traditional punishment should only be employed when a student refuses to comply. "Always remember," I emphasize, "there's no such thing as a bad kid, only bad *situations* that need to be corrected."

I gaze out into the audience. Gone are the hesitant looks and the pall of reluctance that permeated this gym when I stepped onto this platform. Taking a deep breath, I prepare to drive my message home.

"Traditional punishment doesn't work!" I cry again. "It accelerates the bullying cycle and when the outcast finally snaps, we blame everything else, from the availability of guns and the overprescription of antidepressants to bad parenting and government budget cuts. While these elements contribute to adolescent rage, none of them are the cause. We need to face the truth, that it's our archaic disciplinary system that's feeding the baleful impulses in students. We want our kids to be more loving and tolerant but when we punish them, we reinforce the consequences of being cruel, instead of exposing them to the rewards of being kind. We hand out detentions and suspensions as if they're the solution, when they're actually the problem! It's *time* for change! It's time for enlightened, innovative strategies that exercise the empathy muscle instead of destroy it. It's time for Compassionate

Discipline Driven by Curiosity."

Everyone cheers. One of the school-board members has just stood up and raised her arms high in the air and as if she's rooting on a marathon runner approaching the finish line. I pause and savor the sweetness of this moment.

Today is finally the last day of the tour and I'm itching to get home. I'm standing on a stage in a small auditorium, speaking to a group of two hundred faculty and administrators. The district superintendent extended an invitation to the all the police precincts in the area, and the local DARE officers, and they're occupying the first five rows of seats. I've never had the police attend one of my workshops before, and I know the Little General is already contemplating how we can reach out to more law enforcement officials.

"Now, let's talk about the two types of bullies." I explain how the school-yard bully who steals everybody's lunch money isn't doing any long-term damage to anybody because he's picking on everyone indiscriminately. "The problem occurs when a group of students whom the teachers adore and other students look up to, single out one person, usually the Ancient Child, and make that kid's life a living hell. They treat him as if he's invisible; let him sit alone at lunch, walk to class alone, and never invite him to anything. It's called *Aggressive Exclusion*, and it's the most damaging type of bullying because, unlike more overt forms of abuse where the victim can say to himself, there must be something wrong with *them*, this makes the victim say to himself, there must be something wrong with *me*. It's apparent how to discipline a student for the mean things he does, but how do you discipline a student for the kind things he doesn't do?"

Smiling as I remember my interview with *Chicago Tribune* reporter Barbara Brotman, I tell the audience that the student who engages in Aggressive Exclusion is the second type of bully, the Elite Tormentor. As I review the characteristics of the Elite Tormentor, I can feel the pull of the past trying to suck me in. Clarke and Nadia and Shelly and the rest of the gang are laughing at me in the school cafeteria, delighting in my embarrassment. I close my eyes and conjure an image of who they are today to push the thought away.

"Beware of the Elite Tormentors in your classes," I warn. "They're the ones who *seem* to epitomize the ideal of the perfect American teenager, but beneath the façade is the worst kind of bully." Early this morning before breakfast, Eileen and I typed out all the new ideas that have been coming to me during these workshops. I've never experienced anything like this before. They're like a series of mini-epiphanies.

"'The other form of bullying Elite Tormentors use," I point out, "is *Arbitrary Exclusion.*" I see everyone writing it down and I can't help but marvel how far I've come from that first workshop when more than half the audience walked out.

"You see it more with female students," I say. "It's when a best friend or group of friends inexplicably turn on someone and persuade everyone else in the clique to follow suit." I hear this complaint more than any other from students during the one-on-ones. "Arbitrary Exclusion rarely precipitates any specific act, but seems to come out of nowhere, which is what makes it so devastating," I continue. "Classmates you may have been close with for years will suddenly want nothing to do with you anymore."

It's amazing the relief people feel when you label something, like when you visit the doctor complaining of certain symptoms, and the comfort you get when he gives you his diagnosis and there's a name for what you've got.

"Let's talk about what schools can do to create an environment where these and other behaviors can't flourish," I say.

"First I have a question. Who here decides what fashions are cool, and which ones considered geeky? Who determines what recording artists are hot, and which ones are not? Who sets the social trends? Is it you?" The audience laughs. "The popular kids define student culture. Rather than fighting the power of the popular student, why don't we harness their influence and use it?" I suggest. "Not all popular kids are Elite Tormentors. The *Elite Leader* is the caring, natural born leader who's also a member of the cool crowd. These are the kids we have to enlist as our frontline defense. What's our strategy?"

I launch into my call to action.

"The *Hero of the Week* is an awards program that celebrates bystanders who stand up against the Elite Tormentors in defense of an underdog," I say. "Every week, students and faculty cast their votes for the student who they think displayed the greatest act of bravery that week in sticking up for a fellow classmate. Three winners are chosen weekly and handed a certificate of merit in front of the entire student body. But here's the kicker!" I explain that instead of a teacher or administrator formally presenting the award certificates, the school's Elite Leaders are given the honor on a rotating basis.

"You'd be surprised how quickly students start wanting to do the right thing and take a stand against cruelty when they see members of the cool crowd publicly behind it." I say that it typically takes three quarters, or a semester and a half, before a school can measure the impact of this initiative. "I've got hand-outs today with details on how to implement the program as well as assessment guidelines that will allow you to measure its result on your school." I also state that none of this costs anything except the price of a lost opportunity if you choose not to try it.

Next, I tell them about the *It's NOT Just Joking Around!™ Encouragement Club* or *INJJA*, a weekly after-school club comprised of Elite Leaders, and students who struggle to fit in, plus a faculty adviser. "By the way," I add, "you might want to consider an Irreverent Educator for that job." Several people smile.

I go on to explain that the purpose of INJJA is to create a neutral environment where these students can engage in a broad range of activities that help them discover things in common. I explain that the club's curriculum is divided into twenty-six one-hour sessions that include activities ranging from writing movie and book reviews and community service projects to youth discussion groups and town hall meetings on relevant issues.

"In addition to the social function of this student organization, it has the potential to save lives," I announce. Several teachers look at each other hopefully. "At a discreet location somewhere inside the school, the club places a large drop box where bullied students who need help or students who think they know someone who may be on the verge of committing a violent act can anonymously reach out." I explain that there's a method I've devised by which the faculty advisor can respond to these cries for help while still protecting the privacy of each student. "In addition to the drop box," I go on, "you set up an anonymous e-mail address through the school computer lab that functions as an electronic version of the drop box."

The superintendent, who had told me earlier that he could only stay for the first few minutes of my workshop, has just popped open his laptop and I hear the clicking of keys. Feeling triumphant, I move into the final section of the presentation, knowing I've opened enough hearts that the message will sink in.

"I want to thank every one of you for dedicating your life to kids," I say. "I also want to thank you for listening to me and giving my ideas a chance. Before we conclude, there's only one more thing we need to cover." I share what I imparted to the faculty at Samuels, and to virtually every educator I've met since I started this journey. I beg them not to get so caught up in the academic lessons that they forget that it's the life lessons their students will remember them for most. I tell them there's a way to incorporate those life lessons into their syllabus that will increase comprehension tenfold. "Kids are solipsistic," I continue. "They tend to pay more attention when something is personal. That's the secret to reinforcing social responsibility."

I've never seen this many expectant faces in a single audience before.

"Let's say you're a biology teacher and you're giving a quiz on the food chain," I say. "In addition to the typical questions you might ask such as the year the concept was introduced and the name of the person who originated it, consider adding another one like, 'Compare the social life at this school to the food chain, and describe where you fit in and why.'" I explain that not only would this question allow teachers to determine whether or not the student was absorbing and assimilating the material, but they'd find out if he was feeling shunned by his peers, as well as learning about the bullying situation at the school itself. "A good teacher knows how to excite and nourish the mind," I say. "The unforgettable teacher knows how to engage the soul. Does anyone have any questions before I leave?" I ask.

Half the audience raises their hands. I look at the clock and realize if I answer all these questions, I'll never make my flight tonight. I envision the romantic dinner Mitch had promised me this evening, the scent of the candles when I walk in the door, the feel of his arms around me. I ache to get out of here and be on that plane. But I also know I'll feel worse if I don't stay and finish what I started. I glance over at the Little General, who's pointing to her watch and gesturing for me to wrap it up. I shake my head. Home will have to wait until tomorrow.

chapter seventeen

The Moment
of Truth

March - April 2004

I've been back for nearly a month, and I'm just now starting to feel like myself again. Though the tour was rewarding, it took its toll. After Eileen and I left that final teacher workshop, we missed the last flight and were left stranded at the airport all night because we'd already checked out of our hotel and every place was booked. By the time I arrived home the next afternoon, the strain of having pushed myself to the point of emotional and physical exhaustion every day for four straight weeks had finally caught up with me. I couldn't wait to curl up on the couch and watch reruns of *Bewitched*.

Before I could finish unpacking, there was an attempted school shooting on the East Coast and I flew to New York to do a national television show. The host lambasted me on air for insisting that bullying damages people for life. In his opinion, anyone who can't handle a bully is a wimp, and wimps get what they deserve. "It's just too bad some of them have to snap," he said. I tried to reason with him, but when you've got less than three minutes on camera and you're being interviewed by someone who's a bully himself, it's hard to get any message across. I felt beaten up when I left the studio and was convinced I'd blown it. Ironically, being abused on live television reinforced my standing as an activist, generating support from irate educators and parents who wanted to kick that host in the butt more than I did. Though I don't know it now, this wouldn't be the last time the American media put me through the wringer. In fact, it will be nothing compared to what's coming.

I'm in the office on a conference call with Eileen and her friend Terri, who, thank God, has come on board part-time. Between the unexpected media exposure and the success of the recent tour, the volume of letters and e-mails has quadrupled. The speaking requests have intensified, too. In addition to more schools wanting to bring me in, word of mouth has been spreading about my teacher workshop, and now, some of the nation's largest educational organizations are inviting me to host workshops for their memberships, as well as keynote their annual conventions.

"Can you believe it, the NCEA!" Eileen says.

I've never heard her this excited before.

"The National Catholic Educational Association is the largest private professional education organization in the world," she explains. "They represent two hundred thousand educators and over seven million students."

"And they want *me*?"

"Yes! They want to feature you as a speaker at their international conference and they've also asked if you'd host a couple of workshops."

"When is the conference?" Terri interjects, already anticipating the e-mails.

"Right after the start of summer break," Eileen says. "And they want you to write an article on Compassionate Discipline Driven by Curiosity for their magazine.'"

"That's fabulous!" I reply.

"And that's not all," Eileen adds.

"Tell me," I say, trying to absorb all this.

"The Illinois Association of School Board Members contacted us. They also want you to host a workshop for their conference."

"Maybe our hard work is finally starting to pay off."

"From your lips to God's ears," Eileen says.

After we hang up, I run into Mom's office to let her know the good news.

"Oh, angel, that's wonderful!" she says.

"Can you believe it, Mom? The educational world is finally starting to take me seriously."

"Did you really think they wouldn't?" she asks.

"Honestly, for a while there, I wasn't so sure," I respond.

As Mom and I are chatting, my cell phone rings. It's Mitch's daughter Amber.

"I've just booked you a speaking engagement," she announces proudly.

"Thank you, honey! Where and when?"

"At my school," she answers. "You can pick the day as long as it's after spring break."

"How did you make this happen?" I ask. This kid is nine going on forty. It's like I'm talking to a peer.

"It was easy," she says. "I told my counselor there are too many bullies at our school and she needs you to fix it."

"Amber, I'm so proud of you," I respond, touched.

"There's only one thing," she adds, hesitantly.

"What's that, sweetheart?"

"I told her you'd do it 'co bono.'"

"You mean *pro* bono," I say, smiling. "And yes, I'd be honored to."

After promising to call her counselor to review the details, we hang up. Though I'm delighted to be doing this for Amber, there's also a part of me that's nervous. I love this little girl and I want her to think well of me. Thank God I have no idea what I'll be up against at that school.

The days pass quickly, and soon, it's spring again. My relationship with Mitch is deepening, and though I haven't admitted this to anyone yet, whenever I pass a jewelry shop I peek through the window at the engagement rings. I've never felt as comfortable with anyone as I do with Mitch. When I'm with him, the kids, and of course snuggly Shadow, it's as if we're already a family. I used to have this yawning emptiness inside me that would sometimes threaten to swallow me whole. It's finally gone and in retrospect, I don't know how I was able to live with it for so long. I never realized how miserable I was until I found happiness. They say you can't miss what you've never had, but that isn't true. The blessings God has recently bestowed—Mitch and the children, my new friendships, being back home near Mom again, having a purpose in my life—I ached for all of it. I just didn't recognize it until now.

That isn't to say it's been easy. I'm discovering that there are still people in my hometown who resent me for the same reasons they did when we were kids. Though I know I shouldn't let them get to me, sometimes, I won't see it coming, and before I can protect myself, the damage will have already been done. Last week, Mitch and I went out for dinner at our favorite Italian restaurant. While we were waiting for a table,

Darren, one of Mitch's old wrestling buddies from high school, walked in.

Darren was ruthless when we were classmates. He didn't spit at me or slam me into lockers the way his friends did. He'd simply shove the truth in my face, knowing it would make me feel hopeless and ashamed. My body image was the focus of his verbal target practice. He'd corner me in the hallway between classes and fire away with the insults until my eyes welled with tears. Then he'd laugh, a sound so loud and callous that when I went to bed at night, I could still hear it in my head.

When I saw Darren at the reunion, he was warm and affable, as if we'd always been friends. I assumed he had no recollection of his past behavior toward me, which was fine, because I was content to forget it as well. Apparently, he was just in a good mood that night, or perhaps, he'd since read my book and thought he recognized himself in one of the characters. Whatever it was, the Darren at the reunion was gone, and the one who made me cower in high school was back and in full force. He immediately came over and said hello. I could tell he was slightly tipsy already, and when he asked to join us for a drink, I felt a foreboding, but foolishly chose to ignore it. Everything was fine until Mitch started talking about my book and how proud he was of the work I was doing with bullied students. Darren looked at us both and rolled his eyes, insisting I was wasting my time, that the normal kids will always pick on the weirdoes, and who was I to try and change the world.

"School bullying is like the balance of nature," he professed. "Or do *you* think you can prevent that, too?" he added, laughing.

My stomach lurched. I fantasized about slapping him but was too paralyzed to move. Worse, I felt as if I was the biggest hypocrite on earth. All those student presentations, telling kids to stand up against the bully, yet there I was allowing this arrogant ass to humiliate me again. Why couldn't I find the same courage in me that I was always able to inspire in others? As I stood there impotent with rage, silently cursing myself—

"I'd like to hear what *you've* done with your life since graduation, Darren," Mitch interjected, his voice cold and hard.

No response.

"How many *New York Times* bestsellers have you written?" Mitch pressed, his volume rising. "Do thousands of kids consider *you* their personal hero?" By now, people around us were starting to stare.

I had been waiting my whole life for a classmate to stand up for me.

"This woman puts you, me, and everyone else in our class to shame," Mitch continued. "Instead of putting her down, you should be thanking her for being the one person we went to school with who's trying to make a difference."

"Hey Mitch, take it easy, I was only kidding," Darren said.

It was time to show the Darrens of this world I wasn't that whimpering outcast they once knew, that she'd been replaced by a strong, confident woman no longer willing to permit abuse. Taking a deep breath, I reached over, squeezed Mitch's hand, and then did what I should have done two decades ago—fought back.

"Darren, you have two choices right now," I said. "You can join Mitch and I for dinner and act like the decent guy I still want to believe exists underneath that ignorant buffoon, or you can leave. But, what you *can't* do is stay here and insult me."

Darren stared at me, incredulous. When he was finally able to open his mouth, he politely declined my invitation. "Well then, enjoy your evening," I said as Mitch and I walked arm in arm out of the bar.

"What a jerk," Mitch mused, as we made our way toward the dining room.

"He was drunk."

"Maybe we should eat at another restaurant," Mitch suggested.

"Are you kidding?" I answered, flagging down the hostess. "I'm done running away from bullies."

Though the episode with Darren was empowering on one level, it also shook me to the core on another. I felt like Daffy Duck in one of those old Warner Bros. cartoons, where he looks down the barrel of Elmer Fudd's gun in a fearless stand off, and then, after scaring his enemy away, it dawns on him that he had a loaded rifle pointing straight at his fuzzy head, and that's when he faints.

These odd incidents with former classmates seem to be on the rise along with the temperature. Mitch and I attend a local carnival, and bump into several girls from his old neighborhood, who accuse me of being a liar in front of dozens of onlookers. They make such a scene, claiming if I was bullied the way I describe in my book, they would have known about it because they were popular, and nothing slipped past them in school. Their nastiness made me snap. All I remember was feeling profoundly indignant. How dare they accuse me of lying? Why would anyone resurrect all this pain if it wasn't the truth, and if the truth didn't have a purpose? Unable to listen to any more, I ran off in a rage. Mitch finally found me sitting alone on a bench. He and I got into a huge fight that night, because he thought I overreacted, and I was angry that he didn't put those women in their place. It was the worst argument we ever had, and I realized if I didn't get my emotions in check I wouldn't only be jeopardizing my future with Mitch, but my own mental and physical well-being. The next day I called Dr. Winter and made an appointment to see him the following week.

Though Mitch and I had made up by morning, there was a wall between us now, one that scared me. Thank goodness, I had enough to keep me distracted. In addition to preparing for my day at Amber's school which was coming up rapidly, I was also informed that the mayor of Chicago, Richard M. Daley, had started a teen book club and that my book was a selection. I was asked to be the keynote speaker along with the mayor himself and the chancellor of schools at their big annual event. It meant a lot to me, because now, in addition to being recognized by educators, I was also being acknowledged by the city I grew up in. Despite the personal chaos I was going through, professionally, I was dancing on air.

It's the morning of my talk at Amber's school. I'm at Mitch's house. Our puppy Roxy, whom we recently adopted as a companion for Shadow, is dashing about the kitchen barking and chasing her tail. Shadow is licking my legs. Mitch is assembling Amber and Val's lunches as I hurriedly make coffee. The girls are staying with him this week, and I'm helping out.

The tension between Mitch and me isn't as bad as it was in the days immediately following our fight at the carnival, but we're not back to where we were before it happened either. It isn't so much the disagreement we had, but the larger issue of my doing anti-bullying work at all that's the problem. This is the longest I've been home since Mitch and I started dating, and he's beginning to see on a more daily basis what reliving my past for a living does to me emotionally and psychologically. I have to admit, he's not wrong. There are days when I'll be at the mall or the gym and will see someone from school, and it will rattle me as if I'm waiting to be attacked, even if they're being perfectly friendly. Mitch thinks I should finish up the speaking engagements Eileen has already booked, and then leave this work for good. Part of me would like nothing better than to resurrect my consulting career and have a normal life again. Another feels obligated to see this enterprise through until my job is done and it can continue on its own. What scares me though is at what cost? How much will I have to sacrifice? It was one thing when I asked these questions of myself. It's another now that Mitch is asking them, too.

"Good luck today," Mitch says, kissing the girls and me goodbye as we're getting into the car. "I'll see you tonight at the family seminar."

As I'm driving the girls to school, I can't help but feel concerned. If I don't do a good job today, Amber and Val will be embarrassed in front of their peers — the worst fate of all to a child. Amber notices my distress. As we're pulling into the parking lot, she reaches over and hugs me. "You don't have to be worried," she says. "Val and I will be there and we'll make sure everyone claps really loud." Too pleased to speak, I kiss her forehead, and then, together, the three of us make our way inside the school.

I'm scheduled to talk to the elementary students first, and then the middle school students. For the younger kids, I use the speech I gave at Kyle's school. It's a hit, with dozens of little ones raising their hands, eager to participate. Val is beaming the whole time. Now I understand what Mom always meant when she would tell me how good it felt whenever she did something that she knew made me proud.

Amber's classmates are equally as receptive as Val's. I do my standard student presentation for them, emphasizing that all the experiences I describe happened less than a mile away. I know I'm making an impact when I notice several students in tears, and friends reaching out to comfort them. At one point, Amber catches my eye and smiles. There's so much love in the look she gives me that it's hard to keep talking, and I have to clear my throat before continuing. After I conclude the presentation and finish answering questions, I request everyone's attention. "Do you think you learned something today?" I ask. Everyone nods their heads vigorously. "I want you to join me in thanking a very special person who was responsible for making my visit possible," I announce. "Amber, could you please stand? Everyone, let's hear it for Amber!" There's an explosion of applause. Kids are shouting her name and cheering. I look over at Amber, who's on cloud nine. I close my eyes and commit every detail of this moment to memory.

Still on a high from knowing I was a hit with Mitch's daughters' friends, I walk into the teacher workshop full of optimism and excitement. The faculty and administration for the whole district are in attendance, and what makes it rewarding is that they're here voluntarily. They weren't required to show up. This is the largest turnout I've had on a non-mandated workshop, and I'm out of body with delight.

This is a great crowd, too. They're open and receptive to my ideas, and make me feel appreciated. When I get to the part about Jerry and what his principal should have done to help him, I can see the anguished expressions, and know the message has gotten across. None of the administrators are reacting defensively, either, but instead seem to be absorbing what I'm saying as if it were the natural conclusion to make. I feel a connection to this audience unlike anything I've experienced at my other workshops. What I don't know is that there's someone here preparing to ambush me.

As I'm concluding the presentation, a middle school teacher pushes her way toward me from the back of the gym, a scowl on her face. I immediately recognize her: Betty Luna. She tormented me when we were classmates. The character of A.J. in the book was partially inspired by Betty. She wasn't just psychologically abusive, but would assault me physically when no one was looking. I hated her for the fear she made me feel, a fear that's choking me again now.

It's strange how a person's body language rarely changes. When Betty used to bully me in school, she would put her hands on her hips, get in my face, and begin threatening me, relishing my terror. Now, twenty-five years later, here she is again, her eyes full of contempt. No, I can't let her do this to me, I tell myself. Before I can stop her, she goes in for the kill.

"I've known you since seventh grade, and *I* don't remember any of the incidents of abuse you describe," she says imperiously, making sure her voice is being picked up by the open mike. Now my fear turns to fury. How *dare* she accuse of me of lying, in front of hundreds of people?

"You were *never* bullied," she hisses, glaring at me. "I don't even know why the district thought it was necessary to bring you in. Besides, I *know* there's no bullying in my classroom."

"Betty, you're entitled to your own memory of events," I reply. "I only have one question."

Dear God, please make my knees stop trembling.

Taking a deep breath, I concentrate on the image of Darren laughing at me and the sound of those girls berating me at the carnival. As remorse washes over me, I find the strength to finally stand up to the dreaded Betty Luna.

"If you didn't see the abuse I endured when we were both students on the *inside*, imagine what you're missing in your own classroom now that you're an adult on the *outside*? How many kids are being bullied right under your nose and you don't see it, just like you didn't see it when it was happening to me all those years ago?"

Several of her colleagues echo my concern, showering her with dismissive looks.

"Get out of my way," Betty barks, shoving me aside and stomping out of the gym. Like most cowards, when confronted she runs away. I wish I had known that when I was a kid. The outcast inside me that's just been reawakened is about to throw up, but the adult *survivor* is having to bite her lower lip to keep from smiling.

As I'm leaving the school, the vice principal approaches. She hands me a box full of handwritten letters, all with today's date. "These are only the first batch," she says.

"What are they?" I ask.

"Letters from students who are being bullied and several from bullies who feel guilty about what they've been doing. They're grouped according to homeroom."

As I'm flipping through them, not surprisingly, some are from Betty's class. I shake my head, knowing that no matter what I or anyone else tells her, she'll never change. With some people, once a bully, *always* a bully.

The evening seminar is standing room only. There are many familiar faces scattered throughout the crowd. Clarke and Shelly are here. Kaye and her husband are sitting with Mitch and the kids. My mom and Jeanine are near the front. Having their support is like a shot of adrenaline, and I sail through the seminar with energy to spare. As I'm signing books afterward, several parents approach me and tell me they heard what happened with Betty Luna and that they plan on talking with the principal about setting her straight.

Though I try to convince myself the run-in with her didn't affect me, I'm unable to sleep because I can't get her face out of my mind. By the time I see Dr. Winter the next morning, I'm beginning to think Mitch is right, that I have to give up this work.

Dr. Winter's office is cozy and quaint. He hasn't changed the décor since I was a teenager, and the familiar surroundings calm and comfort me. Though I've seen him a couple of times since the holidays, admittedly, I held back during our sessions together. I addressed the flashbacks, but I sugarcoated the extent of the problem, because I was nervous he would come to the same conclusion as had Mitch. But now that I'm experiencing night terrors, I can't keep kidding myself that this will pass.

"Just say what first comes to mind," Dr. Winter urges, settling into his wingback chair.

I bring him up to speed on the events since my return from the tour, focusing on my concerns about the effect all this is having on my emotional health. He listens intently and takes notes. I try not to skip any details, knowing that what may seem irrelevant to me might be a vital clue he needs to diagnose what's wrong. After an hour, I'm out of words. I feel better that I've admitted these fears, but I'm still worried I may not like what I'm about to hear. Dr. Winter closes his notebook and looks at me, his face radiating warmth and compassion.

"What do you know about post-traumatic stress disorder or PTSD?" he asks.

"My parent's best friend Don was diagnosed with it," I say. "He's a veteran of the Vietnam war."

"Did he ever talk to you about any of his symptoms?"

"He gets horrible flashbacks when he hears certain loud sounds," I answer. "My mom says he struggles with depression and anxiety, too, and that sometimes the past sucks him in and chokes him."

Oh, my God, why I didn't see it before?

"I have PTSD, don't I?"

"Yes," Dr. Winter states. "Though most people associate it with war veterans, it can affect anyone who suffers a shattering experience or is exposed to chronic trauma."

"Don't a lot of rape victims have it?"

"Rape victims, battered wives, child-abuse victims," he replies. "There are varying degrees of affliction, though."

"From what I understand from Don, there really isn't a cure?"

"It can be managed quite effectively, but many people believe there's no cure."

"Has anyone ever associated PTSD with school bullying?" I ask, already envisioning the implications.

"Not formally, or at least, not that I'm aware of," he says.

"But now that we know what's wrong with me, we can deal with it, right?"

"Jodee, most people with PTSD don't make their living revisiting the events that *caused* it," he explains. "On top of the pain from your own past, you're also dealing with thousands of kids who are experiencing the same pain, which is a much larger burden on your psyche than you realize."

"OK, I admit it. I hate how I feel most of the time when I'm on tour, and there are moments when I'm scared to death I may doing real damage to myself."

"That's a reasonable concern," Dr. Winter says.

"But what am I supposed to do? I can't just walk away from this cause, especially now. Think of all the adult survivors like me who are going through life worried they're crazy too. At least letting them know they might have PTSD gives them something concrete to work with. Half the time, these people are told they're just being overly dramatic, and they need to forget the past and move on. I can't quit now and abandon them or the kids who need me. I just can't!" I don't know whether I'm trying to convince Dr. Winter or myself. Part of me is burning with conviction. Another part wishes I'd never started any of this.

"You don't have to make any decisions right now," he says. "But I do want you to take some precautions."

"Like what?" I ask.

"Limit your tour schedule to four talks per day maximum," he states. "Also, make sure you have sufficient downtime to regroup between presentations."

"That may be difficult, but all right," I reply.

"I also want you to be more self-protective when you get back home from the road, especially the first few days," he continues. "Avoid situations and places that could trigger flashbacks until you've had a chance to recuperate from the strain of the tour."

"I'd have to hide in a cave," I say. "The people who are closest to me now are faces from school."

"Let them know about the PTSD and ask them to help you avoid things that can trigger it," he answers.

"In some ways, I've already been doing that," I comment. "When I get the really bad flashbacks, I call Shelly or Clarke, and they talk me through them. Mitch is great with that, too."

"That's excellent," he says. "I also think it's a good idea to keep coming here at least once every two weeks so we can monitor your progress."

After confirming my next appointment, we conclude the

session. The moment I get home, I start writing ways I can incorporate what I discovered with Dr. Winter into my parent/family seminar, which I now realize must include a special advice section for adult survivors. As I finish typing my notes, I shudder, knowing that once I start publicly talking about my PTSD to other adult survivors, it will help them, but it will drain me even more.

Though I try to relax in the days leading to the Mayor Daley event, I'm haunted by the reality of my situation. I'm scheduled to go back on tour next week, and I feel guilty because I'm dreading it. Eileen and I have had to work so hard to reach this point, and I should be grateful for every booking, not whining that I wished I didn't have to do them. Despite my efforts to shake this foul mood, it permeates my outlook lately. I'm irritable, short-tempered, and driving everyone around me nuts because no matter what the circumstance, I fixate on the wretched aspects first. This isn't me, and I know I'm behaving this way because I feel depleted by everyone from Eileen, who's pushing more speaking engagements on me than I can handle, and Mitch and the kids, who are demanding more of my time than I have to give, to the dogs, who look at me with furrowed brows whenever I come over because I'm not scratching them behind the ears enough. I'm so busy trying to give everyone what they need that I'm disappearing from myself.

The night before the Mayor Daley event, I'm assailed by night tremors. I wake up drenched in sweat, determined that once this next tour leg is over, I'm done. What I don't know is that God has other plans.

I'm seated at the dais with Mayor Daley and a handful of

other local dignitaries, including the chancellor of Chicago's schools. They've all spoken, and now it's my turn. We're in a huge theater, and there are at least two thousand teenagers in the audience, all of whom are members of Mayor Daley's book club. The mayor introduces me. As I take the podium, the crowd roars. Two thousand kids are screaming my name as if they're about to see their favorite teen idol in concert. I've never experienced anything like this before. I search the audience for Mom and Mitch, who seem as overwhelmed as me. Mom is smiling proudly and appears as if she might burst any second. The response from this audience is filling me up like helium and I can feel an enormous grin spreading across my face. I wait a moment for everyone to quiet down.

"Thank you for that amazing welcome," I state. "It made me feel like a rock star." The audience giggles. "I didn't prepare a speech for today because I wanted whatever I shared to be spontaneous and from the heart."

Everyone leans forward, the hum of the air conditioner the only sound in the theater.

"There's something I need to say, and it's not easy to admit." I take a deep breath and let it out slowly, trying to collect my thoughts. "When I woke up this morning, I decided I was done speaking and writing about bullying, that it was taking too much of a toll on my spirit and it was time for me to retire."

"Oh, no," I hear kids murmuring to each other.

I open up about what it's been like for me on tour and how it had driven me to the point of being burnt out.

"Many of you have written me letters thanking me for the effect my book has had on your lives. But it is *you* who have affected *me*, and if it wasn't for how deeply you touched my life, right now, this very moment, I know I would have followed through on my decision to let go of this crusade." I take a sip of water. "But when I got up on this stage and heard your voices cheering and saw the joy and enthusiasm in all of your faces, it was like a jolt of electricity."

People start to cheer.

"You've helped me find my courage and purpose again and I'm humbled. Mayor Daley," I say, turning toward His Honor. "You must be very proud of these kids. Your commitment to enriching their lives is your greatest gift to the future of our city."

Then, turning back toward the audience, "You're remarkable, each and every one of you, and I will carry the memory of what you've given me today in my heart forever. Thank you for listening."

I receive a standing ovation. Some kids are stomping their feet on the floor, and whistling. As I'm stepping off the stage, the mayor comes up to me. "That was some speech," he says.

I smile and kiss him on the cheek.

Once again, God has given me strength when I need it most. Though I don't know it now, my faith is about to be tested.

chapter eighteen

Desperate

Parents

April - May 2004

Parents are the wild card when it comes to school bullying. Even the caring, loving ones sometimes feed off the drama and make the situation worse or they let their anguish destroy their good judgment. They can also be overly protective to the point of smothering. Then there are those parents who inspire me with their wisdom and restraint and who don't allow their personal baggage to get in the way of what's best for their child. All of them are kindred spirits doing everything possible to help their son or daughter, only to keep hitting brick walls. By the time they turn to me, many of them are convinced I'm their last hope. I've learned how to cope with the pressure of their expectations and feel honored by their willingness to trust me. It's the emotionally absent parents that are hard to take. Whether they're burdened with severe problems of their own or they're simply self-absorbed, the reason for their negligence doesn't matter, because it's always the child who pays the price.

Eileen and I have been back on the road for nearly a week. We're in a gym at a school in Florida. It's early evening, and I'm about to take the stage for my parent/family seminar. This is always the hardest lecture because by nighttime, I'm weary from having given presentations all day and intervening with kids in crisis. There are some nights when my vocal cords will be ravaged and I'll croak my way through the seminar.

The parent/family seminars are open to the public. Sometimes, like tonight, they're packed, with people having driven hundreds of miles to attend. Other nights, I'll be lucky to see ten seats occupied. A lot of it has to do with how aggressive the school district is in spreading the word, and Eileen and I are always grateful to those that make an effort. Typically, the audience consists of adult survivors, educators, and students who heard me speak during the day and who return with their parents at night. Sometimes kids will ask me during the one-on-ones if I'd telephone their mom or dad and urge them to come. Eileen and I always honor these requests. Once in a while, a reluctant parent will surprise us. But some kids still come back alone and I can see it in their eyes how much they wished their parents would take an interest in the pain they're going through. If those moms and dads only knew how much this small gesture of their time would mean to their child. After the seminar, I always do a book signing, and then sit down with anyone who needs me to listen. I usually start the evening seminar at 7:00 P.M. and rarely get back to my hotel before midnight.

Tonight, I'm on edge. Earlier in the day, I met with a large number of students in crisis. Some of them are dealing with dysfunction in their families on top of being bullied at school. Most of these kids aren't looking for answers as much as they're seeking an adult to validate their pain. I'm pleased they confide in me, but the responsibility grows more daunting every day. Earlier this afternoon at the middle school, a group of girls approached me, saying that their friend Tammy was in trouble and they didn't know what to do. When I met Tammy, I could tell something was wrong. She was skittish and unsure. Her friends told her that if she didn't tell me what happened, they would.

"Tell me what?" I asked, growing more concerned.

"Go ahead, Tammy," they pushed.

Tammy pulled up her shirt. I gasped in horror. Across her chest down to her stomach, her skin was blistered and peeling from what appeared to be a serious burn wound. "Sweetheart, what happened to you?" I asked, shuddering.

Tammy's eyes filled with tears, but she wouldn't speak. "Tammy, please, you have to tell me," I begged.

"My sister threw a pot of boiling water at me," she finally managed.

"Oh, my God, honey. Why?"

"I don't know," Tammy stuttered. "She was in a bad mood, and sometimes when she gets like that, she does mean things."

"How old is your sister?" I asked, not sure I wanted to hear the answer.

"Fifteen."

"Do your parents know about this?"

"I only have foster parents now, but I told my foster mom," she replied. "Except —" She hesitated, her expression fearful.

"Go on," I gently pressed her.

"I told her it was an accident, that my sister and I were making soup and the pot fell," she said. "I was afraid they'd separate us if I told the truth."

"Tammy, your sister is troubled, and unless you're honest about what she did, she'll never get the help she needs," I explained. "May I have your blessing to call your foster parents and see if they can come to my seminar tonight and then talk with me afterward?" This is where I feel as if I'm always walking a tightrope on tour because even if Tammy begged me to keep her confession a secret, ethically and legally I couldn't, but I don't want to betray her trust either.

"OK," she answered meekly. *Thank God.*

"It'll be all right," I reassured her. "I'd also like to get your school counselor involved, too."

"Please don't let them take my sister away!" she cried.

"I'll do everything I can to prevent it," I answered.

I spoke with the school and with Tammy's foster mom, who upon hearing what happened, was too stunned to speak. While I realize not all foster parents are what they should be, and that some only take on kids to bilk money from the government, there are also those foster parents who are genuinely in it for the love of children. Tammy's foster mom was obviously the latter. I could hear her concern as I relayed my conversation with her daughter. "Anything, I'll do anything," she replied. "I love both girls with all my heart."

I asked her why Tammy and her sister were in foster care, what had happened to their biological parents. She told me that the father disappeared from their lives long ago, and the mother was in rehab recovering from multiple addictions. As I stood there in the counselor's office on the phone with Tammy's foster mom, I couldn't help but wonder how many more stories like Tammy's I could endure before the sadness claimed my spirit. Then again, I told myself, I was a child advocate now, and like it or not, this was part of the territory.

Eileen and I are also expecting a handful of other parents whom we called either at a student's behest or because we were able to persuade the student to give us his blessing to telephone them. Sometimes a student will be afraid I'll get him into trouble by telephoning Mom or Dad. Usually, I'm able to overcome that hurdle by telling the student exactly what I'm going to say to the parent — namely, that I want to meet the person who raised such a remarkable child. This puts the student more at ease and lessons the chance of a parent becoming defensive, but more importantly, it's the truth.

During my student presentation this morning, there was a seventh grade boy in the audience who kept covering his face, and I suspect it was because he was crying and didn't want his peers to see. He was slight compared to his classmates, many of whom were already on the brink of puberty. I made a mental note of where he was sitting so that I could locate him afterward, but it wasn't necessary. The moment I concluded my talk, he was making his way toward me, his eyes red and swollen.

"My name is Justin," he whispered. "Thank you for telling us your story."

"You're so very welcome," I replied, fighting the urge to scoop him up into my arms and hug his hurt away.

"There's something I need to share with you," he said.

Another old soul.

"I should only be in fifth grade, but I skipped two years," he explained. "Now I don't fit in anywhere."

"I'm so sorry you're going through this," I said. "It must

be hard."

"It is," he answered, solemnly. "What I want to tell you is I was going to run away this weekend, but since I heard your story, I feel braver and probably won't now."

I suppressed a smile. "Do your parents know that you're struggling at school?" I asked.

"Yeah, but they say it's because my classmates are just jealous of me and I have to ignore it and be the bigger person," he responded.

"They're wrong," I said.

Justin stared at me wide-eyed. "No one has ever said my mom or dad was wrong before," he stated nervously.

"Part of what I do, Justin, is help parents who have kids that are being bullied understand what that feels like and what to do to make things better," I explained. "I'd like to be able to help your parents, too."

"I don't think they'd come to your seminar tonight," he said, sadly. "Dad always works until late at the office and mom is busy with my sister. She's got autism."

This poor kid.

"Tell you what," I suggested. "Why don't I call your mom and tell her that I'd like to meet the parents who raised such a remarkable son, and that I'm extending a VIP invitation for your whole family to attend my seminar tonight?"

"That would be awesome," Justin said, smiling from ear to ear.

After getting his mom's telephone number and promising to call, I send Justin off to class. As I watched him walk away, I wanted to scream at his parents, "Please don't forget about him because your other child is challenged, Justin won't hold on much longer if you don't make some adjustments." When I talked with his mom, she was polite but reserved. I emphasized how much it would mean to Justin if she and her husband brought him to the seminar tonight. She insisted she would do what she could.

I also spoke with a single dad today, whose daughter, Sally, read my book and has been e-mailing me for months. They live a couple of hours away. Sally is being harassed by a clique of Elite Tormentors who spray painted the word "slut" all over her locker, pushed her down a flight of stairs at school, and posted malicious rumors about her on the Internet, all because she decided she didn't want to do drugs or party with them anymore. What's interesting is that when I e-mailed Sally that I'd be in town and wanted her dad's phone number so I could call and invite them to the evening seminar, she said that her father was stubborn and not to be surprised if he hung up on me. But when I spoke to this dad, he was willing to do whatever it took to help her.

I see this often, where a bullied child, too lonely and frustrated to be rational anymore, makes a perfectly loving parent out to be a monster. One of the most challenging aspects of this work is to remain clearheaded when I'm interacting with a hurting child and not get so caught up in his distress that I vilify an undeserving parent, or worse, assume the child's being overly dramatic and miss the warning signs of abuse. That's why it's difficult when parents don't come, because how can I ever know what's really going on unless I meet them? And even then there's no guarantee, but at least I know I did everything I could. Before I depart a tour city, I always review with each school counselor what I've learned from the students who sought my help and offer suggestions for follow-up. Though most of these counselors are dedicated, committed individuals who would take a bullet for their students, it's still painful leaving these kids, knowing that while I was able to touch their lives, I'll have to rely on others to take it from there. I'll never get used to that.

I hear the principal making an announcement that we're ready to begin. As people are taking their seats, I search for the faces of those kids who were desperate for their parents to return with them tonight. Several are sitting with one or both parents, and I notice Tammy arriving with her foster mom. Others are by themselves. Though I sometimes like to think I can predict who will and won't come, the truth is, whenever you're dealing with family dynamics, it's a crap shoot. The only way I've been able to survive my worry and disappointment over the no-shows is to tell myself that whatever happens is God's will. But there are days when despite how much faith I have, those words are little comfort.

The principal has stepped up to the podium to introduce me. I don't see Justin or his family yet and keep glancing over at the main entrance hoping they'll walk in. The large doors are still open and I can see outside into the parking lot. It's pouring rain and thundering. As the principal concludes his introduction, I see a boy pulling up on a bicycle. He's in a bright yellow raincoat.

Dear God, please don't let that be Justin.

Sure enough, it's him. No parents, no family, no nothing, just this little boy, soaking wet and alone. He catches my eye and smiles. There's a lump in my throat so large that I can't speak. I'm sure the audience is starting to think there's something wrong because I'm standing here silent. I look over at the Little General to get her attention and then gesture toward where Justin is seated. She immediately understands and goes and sits down next to him.

Taking a deep breath, I begin the lecture.

"Hello, everyone. Thank you for being here. I see many familiar faces and I couldn't be more delighted." I wink at Tammy and Justin. They both grin. "Kids, it means so much to me seeing all of you here and I'm going to do my very best to help your parents understand where you're coming from and how they can make things better for you, OK?" The kids nod energetically. Then I address the parents. "Today I relived onstage for your children what happened to me when I was their age, how I was tormented and rejected by my peers simply for being different," I explain. "My primary message was that it's not just joking around, that bullying damages you for life."

A father gently pokes his son, urging him to pay attention. A couple rows down from them, a girl is clutching her mom's arm. She had approached me after my student presentation this morning saying that she thought she was the only person who ever wished for cancer until she heard me admit the same thing. She confided that despite how hard she tries to make friends, no one at school will have anything to do with her. She said that last year she tried to kill herself with an overdose of aspirin, and that now, a group of her classmates keep teasing her about it, saying she couldn't even do suicide right. Both her school counselor and I called her mom and urged her to come tonight. Judging by the mom's strung-out appearance, I wonder how much of her daughter's stress is being further amplified at home.

"First, I'm going to do my student presentation because I think it's important you experience what your children did today so you can talk about it together," I inform the parents. "Then, afterward, I'll give you advice on how you can help your child, whether they be a bully, victim or bystander." People begin pulling out their notebooks and pens. Pleased, I continue.

I discuss Columbine, the same way I do with the students. I see dozens of parents nodding their heads in understanding. Then, I re-enact my school days, allowing myself to go back once more in time to the pain of my youth. The present starts to recede, and soon, I'm the struggling teenager again, lost in the power of the memories. As I chronicle my story, I look out into the audience and see parents whose kids didn't think they cared putting their arms around them in a public show of support. By the time I get to the part in my talk where I recall how no one would let me sit with them at lunch, a mom toward the back quietly begins to weep. Her daughter, who sought me out today admitting to being a bully and asking for advice on how to make amends to her victims, is trying to comfort her. By the expression on this girl's face, I doubt she realized until just this moment that her mom was shunned as a teenager the same way she's been shunning her classmates. I press on, anticipating a long night ahead.

As I delve into the evening of my high school reunion, the students look at each other knowingly, their excitement growing. When I describe how Mitch kissed me in the parking lot, the audience bursts into applause. I notice several women exhale, as if they'd been holding their breath this whole time praying for a happy ending. Next, I take everyone through the empathy exercise.

I read in a book once that "it's easier to open a heart that's already been broken," and I realize as I watch everyone trying to resurrect the memory of the most humiliating moment of their lives that all of us are the same. We are opening each other's hearts because we've had our hearts broken. Our individual vulnerability is our collective strength. By the time the empathy exercise is complete, some of the adults are looking over at their kids, their faces portraits of their own unresolved adolescence. One bullied girl who confessed to me she's been struggling with her mom reaches out and squeezes her hand. Another girl rests her head on her dad's shoulder while he gently strokes her hair, his expression a mix of remorse and relief. Watching these parents and children finding each other again is overwhelming. School bullying just doesn't damage kids, it damages whole families, and whatever I'm doing in this gym tonight is helping to heal those wounds.

Dear God, thank you.

I commence the second half of the seminar, explaining a significant portion of this information is also featured in the faculty workshop so that both teachers and parents are operating from the same perspective. "I can open the students' hearts and enlighten their minds, but if what I do isn't reinforced in the classroom and at home, that which has the potential to be a movement loses its wings," I say.

Enthusiastic nods. I forge ahead.

"I love my parents with all my heart, and though my dad is gone now, I think about him often and how remarkable he was during those turbulent, lonely years that defined my school experience," I say, wishing he was in the audience. "I can't imagine what it was like for my parents watching me suffer every day knowing they were doing everything they could and it still wasn't enough. I'm going to tell you what my parents did that didn't work, what they did that was success-ful, and why," I continue. I look over at Justin, who's leaning forward listening intently, when all of sudden, he glances up at the clock, then turns his head toward the door, straining to see out into the parking lot. Could it be that his parents might still show up?

Taking a deep breath and letting it out slowly, I begin reviewing all the things you should never say to a bullied child from "Ignore the bully and walk away," "They're just jealous," and "I know how you feel," to "Twenty years from now you'll look back on this and laugh," and "Be patient." As I'm explaining as I did to the teachers why each of these statements drove me nuts, I see delighted students grinning at their parents while whispering in their ear, "I told you so." Some parents smile good-humoredly, relishing this camaraderie with their child. Others seem to be struggling, not wanting to accept that the clichés handed down to them from their parents like pieces of heirloom china passed from generation to generation weren't the valuable treasures they thought.

I move on to the difference between authority and Emotional Credibility and how to earn the latter. I describe the steps for how to intervene with a bullied child one-on-one, and warn parents as I warned teachers about making sure that when your child confides in you, you play the role of friend and ally, and not the disciplinarian. Upon hearing these words, Sally's dad stares at me, his eyes tight with concern.

"I know a lot of what I'm saying is hard for many of you to take," I acknowledge, giving him a reassuring smile. "And the more you hear, the more you're beating yourselves up," I add. "Please, don't lose sight of the fact that all of you are caring parents or you wouldn't be here." I pause and look from parent to parent, making sure this sinks in.

I launch into the definition of the Ancient Child, and why most bullied students fit that profile. It never ceases to surprise me how much that concept resonates with everyone. Next, I talk about Jerry to illustrate that the bully is bleeding, too, and that he needs love and patience as much as the victim. Just as in the teacher workshop, Jerry's story moves many in the audience. I address traditional punishment vs. Compassionate Discipline Driven by Curiosity, and cite examples. Then I discuss the warning signs a child is being bullied, like lethargy, depression, self-mutilation, extreme makeover attempts, diminished personal hygiene, lack of interest in social activities, sudden change in weight, overreacting, inexplicable fits of rage, and faking illness to avoid going to school.

"Not all the red flags are easy to spot, nor are they necessarily what you'd expect," I warn. "I never had to fake illness to avoid school," I recall. "Every week I was lucky enough to come down with something else, strep throat, mono, low-grade viruses, head colds, bronchitis, you name it. I was getting sick so frequently that my parents started to think that maybe I *was* faking it, but fevers and swollen glands don't lie." I recount how they took me to a specialist who explained it was possible for someone to will themselves sick, especially when their immune system was already being weakened by chronic stress. "'Address your daughter's emotional health, and her physical well-being will return,' he told my parents." A woman sitting toward the back looks at me her cheeks flush with excitement, as if she'd just been given the missing piece to a puzzle.

"Another symptom that many parents don't immediately recognize is a sudden *increase* in grades," I state, watching all the surprised expressions. "When a kid's grades go down, there's predictable concern, but when they go up, parents tend to perceive it as a sign that everything is fine, when it can mean precisely the opposite for a bullied student." I tell how a significant number of parents I've met whose child either committed suicide or attempted it told me one of the reasons they were shocked was because their son or daughter's grades had never been better, and that they finally seemed to be "doing so well." I explain that while this is not an absolute, and that a drop in grades is the more common sign that a student is being bullied, you should still pay attention to any changes. "Some severely bullied students immerse themselves in academic achievement as an escape, and then feel even more hopeless when they realize they're still lonely." I also define Rejection Junkie Syndrome. As I begin describing its characteristics, I notice a husband turn and look at his wife with suspicion.

"I described some of the signs your child may be a victim, but what if you're worried she may be a bully?" I ask. The mom who was crying earlier whose daughter is a bully sits up straighter. I describe the two types, the school-yard bully and the Elite Tormentor, and why the latter is dangerous. "If you suspect your child may be an Elite Tormentor, you may have to commit the one dreaded parental sin second only to embarrassing your child in front of their friends," I say. "Yes, folks, you may have to invade their privacy!" A group of parents burst out laughing, "I'm not trying to make light of the right to privacy, but when that privilege allows a child to hide acts of cruelty against a classmate, it should be taken away until they earn it back."

"Amen to that," shouts an exuberant father, followed by a chorus of other voices echoing their agreement.

I continue with my advice on how to uncover a possible Elite Tormentor, urging concerned parents to try the following. Casually have a conversation with your child about who's popular at school and who's not, coaxing her into revealing the names of those students who struggle to fit in or who strike her as lonely. A week later, ask her if she'd like to host a party, suggesting it might be nice if, along with her friends, she invited a couple of the forgotten ones, too. "If she agrees despite what her friends may think, she's not an Elite Tormentor," I say. "In fact, she's probably an Elite Leader." I explain what this is. "If she won't because she's fearful her friends would freak but feels badly about it, she's most likely a bystander," I point out. "But if she recoils at the thought or acts indignant, perhaps even laughs, chances are you're living with an Elite Tormentor."

A few kids are glancing at one another guiltily.

"When your child is on the phone, pay attention to her tone and demeanor," I continue. "Does it sound like she's making a joke at someone else's expense or gossiping about another student?

"Lastly, and I know this may anger your child and make you uncomfortable, but remember, if you suspect your kid is one of the mean ones, you may be saving a life by doing this. Keep an eye on her when she's on the Internet. When she instant messages her friends, is she bad-mouthing others? What blogs does she frequent and what are some of the things she and her friends are posting? Does she participate in nasty e-mail-a-thons with other students? The more you know, the more you can protect everyone."

The Little General is pointing to her watch.

"Whether your child is a bully or a victim, if you think she needs help, these are my recommended guidelines for working with any mental-health professional," I state. I use myself as an example, telling them how when my parents started dragging me from one doctor to another, how they'd remain in the waiting room while I went in for my sessions. "I always felt like I was walking the plank, and used to think not only did the kids at school think I was a freak, but now my parents did, too." I emphasize that it's important that everyone in the immediate family attend the first few sessions together with the child, so that he feels like this is a problem you're tackling together as opposed to "I am the problem." "It also gives the therapist insight into any dynamics in the home that could be contributing to the bullying issue at school," I add. I warn parents to thoroughly vet their therapist: review articles they've written for professional journals; ask questions about their background and treatment philosophy; and then weed out any who are proponents of tough love techniques. "Bullied kids have it tough enough," I state. "They don't need their love to come that way, too." Several parents are nodding their heads somberly. I then tackle the subject of psych meds. "I'm not saying there isn't a legitimate need for these drugs," I remark. "But before you let a doctor diagnose your child with attention deficit disorder and put her on Ritalin, or declare her clinically depressed and give her an antidepressant, ask yourself this question. If I spent every day dodging insults and attacks, and cried myself to sleep every night because I was so desperately lonely, isn't it possible I might be distracted easily too or not feel like washing my hair or going out?" There's a collective gulp. "I advise that before you let any doctor prescribe anything, he screens your child for bullying or other daily traumas of this type, and even then, it wouldn't hurt to obtain a second opinion."

Now Eileen has removed her watch and is waving it above her head.

"Everyone, my manager is letting me know we're nearly out of time," I say, gesturing in her direction. The audience chuckles. "Before I conclude this presentation and take some of your questions, there's a group of people here I need to recognize." Everyone begins looking around. Designating myself as an Adult Survivor of Peer Abuse, I briefly describe what that means and some of my struggles including the diagnosis of post-traumatic stress disorder. I then ask those who would define themselves as kindred spirits to stand up. Nearly three-quarters of the audience rises, including Tammy's foster mom.

"This is my call to action," I state, my voice strong. "No one knows the hell these kids face every day more than us. We need to use our experiences and the miracle of our survival to help them find their way out. Parents, adult survivors, I invite you to start an *It's NOT Just Joking Around!*™ *Community Coalition* in your district and help lead the charge in the movement against school bullying. Those of you that are interested, please see the Little General at the conclusion of tonight's presentation. Now, are there any questions?"

"I know you encourage victims to stand up to the bullies, but what if you have a child who doesn't have the confidence?" asks a mom in the front.

I tell her to rehearse the confrontation with the child the same as if it were a scene in a play, writing a script, and memorizing the lines. "You or your husband could play the bully, your child plays himself, and someone else in the family acts as director." I explain that not only will this give the child a sense of control because he's practiced what he's going to say and do, but the mild disassociation of approaching it like an actor portraying a part makes him feel less vulnerable.

"Next?"

"My daughter is getting harassed by a group of Elite Tormentors," a woman says. "My husband and I have been getting the runaround from the school. What should we do?"

"Start with the counselor and work your way up the chain of command," I instruct. "If the principal and the superintendent are unresponsive, present your case at a school board meeting, and if that doesn't work, contact the education writer at your local paper. The same applies if you're dealing with a teacher who's a bully and are getting stonewalled by the school administration. You'd be surprised how quickly people come to attention when they start getting phone calls from journalists.

"Any other questions?" I say, vibrating with the energy of

my second wind.

"What about the parents of bullies?" someone shouts. "What's the best way to deal with them?"

I offer advice similar to what I gave teachers on how to approach them, that rather than initiating the conversation on an accusatory note likely to make them defensive, start out by emphasizing what you have in common as parents as opposed to what separates you. "You might try something along the lines of 'our kids are struggling with each other — why don't we get together and discuss how we can work together to help them both?'" I see parents taking notes. I'm about to conclude when I hear a tiny voice in the front row.

"Please, just one more question!" Justin begs.

"Yes, sweetheart?"

"My sister has autism," he says. "A lot of kids at her school are mean to her and I was wondering if you had any advice you could give me to help her."

The gym is silent. This little boy has just captured every heart here.

I pause for a moment to ponder my answer, when it hits me in the form of a memory of another remarkable child. I recount the story of a fifth grade girl named Darla I met on tour. I saw her chatting with her friends by the locker, joyous and full of laughter, and I could tell by the way they were hanging on her every word that she was one of the most popular girls at school. She was also afflicted with a rare form of primordial dwarfism and stood less than three feet tall. As I'm telling the story, people are listening wide-eyed.

"It was one of the most inspiring things I'd ever seen," I tell the audience. I describe how this example of unconditional acceptance for someone who was different was achieved. I explain how Darla's mom prepared a slide presentation which she gave in every science class explaining what primordial dwarfism is and why some people are born with it. Then Darla answered all her classmates' questions about what her life was like, including some of the unexpected advantages of being tiny. The mom also wrote a letter to parents explaining the presentation, and asking them to reinforce the message of acceptance at home, which the principal printed on school letterhead and made sure was sent home with every student. "Kids tend to reject what they don't understand because it frightens them," I explain, looking at Justin. "When Darla and her mom took the mystery out of her dwarfism for her classmates, they also took away the fear."

"I'll tell my parents about Darla and maybe they can do something like that for my sister," he says, hopefully.

I announce that I'll be signing books in the foyer, and afterward am happy to sit down with anyone who wishes to talk with me. There's a flutter of activity as everyone makes their way to the autographing table and forms a line that soon reaches clear to the other end of the hall. As people come up to me to personalize their book, they begin pouring out snippets of their past. Sally and her father both embrace me, and then Sally's dad takes a picture of Sally and me. Next, Tammy and her foster mom reassure me they'll keep me posted on their progress. "Can I hug you goodbye?" Tammy says. I motion for her to come around the other end of the table. She wraps her arms around me, burying her face in my neck. "I'll never forget you," she whispers. One after another, people keep coming, some of whom say they'll wait to talk to me. Justin is the last in line. He hands me a scrap of notebook paper and asks if I would sign it.

"Honey, why don't you let me autograph a book for you?" I say.

"I don't have enough money to buy one," he replies, ashamed.

I grab one off the stack, telling the book store clerk as always that I'll take care of it, and then I sign it.

Justin smiles as he reads my inscription. "To Justin, I wish you were my son."

"Oh, thank you," he says.

Unable to even think of him riding his bike home alone at this hour, and furious that his parents aren't here, I grab Eileen, who says she's already arranged it with the principal. He'll drive Justin home and drop off his bike tomorrow. I tell Justin goodbye, biting hard on my lower lip not to cry. I make him promise to stay in touch, assuring him that Eileen and I are never more than a phone call or e-mail away. These are the kids that haunt me. They're a paradox in my life because they validate and deplete my soul at the same time.

For the next ninety minutes, I do one-on-ones. As I suspected, the mom whose daughter tried to overdose on aspirin is a piece of work. She goes on nonstop about her break up with her boyfriend, her gambling problems, her issues with weight control, until finally, I have to stop her and remind her that she's supposed to be focusing on her daughter tonight, who's sitting beside her, looking mortified. When I chastise her mom, her mood brightens. I give them both a heartfelt mother/daughter pep talk, encouraging them to seek family and individual counseling. The adult survivor mom and the daughter who's a bully are the last two people waiting for me.

"Talk to me," I say, sitting beside them.

The daughter speaks first. "I'd like to start an INJJA Encouragement Club at this school," she says. "And mom wants to do that coalition thing you were talking about."

"Little General," I shout, so excited I could burst. Eileen comes running over.

"What is it?" she asks, out of breath.

"I'd like you to meet two heroes."

The weeks following the tour are a blur with the National Catholic Education Association and FCCLA events approaching rapidly. Eileen and I are frantic preparing all the hand-outs and promotional packages both entities have requested for their members. The morning of the NCEA engagement, I'm vibrating with nervous energy, eager to take the stage. When Eileen and I arrive the convention center, I'm immediately impressed with this organization. It's one thing to read how influential they are, it's another to be standing in the middle of it. There are rows and rows of tables at the main check-in center, with hundreds of volunteers darting in and out of dozens of conference rooms where the various work-shops will be held. This is the largest event I've ever been asked to participate in as an anti-bullying activist, and I'm enjoying feeling like Eileen and I are finally starting to get rec-ognized for the strides we're making in schools. There's an announcement over the PA system that the first round of workshops will begin in ten minutes. As Eileen and I are making our way to the room where I'll be hosting mine, she pulls me aside for a moment.

"You're competing with a lot of other workshops," she says. "I don't want you to be disappointed if there's not a good turnout."

The room has fifty seats and they're all empty when we walk in. I sigh, not wanting to face the embarrassment. Suddenly, people start filing in quicker than I can count them. Within minutes, the space is standing room only. There are educators sitting in the aisle. A group of nuns in habits, unable to find seats, have plopped themselves down directly in front of the podium, their navy blue skirts hiked around their middles, their underwear peeking out from underneath. They're laughing and chatting. They remind me of my first grade teacher Sister Rose Agatha, who always makes me smile whenever I think of her. By now, the Little General has gone from worried no one would show up to sweating there may be too many. A priest standing toward the back asks if the adjacent conference room is being occupied. When no one seems to know for sure, he walks over to the slatted door separating the rooms and slides it open, the clacking of slats echoing down the hall. "It's ours now," he states triumphantly. Then he opens the door to the foyer, peeks his head out, and says, "OK, everyone, come on in."

To my utter amazement, more people begin filling the adjacent space until it too is packed. Eileen is euphoric. As the person who's supposed to introduce me is climbing over the people on the floor, making her way to the podium, the fire marshal bursts in, announcing we're creating a fire hazard and need to disperse. The Little General, putting on her fiercest face, convinces him to look the other way. To this day, I have no idea how she did it.

With everyone settled, I do my teacher workshop. I have never experienced such an engaged crowd of educators. They cheer and during some of the more emotional parts, they cry openly, unafraid to show their feelings. At the conclusion of the seminar, Eileen and I are bombarded by grateful educators eager to bring us to their schools. It is a triumph unlike any other so far.

The rest of the day only gets better. Word of mouth about what happened spreads, and the NCEA, concerned the room they've reserved for the afternoon workshop won't be big enough, switch me to a conference hall, which also fills to capacity. By the time we leave the convention, we're the talk of the event.

The FCCLA keynote is equally successful. For this event, I'm scheduled to speak at a concert hall that seats five thousand people. I don't know this beforehand, and when I walk into the theater, I nearly fall over. The stage is enormous, and the sound engineer's booth is larger than my kitchen. After he mikes me up, the production engineer does a technical run-through making sure the cameras, which will be projecting my image onto two large video screens located at either end of the stage, are in working order. After my speech, I'm scheduled for an autographing.

As I'm waiting backstage for my cue, I call Mom, who says she's proud of me and to break a leg. Then I dial Mitch, filling him in on what's happening. "Tell the Little General I better not hear she let any groupies in your dressing room," he teases. After we hang up, I close my eyes and imagine his face, the timbre in his voice, and realize, that once again, despite how excited I am to be here, I can't wait to get back home to his arms.

An announcement is made that we're about to begin. As people are making their way to their seats, vibrant, pulsating music is being piped in from huge speakers located throughout the theater. A hush falls on the audience as the FCCLA president steps onto the stage. He introduces me, and takes his seat. I feel the heat of the lights bearing down on me. I walk to center stage, gaze out into the audience, and gulp. I'm staring at several thousand expectant young faces. I've been asked to give my student presentation with a motivational twist.

As I launch into the performance, I can feel a connection with the audience. For the next hour, I pour out my heart as never before. When I get to Mitch's kiss, the crowd goes wild, my ear drums hurt from their enthusiasm. By the time I reach the end of my presentation, I'm damp with perspiration and utterly spent. I've also never felt so alive in my entire life.

When I return home, Mitch has a surprise waiting for me. He's purchased two tickets to Santorini, Greece, knowing that I miss my friends there. The trip is wonderful, full of romantic firsts. The last night he tells me he has a few errands to run, and asks me to meet him at the jewelry shop of an old family friend. When I arrive before Mitch, everyone is staring at me, and I wonder what's going on. Costa, who owns the shop and who grew up with me during summers on the island, places a diamond and tanzanite ring in my hand, saying that a customer was thinking about getting it for his wife, and do I think this woman would like it. "Costa, *eenai thavma*, it's gorgeous," I answer. "I think any woman would be foolish not to love it."

At that moment, Mitch walks in. Costa hands him the ring. Mitch approaches me, gets down on one knee, slips it onto my finger, and says, "Jodee, in front of your dad, who I know is watching us from heaven, here on the island that has long been the home of your soul, will you marry me?"

"Yes, yes!" I cry. Mitch picks me up and twirls me all over the store.

"*Opa*," Costa yells, popping a bottle of champagne. As Mitch and I toast our engagement, out of the corner of my eye, I could almost swear I see my dad winking at me, and my best friend Niko—who died tragically last year and who I dedicated my book to, looking at me and smiling.

The next day, on the airplane back home, thinking about all the wonderful things that have happened these past few months, I feel a contentedness I've never known before. It won't last long.

chapter nineteen

Slammed

September 2004

Summer flew by. I dedicated myself to getting as much done as possible in my personal life knowing that once autumn arrived, marking the start of another school year, I'd again be consumed by the demands of my career. I immersed myself in all things domestic — working on the house with Mitch, activities with the kids, catering to pets (we've now added two floppy-eared bunnies to our brood), and preparing for the wedding and marriage. My mom and Jeanine have been helping Mitch and me plan the wedding. I've asked Shelly to be in my bridal party along with two other of my dearest friends. Amber and Val are junior bridesmaids. Mitch has asked his brothers to stand up for him. And Clarke has volunteered to jump out of a cake for my bachelorette party, which Mitch is eager to see. We're exchanging our vows at an historic church in Pason Park, and then having the reception at Courtrights, an elegant restaurant surrounded by lush forest preserves. The owner, Rebecca, is a family friend and one of the most imaginative women I've ever met. She reminds me of Glinda, the Good Witch of the North from *The Wizard of Oz*.

Mitch and I have decided not to have a traditional wedding. It'd make it too hard with my dad and Mitch's mom being gone, and besides, I want something whimsical and different. Mitch, God bless him, says he'll go along with whatever makes his bride happy. I hope he still feels that way when we're saying our "I do's" in Munchkinland, and cutting our wedding cake at the Emerald City. When I sprang the idea of a *Wizard of Oz* themed wedding on my fiancé, he didn't blink. He just smiled and asked if he'd need to rent a scarecrow costume. I told him I wasn't sure yet, but to keep an open mind.

On top of everything at home, work has been chaotic. The National Association of Youth Courts has asked to interview me for its publication. A Superior Court in Indiana has invited me to give a series of lectures at its annual conference for family court judges. Educational organizations in half a dozen different states with memberships ranging from social workers and school administrators to mental-health professionals are requesting seminars. Special Olympics has offered me an advice column in their magazine *Spirit*, and a senator, eager to push through anti-bullying legislation, wants my assistance. Between trying to accommodate these new opportunities and honor our current obligations, Eileen and I are stretched to the limit. Next week we're back on tour and it's our most ambitious yet with bookings from the East Coast to the Pacific Northwest.

I'm still seeing Dr. Winter. I'm working with him on managing the flashbacks as well as trying to learn how to cope with the emotional side effects of tour. I feel bad that when I come home, Mitch and the kids walk on eggshells because they don't know what might set me off. Part of the problem is that it's hard for anyone to understand what it's like to have desperate, distraught children begging for help. My nerves are raw by the time I get home. All I want is quiet. During the spring, this became an issue. I was returning from an especially grueling tour and it was Friday, the night the girls usually invite their friends for a sleepover. Mitch insisted he understood why I didn't feel up to catering to a house full of kids and would ask the girls to schedule it for another night. I even gave him an out, saying I could go to my condo if it was a problem. "No, we really miss you, come straight here," he said. I couldn't believe it when I walked in and found eight screaming twelve-year-olds running around the living room in their pajamas playing tag. I could feel my temples start to throb.

"Mitch, how could you be so insensitive?" I cried. "I thought we agreed, you, the girls and I would spend a quiet family night together."

"I'm sorry, honey. I didn't have the heart to disappoint them."

"Amber and Val have their friends over all the time," I said. "One night alone with us wouldn't have killed them, but it certainly would have meant a lot to *me*."

"I don't understand why you're making such a big deal out of this," he responded. "I could see it if their friends were in crisis hanging all over you."

"That isn't the point," I replied, hurt. "Why is it so hard to accept that I can't handle a ton of kids right now?"

"Do you want me to take them home?" Mitch asked, his voice softening.

"No, that's OK," I answered. "But could you maybe ask them to tone it down a little?"

"Sure," he said, pulling me into his embrace.

"Honey, I really am sorry," he apologized. "I didn't realize how important this was to you. I promise, next time the girls and I will be more considerate of your needs."

"Thanks," I responded, snuggling into him.

Though we're finding ways to compromise, it's a struggle, and there are nights that no matter how hard all of us try, everything still gets on my nerves. Despite these personal challenges, professionally, Eileen and I have gotten touring down to a science. That doesn't mean that occasionally we're not hit with a surprise, but when it does happen, we're much better at knowing how to handle it. We've also come a long way on the business side. Our information package is a far cry from what we started out with, that though respectable, wasn't anything like the sophisticated communications tool it is now and we're adding to it every day. But nothing shouts of our progress more than the most current version of our contract, which protects us from things we didn't even know we needed protecting from until we learned it the hard way.

We set out for the fall tour focused and confident, but it won't be long before I start to crack. It's an intensive first couple of weeks during which we hit dozens of schools with little time to breathe. It proves to be a precarious balancing act trying to stay on top of everything that's going on at home while still giving my all on the road. The stress gets to me and I find myself calling Mitch in tears all the time, wanting to fly home. He's always patient and loving and manages to talk me through it, but I can tell that underneath, he's worried sick. I'm also receiving a lot more local media attention now and while it's rewarding speaking at a school and then seeing it all over the local news the next morning, it also puts more pressure on me, too.

Every day so far I've been squeezing in interviews between my talks. I wouldn't mind the hectic pace if I didn't have to start so early. Most of the morning television shows request a 5:00 A.M. arrival and because I rarely get back to my hotel before midnight due to the parent/family seminar, it doesn't leave me much time for sleep. There have been days that I didn't think I'd make it until the evening seminar.

As the weeks blend into one another, I keep hearing Dr. Winter's voice in the back of my mind warning me about the importance of including adequate downtime in my schedule and I have to fight the anger that's been slowly boiling up inside me that Eileen hasn't been doing this. I understand why, because when I did her job, I was exactly the same way. I'd push my clients to the point that it was inhumane, knowing the media and public are fickle and you have to grab what you can when you can get it because the opportunity won't last. Now that I'm in their shoes, looking back, I wish I hadn't been so hard on them.

There aren't many breaks this tour. I get to go home for a day here and there, but that's it. The wedding pressure is becoming almost unbearable and it's getting so that whenever I'm with Eileen I feel myself growing more irritable because she's the one scheduling all these bookings that are making it impossible for me to be able to enjoy preparing for my wedding. I'm also scared for my health. Lately, I've been constantly sick: strep throats, bad colds, bronchitis. My doctor says it's because in addition to the battering my immune system takes on tour, having thousands of kids hugging me and breathing on me all the time is exposing me to every ailment imaginable. He suggested I consider wearing a mask when I get offstage. *Yeah, right.* He also said I should keep a small bottle of antibacterial gel in my pocket and use it on my hands throughout the day. I've started doing that and I pray it helps.

During one of the periods I'm home, something happens that unsettles me. A high school junior pulls a knife on a room full of his classmates, critically injuring several students and a teacher. Rumor has it that the kid was badly bullied and shunned at school, and the media is eager to interview me, hoping, as a former victim, I can shed some light on this "inexplicable act of violence." Though I never tell the media, the boy's family contacts me looking for possible insights into their son's state of mind. They drive out to Chicago to meet with me. It is one of the most moving and disturbing conversations I ever experience, as I listen to this family's story and realize the only difference between this boy and me is that my mom found the knife that I had hidden in my book bag before I had a chance to use it.

With the family's blessing, I honor the media interview requests and get skewered on live national television.

"It sounds to me like you're saying this kid was justified in what he did," one anchor says.

"No, I do not condone violence," I respond. "But the entire school knew how this kid was being treated, yet did nothing about it, and now they're wondering why he snapped?"

Cut to another studio where I'm on with a panel of experts.

"Aren't you just making excuses for an angry kid because you were one, too, and couldn't handle it, either?" asks a prominent adolescent psychologist.

"You can't expect teachers to fight every battle for their students," interjects someone from the local school board. "Kids have to learn to fight their own battles."

It dawns on me that I'll always run the risk of being attacked by the mainstream because I'm speaking on behalf of the person no one wants to take responsibility for hurting. How many potential student killers are out there? Almost as many as get ignored by the adults they trust to help them.

"It's that kind of antiquated logic that caused the tragedy which has brought us all here today," I answer. "You talk about what kids need to learn. I think it's the adults in our schools who need to do the learning!"

Cut to a soundproof booth where I'm doing a radio interview.

"Every once in a while, some tough kid would pick on me at school but that's just a normal part of growing up," says the host. "I ignored it and walked away."

My gorge starts to rise. Doesn't *anyone* get it?

"There's a significant difference between having friends and only getting bullied occasionally by one student, and being the outcast who's put down daily by all his classmates," I explain. "The kid who's like you were can say to himself that there's something wrong with the bully. The outcast thinks to himself there's something wrong with *me*," I explain.

In how many media interviews will I have to say this before America catches on?

"Maybe there *was* something wrong with you," he proposes, laughing.

Seething, I decide to *use* this opportunity instead of allowing it to make *me* feel used, and give the hundreds of thousands of listeners something meaningful to ponder. "Excuse me," I interrupt, "but I can't help thinking how ironic it is that here I am twenty years out of school, still getting pounded by ignorant bullies like you for taking an unpopular stance. Back then, it was my commitment to standing up for the underdog." The host is dyspeptic. He starts to respond, but I cut him off. "When will America realize what every adult who was once a forgotten student has always known?" I say. "Inside every lonely child is a potential time bomb. And as long as people like you cling to the misguided belief that teasing is just a normal part of growing up, our schools will *never* be safe and our country will continue to be run by people who aren't whole inside."

Though it felt good to give this guy a piece of my mind, by the time the day is over and I've endured others as bad as him or worse, I'm exhausted and seriously beginning to think that as much as Eileen and I are accomplishing, it will never be enough. The next morning when I wake up wishing I could cancel the rest of the tour, I tell myself that I'm just exhausted from being pulled in too many directions these past few months, and that once I get some rest, I'll be back to my determined self.

chapter twenty

The Wounded
Healer Reconsiders

October 2004

I wish I could hide. I can't stop thinking about that phone call from Styx asking me to spearhead the public relations for their comeback tour. It sounds so wonderful.

It's the last leg of the fall tour, and Eileen and I are in California. The school district we're currently working in is one of the largest in the United States, encompassing scores of schools. We've already been here a week and we've another ten days to go. This booking has been prickly from the start. Callie, the director of student activities who spearheaded the effort to bring us in, is new to the district and has been making promises she doesn't have the authority to grant and mishandling those that she does. The tour's been riddled with complications from sound systems that garbled my voice so badly students couldn't understand me, and last-minute venue switches that had parents showing up at the wrong schools for the evening seminars, to botched media alerts that created havoc. To make matters worse, Callie tries to cover up her mistakes by passing the buck to colleagues who then blame Eileen and me! She's also been pitting Eileen and me against each other. This entire experience is putting a real strain on our friendship, not to mention making what was already a horrendous tour even harder.

Callie has a lot riding on our success, and on top of everything else is trying to make Eileen and I prove to the superintendent my coming here has been worth the investment. Normally I'd be OK with that, except now she wants me to start lying to the press about the bullying problem here, saying it's minimal when in fact it's profound, and that I was only brought in as a "preventative measure." The whole notion is ridiculous. Parents have a right to know what's happening in their children's schools, as does the community, and sometimes, a little bit of embarrassment is worth the change it can inspire. Unfortunately, this superintendent is as slick as he is powerful and makes no secret of his political aspirations. I get the feeling this job is just a stepping stone to him and that he'd sacrifice his own mother, let alone a student, for a favorable mention in the newspaper. I want to be wrong about him and am reserving final judgment, but unless he reveals a side of his character that makes me believe he isn't cold and calculating, I think the verdict's pretty much in on this one.

It's early morning, and Eileen and I are just pulling into the parking lot of the district's largest high school, with a student population of nearly four thousand. Callie is waiting for us by the entrance and escorts us directly to the gym. The superintendent is there along with several members of the school board and the principal. Clad in saggy brown pants and a pale yellow shirt that's seen better days, this principal looks like the poster child for the tired and downtrodden. I could almost feel sorry for him if he wasn't so rude, barely acknowledging me when I introduce myself. I haven't presented at any of the high schools here yet as everyone thought it would be better if I got the middle schools in the district done first. This presentation is for the juniors and seniors, and I'll be speaking to the freshmen and sophomores later in the day. This high school has had some mixed publicity in the recent past. Earlier in the semester there was a gang-related shooting on school grounds involving several students. The press is intrigued by my visit, wondering how the kids will react to an anti-bullying expert in light of this recent tragedy, and reporters have come out in droves: every major network-affiliate television station is here, all the major daily newspapers within a fifty-mile radius, and half a dozen talk-radio stations.

This is the most media attendance I've had at any presentation. The fact that it's in this part of the state has special meaning for me, because when I was a publicist I used to send touring authors through here all the time because of the abundance of bookstores and A-list media. I never thought then that one day *I* would be the author and the media here would be interviewing *me*. In addition, while Eileen and I have been getting more media exposure on tour, most of the markets are small. This is the first major urban market to give me this kind of attention.

The students are beginning to file into the gym. As I watch them fill the bleachers, I swallow hard. Many of these kids look like the juvenile delinquents of documentaries like *Scared Straight!* before the term became politically incorrect, their anger as much a part of them as their skin. Some seem fresh from the hood, with their stony demeanors and their bandannas wrapped around their foreheads. Others are loud and unruly, making obnoxious comments as they pass. A girl with an elaborate tattoo on her arm, in skin-tight low-cut jeans and a Marilyn Manson T-shirt, yells out to a group of her friends sitting at the other end of the bleachers, who are similarly dressed, asking them to save her a smoke. To her left, a gaggle of gossiping females are pointing to an over-weight girl who's walking past them and laughing. Several rows down, the football players in their lettered jerseys are jousting with the cheerleaders who are flirting with them. I also see groups of "skater kids" scattered throughout the bleachers, a handful of "goths," most of who are sitting off by themselves, and though I can't be sure, a number of what appear to be transgender students, their physical features inconclusive of their sex. Then there are the bookworms, minding their own business quietly studying waiting for the assembly to begin.

In a cordoned-off section at the front of the gym is the press area, where I see lighting engineers and cameramen adjusting their equipment, anchorwomen applying lipstick and powder, radio hosts reviewing notes, and reporters and photographers ready to record whatever unfolds. There must be over two thousand students in this gym and they're grow-ing more restless by the minute. I don't like this. The princi-pal or someone on the faculty should have made an attempt to quiet these kids down by now. The adults are just standing around talking, like this is all perfectly normal. I look over at Eileen, who appears to be having words with Callie, their eyes locked in stalemate. For the first time in my life, I'm standing in front of an audience and I don't know what to do. One group of students has begun shouting obscenities and mak-ing vile gestures, their hostility igniting those around them to do the same. Several teachers make a weak attempt to control this challenge to authority, which threatens to become a riot. As I scan the crowd, one girl catches my eye, and when she realizes she has my attention, pulls a ballpoint pen from her bag, breaks it in half, and throws it at me, ink streaming out. Then she laughs.

A.J., no, don't! Please stop laughing at me. . . .

I can feel the flashback welling up inside me, trying to take over. I hear Dr. Winter's soothing voice telling me to inhale deeply and let the breath out slowly. This simple exercise immediately allows me to relax. I'm conquering the demon. Just then, the principal approaches me, asks if I'm ready, and before I can even reply, switches on the microphone to introduce me. The screech of feedback from the speakers is painful. As he begins to speak, the inadequate sound system muffles his words, making them unintelligible. Students begin booing.

"You suck!" shouts one.

"Kiss my ass!" calls out another.

The principal stands there, his shoulders slumped, saying nothing. His silence and his body language scream defeat, which only feeds the fire. The superintendent is glaring at him but making no move to come to his aid. Eileen is wearing a terrified expression.

"Please, you're shaming this entire district with your behavior," he finally manages, his words barely audible.

Someone crumbles up a piece of paper and throws it at him.

"Come on, you guys, don't do this," he begs. He tries one last time to introduce me. More booing. He hands me the microphone and leaves. I scan the bleachers, trying to figure out what to do. Some students are looking at each other, uncomfortable but helpless. Others watch me struggle with a knowing grin on their faces. They've seen this before. I feel for them all. I can't imagine what they must go through being forced to attend school here. I glance at the press section and, to my alarm, cameras are rolling. If I walk out, I become the anti-bullying speaker who allowed an audience to bully her off the stage. I need to do something dramatic. I remember how Judy Garland could take charge of a hostile audience with a grand gesture. I deliberately cast the microphone aside, walk into the middle of the gym, and begin speaking in my most full-throated voice. Some of the students smile, others seem stunned, but enough become quiet that I can begin the presentation. I realize that I've lost some of the audience and can't get them back, but the ones who are now quiet appear rapt, perhaps the most attentive group of individuals I've yet addressed. The next hour is unlike anything I've experienced before or since. Half the audience seem mesmerized by my reenactment. The other half might as well be in the parking lot trading tunes on their iPods.

The rest of the day, I sweat out the media coverage not knowing how they're going to spin this. The television news stories begin at 5:00 P.M. First I'm relieved, then dumbfounded. They're treating it as victory in the face of adversity and their description of my talk is remarkably fair, even sophisticated. The treatment is so good that Eileen facetiously suggests that we put some of these news clips onto a disc and send them out to schools we're soliciting. No one could say the same for the administration at this school district. Its reputation is in tatters, and I wouldn't be surprised if some jobs were in jeopardy.

This ordeal escalates the tension between Eileen and me. She blames herself for what went wrong on the tour, and in truth, she did seem distracted from the moment we arrived. She wasn't her usual self, nor did she stand up to Callie in the way that earned Eileen her nickname. By the time we're on the flight home, we're not speaking and I'm beginning to think that our falling-out may be the excuse I need to cut short my career on the bullying circuit. Eager to be home and forget the last three weeks, I make myself a promise on the plane to take some time off and focus on Mitch and our wedding. My hopes for a much-needed respite are dashed the moment we land and I start checking my voice-mail messages. There are dozens of threatening messages from Crystal, each one more terrifying than the next. They all relate to last Thanksgiving, the one I didn't spend with her. It's as if she's been festering with rage ever since and has now become psychotic. In one of these messages, she says that she's going to come to Chicago with a knife and cut out my heart. The last time I spoke with Crystal's mother, several months ago, she said Crystal was in therapy and doing well. Apparently, her daughter has taken a turn for the worse. Instead of being able to go home from the airport, Eileen and I spend the next three hours back and forth with Crystal's mom on the phone, managing the crisis from the arrival gate.

By the time I get home, I'm feeling disgusted with everything. Even the embossed envelope that arrives from the Illinois Association of School Boards doesn't lift my spirits. I toss it into my overnight bag unopened. I go to bed more convinced than ever that maybe it really is time for me to retire from this crusade. The universe conspires to agree with me.

The next morning, I receive a phone call from a distraught mother whose daughter, Mallory, is a student at Samuels. The mother tells me that a group of Mallory's classmates set her up in the most unspeakable way. They invited her to a party which was just a ruse to get her alone and vulnerable. Then they pinned her down and started beating her senseless, videotaping the entire attack, which they then copied and passed around at school. "The school administration, instead of doing something about it, is giving my husband and me the runaround and treating Mallory like she's the one at fault," the mother says. "Please help us." I appear before the school board with Mallory and her mom. The superintendent publicly dismisses Mallory as being overly dramatic and castigates me for interfering in matters I don't understand. I find this deliberate public humiliation tough to take, except I know something the superintendent doesn't. In the audience, at my invitation, are reporters from the *Chicago Tribune* and the largest local suburban newspaper. The next day, the story dominates the front pages, depicting Mallory and me as the heroes and the superintendent as the villain of the piece. If it weren't for what the superintendent had done, I'd actually feel sorry for him.

Though I was able to help this girl and her family, it was too hard on me and made me realize that I can't do this anymore. If as a recognized authority, I could still be treated by

Samuels as badly today as I was twenty-five years ago as an ordinary student, the change I envision for America's schools may be more than any one person could hope to effect. It's time to resurrect the consulting business. Now, where's my Rolodex?

chapter twenty-one

Dorothy's Rainbow

November 2004 - February 2005

Since I've returned from California, I've been feeling frantic and numb all at once. I ended up calling Styx back, as well as several of my other old consulting clients, letting them know that come the first of the year I'll be available again. It was a difficult, bittersweet decision to let go of my anti-bullying crusade. But after everything that's happened recently, I realized that not only was this work ripping me apart, but in another few months I would no longer be a single woman who didn't have to worry about anyone but herself. Though Mitch and I are a couple, when I want a night to myself I can still take it without having to worry about who's cooking dinner or which one of us is dropping off the dry-cleaning. A fiancée can do that. A wife shouldn't. Besides, it's hard enough being married and having a normal job, let alone what I do for a living. I'm beginning to see that being a wife and an activist will be an impossible combination. I have a series of speaking engagements before the wedding, and then I'm moving on. To Mitch's credit, while he's relieved over my decision to relinquish my role as an activist, if I were to change my mind he'd understand and support me.

Times passes quickly and soon the day of my bridal shower arrives. Shelly and Mitch's stepmom host it. The theme is winter in Oz, and they go to extravagant lengths to transport guests to a whimsical place that would inspire the Wizard himself to buy a pair of snow shoes. It's a festive, wonderful party filled with laughter and warmth. I don't think I've ever seen my mom as bubbly and joyous before. The highlight of the day is when Shelly presents the gift from the bridal party—an enormous, red velvet lounge chair they had custom-made that's an exact replica of one of Dorothy's ruby slippers!

In the weeks following the bridal shower, I find myself just going through the motions as I honor these last speaking commitments. Though they go well, my heart isn't in it anymore. When I'm onstage, I feel like I'm trying to pull something out of me that's no longer there, and by the time I get to the parent/family seminars at night I'm practically a zombie, I'm so tired. I shouldn't have allowed things to go this far. Maybe if I had been more honest with both Eileen and myself, I would have insisted that I needed a sabbatical, even if it meant having to cancel some appearances. My biggest regret is that in my zeal to make a difference in America's schools I let everyone and everything drain me dry and never once just said, "Stop, I need a break." Now it's too late. All the vacations in the world wouldn't be enough to replenish what I've lost.

Things with Eileen are still strained, too. We're both making the best of it when we're on the road together, but I can tell she wants out as much as I do. Though she hasn't said anything yet, I have a feeling she's been offered another position. She deserves a great job, one with fewer frustrations.

It's late at night and I'm curled up on the couch with Shadow and Roxy, watching a DVD of episodes from

Bewitched, a present from Mitch. Shadow is sound asleep, with his head on my lap, snoring. Roxy is chewing on a bone. Mitch is in the kitchen making us grilled-cheese sandwiches.

"Honey, one or two slices?" he calls out.

"Two," I reply. "Make it gooey and crispy, OK?"

"Sure," he says.

As I sit here comfortable and safe, enjoying the sound of my husband-to-be cooking — the clanging of pans, the hiss of frying butter — I close my eyes and envision a lifetime of these moments. I feel so peaceful and warm and I know that if I hadn't made the decision to end my career as an activist I'd be agonizing over how many of these moments I would miss on my next tour. I did the right thing, I tell myself.

The holidays are a blur. The week before the wedding, I conclude the final speaking engagement, a two-day booking at a school district in Wisconsin. At the end of the parent/family seminar, I feel profound relief. *Freedom.* My family and friends keep asking me if I have any second thoughts about my decision to walk away from school bullying. Any that I might have entertained are erased when, the day after I get back from Wisconsin, I discover that I picked up a horrible bug there. By midafternoon, I'm burning up with a 103 degree fever, so sick I can't get out of bed. Everyone is worried that I won't make it to my own wedding. The night of the rehearsal dinner, my fever breaks. But it's the final straw for me. Instead of being able to enjoy those precious few days before my wedding, seeing friends and shopping for the honeymoon, I was sweating out whether I'd even be able to get hitched. I hope I never see the inside of another school again.

It's late morning the day of my wedding. By this time tonight, I'll be Mitch's wife. Hooray! I'm at Mom's having coffee with her and Jeanine, reviewing last-minute details before I leave for the beauty salon, where I'll be spending the afternoon. I thought I would be nervous today, but what I feel most is a sense of awe. I never would have believed that the boy I sat next to in class and passed in the hallways all those years ago, the one that every girl wanted and who I thought would never want me, is the man who'll be my groom. The bullies who once told me that no one would ever want to date me, let alone marry me, will be sharing in the joy of my wedding. The girl who saw an ugly duckling whenever she looked in the mirror has finally become a swan.

The day passes quickly and soon it's time to leave for the church. I'm wearing an exquisite full-length backless dress that isn't traditional, except that it's all white and my girl-friends say it reminds them of Katharine Hepburn's wedding gown in *The Philadelphia Story*. On my feet are a pair of red sequined shoes that I had made to look like Dorothy's ruby slippers. My "something blue" is a garter belt made out of the same fabric as Dorothy's blue-and-white checkered dress. As I'm waiting for my bridal party to arrive for pictures, the doorbell rings. When I open it, there's a delivery man stand-ing there with the largest, most fragrant bouquet of red roses I've ever seen. He hands them to me, along with a tiny box and a card, a huge smile across his face.

"Goodness," says Mom as I carefully place it all on the dining-room table. "I wonder where that came from!"

"Very funny," I reply, chuckling. I open the card first. It reads,

> *To my bride, I can't wait to skip down the yel-*
> *low brick with you tonight.*
> > *Love, your very soon to be husband,*
> > > *Mitch*

Then, with trembling fingers, I open the box. My breath catches. Inside, resting on plush white velvet is a pair of sparkling diamond earrings.

"Oh, my God," I whisper. "I have to call him,"

"No, you can't!" Jeanine says. "It's bad luck."

"For the groom to *see* the bride before the wedding, not *talk* to him," I reply.

"Oh, that's right," she says, remembering. Mom and I look at each other and smile, shaking our heads.

As I'm on the phone with Mitch, Shelly arrives with Lissy and my old friend Candice, who's also standing up for me. I can hear them commenting to each other about Mitch's gift, saying how lucky I am to have found such a wonderful guy, and I can't help but think, but I didn't find him. He was there all along.

After we take pictures, the limo arrives to whisk us off to the church. As we're driving and sipping champagne, toasting my last moments as a single woman, I notice Shelly's face clouding over. I ask her what's wrong.

"There's something I need to get off my chest," she says, shakily.

"OK," I respond, wondering what could be bothering her so much.

"Last night at the rehearsal dinner, I was listening to your mom talking to someone about what you went through at Samuels." She hesitates, her eyes moist with regret.

"Go ahead, it's OK," I gently reassure her.

"Suddenly, I remembered Nadia and me walking to class one morning with a group of our friends," she recalls. "We saw you coming toward us, smiling, and all that kept running through my head was there comes that weird Jodee again. I looked at everyone and rolled my eyes, and we all laughed in your face. You walked away crestfallen."

Since Shelly and I reconnected, she's consistently denied that she ever shunned me. I didn't contradict her. It's our friendship now that counts.

"Shelly, it's OK, really," I respond.

"No, Jodee, it's not OK. I'm so proud of what you've done with your life. You've come *so* far, and I'm speaking now for all of us who went to school with you. We're honored to be able to call you our friend."

"I'd hug you, but I don't want to get makeup all over my dress," I reply, choking back tears. "You'll never know how much that means to me."

"I do know," she says. "I'm just sorry it took me this long to remember."

The wedding is magical. I walk down a silk yellow-brick road to Judy Garland's original recording of "Over the Rainbow" escorted by my mentor and oldest friend from New

York. Mitch and I exchange vows under a rainbow of carnations, surrounded by those we love most. Then we go up to the altar and light a candle for his mom and one for my dad, telling them that we know they're celebrating with us in spirit. Glancing over at Mom, my eyes well with tears thinking how much she and Daddy both sacrificed for me. For a moment, Mom and I lock eyes and I can feel the strength of our family swelling inside me — my grandparents, Daddy, and all the others who have passed on — imbuing my soul with the power of their presence. Next, Mitch and I are pronounced man and wife. I thought nothing would ever compare to the kiss he gave me at our twentieth high school reunion. I was wrong. Then, as "We're off to See the Wizard" plays in the background, Mitch grabs my hand and together we skip arm in arm down the yellow-brick road to the front vestibule of the church, where we ring the church bell together. As the chimes thunder in my ear, I think of Dorothy and smile. "There's no place like home," I hear her saying. "There's no place like home."

When we arrive at Courtrights for the reception, Mitch and I are awestruck at what Mom's friend Rebecca has achieved. The entire restaurant has been transformed into Oz. Mom says Rebecca hired a set designer from a prominent Chicago theater company to decorate, and it shows. There's a yellow-brick road running the entire length of the restaurant. The bar and the main dining room have been redesigned to look like Munchkinland. There's even a façade of a fallen house, tilted on its side, with the Wicked Witch of the East's black-and-white striped stocking feet peeking out from underneath. The dance floor, in another room, has become the Emerald City. The wedding cake looks as if it were personally crafted by Glinda, the Good Witch of the North, complete with a magic wand and a crown. Atop the cake are a figurine of the Scarecrow with Mitch's face and Dorothy with mine.

It is the wedding of a lifetime, full of love and laughter. Half the guests are people I went to school with who made me cry myself to sleep, and now here we are together dancing and celebrating, cherishing every moment of this remarkable night. Gone are the flashbacks, the fear, the insecurity that maybe I'll do something wrong and they won't like me anymore. I'm whole, and so are they. We are no longer those struggling adolescents searching for validation outside ourselves. They are my strength and I theirs. We are friends who love and believe in each other, and I'm a part of them and they of me. *Finally.* I remember when I used to watch *The Wizard of Oz*, thinking, I'll always be just like Dorothy in that moment after the Wizard has given the Scarecrow, the Tin Man, and the Lion what they asked for, and she is looking at the sack from which he pulled their treasures, and says, "I don't think there's anything in that black bag for me." But there is, and there always has been, Dorothy always had the power to click her heels three times and go home. It just took her a while to figure it out, the same way it did me.

As this magical night is coming to a close, I see Eileen darting around the tables, gathering up all the guests who attended Calvin Samuels. "Attention everyone, please gather in Munchkinland for a Calvin Samuels alumni photo," the Little General announces into the microphone. As my husband and I pose for the shot, I realize what a miracle tonight is. In fact, everything that's happened in the past three years has been a miracle. I close my eyes and envision the children who've touched my life, the parents and teachers whose faces will remain etched in my memory, the adult survivors and the hope and strength they inspire, the bookstore employees who came out at night to do the parent/family seminars, the children who rode their bikes in the rain and trudged through snow to hear me, the families who reached out to me with open hearts, the administrators and school-board members who took on the system and fought for their students, the days Eileen and I survived on nuts and trail mix saving lives.

I open my eyes and gaze at Mitch, feeling as if my heart will burst. He leans over and kisses me, his body melding into mine. The hours pass quickly, and soon the last of the guests have departed. Mom and Eileen are waiting to see Mitch and me off on our honeymoon. Mitch and I run into the bathroom to change our clothes. As I'm pulling my jeans and T-shirt out of my overnight bag, an envelope falls out. It's the unopened letter from the Illinois Association of School Boards. I had forgotten all about it. In a very different mood than I was in the day the letter arrived, I open it with bemused curiosity. I read it with surprise and pleasure. We *have* made a difference. I leave the bathroom grasping the invitation. As soon as I spot the Little General, I hand it to her.

"What are you grinning about?" she says.

"It seems as if there's at least one more stop on our journey," I reply.

Eileen looks up from the invitation. "You realize this conference is one of the most influential in the country," she remarks. We smile at each other, both of us knowing that when I return from the honeymoon in two weeks she and I will pick up where we left off and continue our determined quest. Only this time, we'll be ready.

"I guess the retirement's off," Mitch says, sneaking behind me and wrapping his arms around my waist.

"You don't mind?" I ask, worried.

"I figured you might have a change of heart."

As I snuggle into Mitch's embrace in the limo on the ride to our hotel, I think about the future and smile.

—The End—

Publisher's Note

After her honeymoon, Jodee returned to the fight against bullying, visiting dozens of schools and speaking with thousands of students, educators, parents, and adult survivors. The movement continues!

Addendum

Advice for Students

1. If you're a victim of bullying, remember, there's nothing wrong with you. It's everything that's right about you that makes you stand out from the crowd. Don't change for anyone. It is those who put you down and exclude you who need to change.

2. Never ignore the bully and walk away. You must look the bully in the eye without any emotion or fear, command him to stop, and then stare him down just long enough to let him know you mean business. Next, begin walking away, and then turn briefly back toward him and say "See you later." The first few times you employ this method the bully will probably get meaner because you're taking away his power. After a while, the bully will likely begin to see you in a new light. But even if it doesn't work, at least you know that you defended your dignity and your pride. Remember, standing up for yourself nonviolently in the moment abuse occurs is your human right. Seeking vengeance later on is the mistake.

3. Don't suffer in silence. Confide in an adult you trust that you're being bullied and need help.

4. School doesn't have to be your whole world even though it may sometimes feel that way. Seek an alternative social outlet through the local park district, community center, or public library. Call or visit these organizations online and research what youth activities they have available.

It's important, however, that you reach out to organizations that are one town away from where you attend school, because the purpose is for you to make friends with kids outside of your school network who will have no preconceptions about you.

5. If you see someone being bullied and don't want to be a bystander, you have two options. Intercede on the victim's behalf and tell the bullies to stop or devise a clever excuse to pull the victim away from the situation. For example, you might say something like "Susie, my locker is stuck, could you help me?" or "Jaime, there's a phone call for you in the main office."

6. If you think you may be a bully or an Elite Tormentor, recognize that it's not just joking around. You may be damaging someone for life. Think about that the next time you abuse or shun another classmate, or worse, treat her as if she's invisible.

7. Always remember that bullying isn't just the mean things you do, it's all the nice things you never do on purpose. Letting someone walk to class alone or sit by themselves at lunch, excluding the same person repeatedly from parties and other social activities, choosing the same student last whenever you divide into teams in class or gym, are the worst forms of bullying. It makes the victim say to himself, "There must be something wrong with *me*," and he may believe it the rest of his life.

8. If you see a classmate is struggling to fit in or being maligned, tell a teacher or counselor. It could change this person's life and it could save yours because what happened in Columbine could happen at your school, too.

9. Don't be afraid of professional help. If your parents want you to see a psychologist or counselor, ask if they would attend the first few sessions with you — explain that it will make you more comfortable because you'll feel like you're dealing with the circumstance as a family and not "you as the problem." One tip — be honest with everyone, including yourself, and you will find the experience very worthwhile.

10. Pay attention to other classmates who may be experiencing some of the same loneliness and rejection you are and reach out to them in friendship. You could end up forging bonds that will last a lifetime.

Advice for Educators

1. Never say to a bullied child: "Ignore the bully and walk away; they're just jealous; twenty years from now those bullies will probably be in jail and you'll be successful; I know how you feel; or be patient."

2. This is what you should say to your bullied student and do: Step one: Say, "I don't know how you feel. I can't imagine what you're going through. It must be awful." Step two: Say, "Let's talk about an action that we can take together today to help solve this problem of bullying that you're facing." Step three: Contact the local park district, public library, and community center one town over and ask them to send you a list of their youth programs, then review this information with your student and help him choose something he can participate in. Step four: Contact the parents and explain from a constructive

point of view so as not to put them on the defensive that their child has been encountering some challenges but that both you and their child have come up with some exciting solutions that you're eager to share with them.

3. Before you let any student confide in you, close your eyes and visualize that you're switching hats from that of teacher to friend, and promise yourself that no matter what you hear you'll approach it from the perspective of an ally, and not the stance of an authority figure.

4. Don't chastise an Elite Tormentor in front of the entire class. Devise an excuse to pull the victim out of the line of fire and then approach his assailants individually at a later date.

5. Traditional punishment doesn't work. It only makes an angry kid angrier and is best employed as a last alternative. First, try compassionate forms of discipline that help the student access the empathy inside him. For example, in lieu of a detention for bad behavior, require a student to do one nice thing for a different person every day for two weeks and to record in a notebook each evening how the recipient responded and how the response made him feel. Make sure he has each recipient sign and date his entry and include a phone number so you can verify your student's compliance in this exercise. If the student is remiss, then use traditional punishment as a consequence.

6. Remember, the bully and the victim are flip sides of the same coin. Both are bleeding emotionally, both need love and support. When approaching the bully, begin the conversation on an encouraging note with something like,

"Johnny, I enjoy being your teacher and I know you're a really good kid, that's why it surprised me when you. . . ." Then, launch into the issue you need to discuss, trying to be as general as possible and only using the victim's name if there's no other alternative. This will help to prevent retaliation later on.

7. If you're a teacher trying to help a student and administration is giving you the runaround, plead your case to the school board, and if that doesn't work, contact the education reporter at your local daily paper. Conversely, if you're a principal struggling with a tenured teacher who's a bully, keep going up the chain of command until someone pays attention, even if that means turning to the press yourself.

8. Try to creatively incorporate anti-bullying messages into your required subject matter. For example, if you're teaching students about the food chain in science class, add a quiz question that asks them to compare the social environment at school to the food chain. You can also have students study great leaders in whatever subject you teach who were maligned and shunned for being different or ahead of their time. Their life stories will inspire students who are being bullied, and help to ignite spirited discussion.

9. Develop a code of conduct for your classroom and reward those students who uphold it.

10. Never forget why you became a teacher, and don't let government policies, administrative bureaucracies, or anything else get in the way of your love for your students or your commitment to protect and empower them. And if

you're an Adult Survivor of Peer Abuse yourself, don't minimize what happened, find a therapist and talk about it so it doesn't hinder you as an educator.

Advice for Parents

1. Never say to a bullied child: "Ignore the bully and walk away; they're just jealous; twenty years from now, those bullies will probably be in jail and you'll be successful; I know how you feel; or be patient."

2. This is what you should say to your bullied child and do: Step one: Say, "I don't know how you feel. I can't imagine what you're going through. It must be awful." Step two: Say, "Let's talk about an action that we can take together today to help solve this problem that you're facing." Step three: Contact the local park district, public library, and community center one town over and ask them to send you a list of their youth programs, then review this information with your child and help him choose something he can participate in. It's important you go one town over so your child meets new faces and isn't interacting with the same kids from school. Step four: Contact your child's school counselor and calmly explain what's been going on with your child. You might want to start out with something like, "My child's been encountering some challenges with his classmates and I'd like to sit down and discuss possible solutions with you."

3. Don't advise your child to ignore the bully. Tell him to confront the bully nonviolently and tell him to stop. If your child is too timid to do this, rehearse the confrontation

with him the same as if it were a scene in a play, writing a script and memorizing the lines. You could play the bully, your child plays himself, and someone else in the family acts as director. Not only will this give your child a sense of control because he's practiced what he's going to say and do, but the mild disassociation of approaching it like an actor portraying a part makes him feel less vulnerable.

4. If you feel the school isn't being helpful enough, work your way up the chain of command. If the principal and the superintendent are unresponsive, present your case at a school board meeting, and if that doesn't work, contact the education writer at your local paper. The same applies if you're dealing with a teacher who's a bully and are getting stonewalled by the school administration. You'd be surprised how quickly people come to attention when they start getting phone calls from journalists.

5. When approaching the parents of bullies and Elite Tormentors, rather than initiating the conversation on an accusatory note likely to make them defensive, start out by emphasizing what you have in common as opposed to what separates you. You might try something along the lines of: "Our kids are struggling with each other, why don't we get together and discuss how we can work together to help them both."

6. If you think it would be helpful for your child to see a therapist, make sure that you attend the first few sessions with your child, so she feels you're addressing this problem together as opposed to "I *am* the problem." Also, thoroughly research the mental-health professional's background, and request references. Should a psych med

be prescribed, ask lots of questions and be confident of the doctor's diagnosis before giving your child anything.

7. Be alert to the warning signs that your child may be getting bullied. Those signs could include: lethargy, depression, self-mutilation, extreme makeover attempts, diminished personal hygiene, lack of interest in social activities, sudden change in weight, inexplicable fits of rage, sudden increase or decrease in grades, and faking illness or willing oneself sick to avoid going to school.

8. If you suspect your child may be an Elite Tormentor but aren't sure, casually have a conversation with her about who's popular at school and who's not, coaxing her into revealing the names of those students who struggle to fit in or who strike her as lonely. A week later, ask your child if she'd like to host a party suggesting it might be nice if, along with her friends, she invited a couple of the forgotten ones, too. If she agrees despite what her friends may think, she's probably an Elite Leader. If she won't because she's fearful her friends would freak but feels bad about it, she's most likely a bystander. But if she recoils at the thought or acts indignant, perhaps even laughs, chances are she is an Elite Tormentor.

When your child is on the phone, pay attention to her tone and demeanor. Does it sound like she's making a joke at someone else's expense or gossiping about another student? This too could indicate you have an Elite Tormentor on your hands. Also, keep an eye on your child when she's on the Internet. When she instant messages friends, is she bad-mouthing others? What blogs does she frequent and what are some of the things she and her friends are posting? Does she participate in nasty e-mail-a-thons with other students? The more you know, the more you can protect her and everyone else.

9. Traditional punishment doesn't work. It only makes an angry child angrier. Try more compassionate and creative forms of discipline. For example, if your daughter gets in trouble at school for teasing an overweight classmate, take her to the pediatric eating disorders unit of the local hospital to volunteer as a candy striper for a day. If your son puts down some of his less fortunate classmates, spend an afternoon with him at a soup kitchen handing out food to the homeless. The key is to help your child access their empathy and find creative ways to develop it as one would exercise.

10. The typical bullied child is an Ancient Child, an old soul trapped in a young body. This is the child who wants to fit in just as desperately as his peers, but he has an adult sense of compassion and morality that sets him apart and often makes other children perceive him as "weird." If you have an Ancient Child, remember, though he may act more socially and intellectually mature than his classmates, inside, he's still emotionally just a kid, and realize that the rejection he's enduring at school could be cutting a hole in his soul, and it's up to you to do everything you can to help him, even on those days when your patience has run out and you fear your hope may be next. And if you're an Adult Survivor of Peer Abuse yourself, don't dismiss what happened to you. Find a therapist and talk about it so it assists you as a parent in understanding your child.

Advice for Adult Survivors of Peer Abuse

1. Realize that you need to deal with the abuse and rejection you endured in school the same way you would any other trauma from your past. Do not let anyone tell you you're making a big deal out of nothing. Bullying can cause permanent emotional and psychological scars, and acknowledging this is your first step toward healing.

2. Though you can never erase the painful memories, therapy can help you learn how to cope and move forward. When choosing a mental-health professional, review their background and make sure they have experience in this area.

3. Some Adult Survivors of Peer Abuse can suffer from post-traumatic stress disorder. Symptoms can include flashbacks, nightmares, depression, and social anxiety. If you suspect you may have PTSD, be sure and tell your therapist.

4. If you're a married Adult Survivor of Peer Abuse or in a committed relationship, talk about it with your significant other and make sure to include this aspect of your past in any couples counseling sessions.

5. If you're debating whether or not to attend a school reunion, remember that the only way to overcome a fear is to face it. Try and go with a safe person who understands your fears and is there to support you.

6. If you're a parent, pay attention to how you react to any bullying situation with your child and be aware that you don't want to blur the line between your past and their present. You may need therapy to help you keep that line

clearly defined. The same applies with your students if you're an educator.

7. Turn your pain into purpose and reach out to your local school district and ask if you could speak to students about your experiences to help create awareness of how hurtful bullying can be.

8. Reach out to the parents in your district whose children are being bullied and provide insight and moral support. Form a support group in your community.

9. Attend a school board meeting and share your personal insights about bullying. It could generate awareness that saves lives.

10. Always remember, there's nothing wrong with you and there never was. It was everything that was *right* about you that made you stick out when you were a student. It's time to celebrate who you are!

Author Q&A

What is "academic bullying"?
That's when a student or group of students purposely makes it difficult for a classmate to perform academically. For example, if you're assigned a book report and another classmate checks out the book you need and keeps it just so you can't have access to it for your assignment, that's academic bullying.

What role does ethnicity play in school bullying?
When ethnic groups bully each other, it can be hurtful and infuriating, but at least targets can lean on others within their own group for support. It's damaging when the members of an ethnic group turn on one of their own, because that person is not only bullied from the outside, but also shunned on the inside, and that frequently has long-term emotional and psychological consequences.

Can sibling rivalry have an impact on school bullying?
Sibling rivalry can be the early breeding ground for bullying behaviors. I always warn parents not to allow sibling rivalry to flourish, because if children don't learn compassion early on, in the home, they will bring that same lack of empathy to school.

What was your college experience like?
I loved college. I attended New York University, where being a nonconformist was the norm instead of the exception. It was such a delightful shock going from high school, where I was

the misfit, to college, where I flourished socially and academically. It was the best four years of my life.

Do you ever speak at college and university campuses on bullying and hazing, and what advice do you have for students struggling to fit in?
Yes, I do speak at university campuses. I developed an anti-hazing program called *The Desperate Freshman* that helps colleges identify and empower those students who may be more vulnerable to the peer pressure typically associated with hazings. I also work with fraternity and sorority leaders on compassion-based initiatives that honor their Greek traditions. My advice for students struggling to fit in is to get involved in as many clubs and organizations as you can and try to develop friendships with people whom you share common interests, as opposed to trying to achieve acceptance from a large clique or group. Build your social life one individual at a time based on mutual admiration and respect. Your whole world will blossom.

What advice do you have for Adult Survivors of Peer Abuse who are torn about whether or not to attend a school reunion?
Of course I'm probably a little biased, but I think every adult survivor should attend their high school reunion because there's nothing like the satisfaction of knowing that you faced your fears and survived. It almost doesn't matter what happens when you're there, it's the fact that you stood up to something you were terrified of and got through it. If you don't attend, you run the risk of the past always holding you hostage. Just remember, walk through those doors proud of

425

who you are, and have no expectations other than how you're going to reward yourself the next day for your remarkable courage. It's also a good idea to attend with a loving, supportive friend who understands your insecurities and can be there to hold your hand when you need it.

What should you do if you're being bullied at work?
Whether you're a student being harassed by your classmates or a professional getting mistreated on the job, you need to confront the bully nonviolently and tell him or her to stop. If he or she refuses, report the abuse and continue going up the chain of command until you get action. Remember, standing up for yourself in the moment abuse occurs is your human right. Seeking vengeance later on is a mistake.

What's next for Jodee Blanco?
I'll continue trying to reach as many people as possible with my message of compassion and tolerance. Additionally, I've developed a series of motivational seminars and workshops for Adult Survivors of Peer Abuse, corporate America, and other sectors of the populace affected by bullying behavior. I'm also looking forward to whatever surprises the future has in store for me.

About Jodee Blanco

Survivor, expert, and activist Jodee Blanco is one of the country's pre-eminent voices on the subject of school bullying. She is the author of the *New York Times* bestseller, *Please Stop Laughing At Me . . . One Woman's Inspirational Story*. A chronicle of her years as the student outcast, the book inspired a movement inside the nation's schools and is swiftly becoming an American classic. Referred to by many as "the anti-bullying bible," it is required reading in hundreds of middle and high schools and numerous universities throughout the country. *Please Stop Laughing at Me . . .* has also been recognized as an essential resource by the National Crime Prevention Council, the Department of Health & Human Services, the National Association of Youth Courts, Special Olympics, The FCCLA (Future Community and Career Leaders of America), *Teacher Magazine*, and hundreds of state and local organizations from the PTA and regional law enforcement coalitions to school safety groups.

Blanco's highly anticipated sequel, *Please Stop Laughing at Us . . . One Survivor's Extraordinary Quest to Prevent School Bullying*, is written in response to the demand for more information from her core audience — teens, teachers, parents, and other Adult Survivors of Peer Abuse like herself, who have come to know Blanco as the champion of their cause. It provides advice and solutions set against the backdrop of her dramatic personal and professional journey as the survivor who unexpectedly finds herself the country's most sought-after anti-bullying activist.

In addition to her books, Blanco's unprecedented approach to shifting the social dynamic of America's schools is saving lives and making headlines throughout the United States. She's presented *It's NOT Just Joking Around!*™, her acclaimed anti-bullying program, to a combined audience of over five-hundred thousand students, teachers, and parents nationwide at the behest of such entities as the United States Department of the Interior, the United States Department of Justice, the National Catholic Educational Association, the Illinois Association of School Boards, and scores of local school districts, many of whom are adopting her initiatives as part of their core bullying prevention curriculum. *It's NOT Just Joking Around!*™ has also generated tens of thousands of dollars in grant awards for schools and organizations coast to coast.

Blanco has successfully intervened in numerous bullying-related attempted suicides and acts of student retaliation. She is a respected crisis management consultant and expert witness in the areas of school violence and peer abuse, and is frequently called upon by the media as an expert interview. Some of the outlets who have turned to her for commentary include *Newsweek*, CNN, NBC, FOX, *The John Walsh Show*, and National Public Radio. She is also the resident authority on school bullying for Meredith Vieira's popular parenting Web site ClubMom.com. Blanco's life story has been featured in *Parade*, *Teen Newsweek*, *Teen Guideposts*, *Hispanic*, *The Chicago Tribune*, *The St. Petersburg Times*, hundreds of local daily newspapers across the United States and is part of a permanent exhibit at the Chicago National Historical Society.

A tireless advocate for the shunned and forgotten student, Blanco's rare understanding of why kids abuse other kids comes from a deep personal place. From fifth grade through the end of high school, she was rejected and tormented by her peers simply for being different and knows firsthand what it's like to contemplate retaliation. As an adult, she decided to go public with her story because she was frustrated by society's misconceptions about the true cause of the school tragedies such as Columbine.

Since the release of *Please Stop Laughing At Me . . .*, Blanco has committed her life to turning her pain into purpose. Inspired by the thousands of letters and requests she receives for help, she travels around the country sharing her story of forgiveness and triumph. One of the most sought-after keynote speakers and seminar presenters, Blanco's anti-bullying initiatives are redefining the scope of possibilities for curbing suffering in our schools worldwide.

Blanco's work has been published in Japanese, Danish, and Arabic. She lives in the suburbs of Chicago with her husband and family where she is currently at work on a series of anti-bullying related fiction titles for young adults. For more information on Blanco, visit her Web site at www.jodeeblanco.com.

Glossary of Key Terms

Adult Survivor of Peer Abuse — an adult who was chronically bullied and/or shunned by his classmates and who has been scarred by this abuse.

Aggressive Exclusion — the most damaging form of bullying, often used by Elite Tormentors, best defined as a deliberate omission of kindness. Examples include letting someone sit alone at lunch every day, ignoring someone as if he's invisible, always choosing the same person last when dividing into teams in class, letting someone walk alone to class, and never inviting him to participate in social gatherings.

The Ancient Child — the typical profile of the bullied student, best described as an old soul, a kid who's blessed or cursed, depending upon how you look at it, with a stronger conscience and a more evolved sense of compassion and empathy than other kids his age. No matter how hard he tries to hide it, in the end, the sensitive, thoughtful adult inside him usually wins out over the teen who just wants to belong.

Arbitrary Exclusion — when a best friend or group of friends inexplicably turns on someone and persuades everyone else in the clique to follow suit. This form of bullying is rarely precipitated by any specific act, but seems to come out of nowhere, which is what makes it so devastating.

Compassionate Discipline Driven by Curiosity—enlightened, innovative disciplinary strategies that help children discover the empathy inside them and develop it like a muscle. Its purpose is to teach children the joy of being kind as opposed to the consequences of being cruel, which is the focus of traditional punishment.

Elite Leader—the caring, compassionate popular student.

Elite Tormentor—the mean-spirited popular student who employs subtle, insidious forms of bullying such as Aggressive Exclusion and Arbitrary Exclusion.

Empathy Deficit Disorder—a chronic lack of empathy that inhibits a child's access to the compassion inside him.

Irreverent Educator—the teacher with the instinct of an activist. He or she isn't afraid to stand up to authority or challenge the status quo and will break the rules when necessary. The **Reverent Educator** is the teacher who respects the rules and prefers established policies and procedures to get things done.

Note: Both types of educators are equally vital to the system. One is the catalyst for change, and the other the facilitator, and it's the blending of the two that makes a school run efficiently.

Rejection Junkie Syndrome—a form of self-sabotage experienced by many peer abuse victims in which a person grows so accustomed to negative attention from his classmates that when they finally do leave him alone it's like a death, and he finds himself provoking them to bully him again because if he's being ridiculed at least he knows he still exists. It's as if circumstances drive him to make a choice between being a no one and being a target.

Excerpts from E-mails and Letters Written to Jodee Blanco

(*Note: Names, dates, and places have been altered to protect individuals' privacy*)

Students' Voices

I have cerebral palsy that causes me to walk with a slight limp. All through school kids have teased me for it, and one kid even now after twelve years still disinfects the area around his desk whenever I come near it. He gets up and asks the teacher for cleaner and makes a huge scene of cleaning the room. The teacher never tries to stop him either. One day at recess, I fell on the playground. Rather than go around me, many of the kids just walked right on top of me. The school's answer to this was to make me go in another door that was all the way at the other end of the building from where my classroom was. Why couldn't they punish the kids that did it instead of me?

My name is Kim and I am seventeen and in eleventh grade. School has been a nightmare, a living hell...I am very close to my mom but she doesn't know everything. I barely eat and have tried to kill myself. I also wanted to kill my tormentors. Maybe some day I shall write a book on my "hell" as you have. I don't know how you did it, but thank you for writing that book. I admire you. P.S. I learned never to use the bathrooms. I do it at home so I don't get hurt.

I just wanted to say thank you so much for coming to speak at our school. I really loved your story and everything you said. I see bullying in every single way you described every single day at our school, and you made me realize that sometimes I do it too without even thinking I'm doing anything wrong...

Like you, I'm picked on for being myself. I never imagined that school would be like this. Like you I feel for those who have special needs. My brother does. I have spent countless lunch hours hiding in the bathroom because I didn't have anyone to sit with. Cliques of friends I used to have turned on me and tried to beat me. It's so hard when you don't have anyone. Obscenities have been written about me in washroom stalls and my name slandered in ways you could not even imagine. My locker has been broken into, my books stolen, and with no one to turn to, I never dreamed I would be the misfit. Help me!

I'm fifteen years old and have been picked on since the second grade. Even as I type this I'm crying. This year has been extremely rough. I've been hospitalized for depression, anxiety and suicide. It has caused me so much pain to be constantly teased and told I was worthless. Thank you so much for giving me hope that one day I will not be sad or tormented by my peers.

Parents' Voices

My son has been bullied for three years since he entered middle school. He tried to hang himself at the beginning of the month because he just couldn't take it anymore. The work you are doing is so necessary. Please keep it up.

I just finished your book and I am in tears. Tears of joy, sadness, anger, frustration and relief. I have watched my daughter change from a beautiful child full of unconditional love for all to an angry person who has tried to kill herself and disfigure herself. She was always taller and bigger than her classmates and they teased her. They were cruel to her from kindergarten on. If it wasn't her weight and calling her fat, they would tease her about boys, invite her to events at the wrong time and she would show up and be forgotten. She would get pushed in the hall and verbally abused. Repeated trips to the principal did no good. I have watched a child so full of life and promise fade and wither. She won't leave her room. My husband and I have tried therapy, but all the medicines they gave her put weight on her which only worsens the teasing. I only hope it is not too late to revive the deadened spirit of such a young, beautiful woman. Peer pressure and bullying is out of control in our society. For our family it has been a painful journey. I thank God for giving my daughter to me. She has made me a stronger person. If you're ever in the DC area, please, could we have lunch?

I am the mother of a seventeen year old boy who is a junior in high school. In seventh grade, the rumor started that he is gay. That rumor has never died and this kid has gone through daily hell because of it. My son is a nice looking clean cut kid who wants to become a firefighter. He isn't a drinker, doesn't do drugs and stays away from those kinds of parties. Thus, I guess the concensus that he is gay. The kids have refused to leave him alone calling him derogatory names, writing comments on his car in lipstick, egging our house, paint balling our house, and writing comments in shaving cream all over our porch and sidewalk. In our town, the police consider this to be childish pranks and have done nothing to stop it. We have gone to the school, the school board and even the superintendent who also believes this is child's play. All they want is to have my son name the kids but he's afraid it would only make matters worse there are so many of them. Why is it in the workplace this kind of behavior could end in termination, but in school, it's just kids being kids? My son hates school. He is constantly feeling bad about himself. He has no friends. My son is very accepting of everyone and when people put down homosexuals or any other minority, he tells them

that he thinks everyone has the right to be who they are. I
have had it. I can't stand seeing him hurt like this. I don't
know what else to do or where else to turn. My husband
and I are at our wit's end. We love our son and don't want
to see him treated like this in a place he should feel safe
and where he has a right to be respected. Please, help us.

I have been leading a year long fight against bullying for
my son. He was profoundly bullied last year. So many of
the parts of the system failed him in our pursuit to help
him — teachers who didn't let anyone know what they saw,
teachers and students who watched or joined in, a school
administration operating with poorly defined policies, and
a guidance department that didn't help the bullies or the
bullied. I am willing to do anything to make things better. I
am shouting from the rooftops but I am only one voice. The
kids here need your help.

My daughter has been tortured at school since she was in
second grade. The bullying has not stopped and my
daughter is in eighth grade. I worry and cry for her on a reg-
ular basis. She is such a wonderful person and does not
deserve this. When my daughter defends herself at
school, she suffers the consequences. She has taken to
not doing anything and does not want to worry us. It is so
sad. I want to help her. I write this to you as I get ready to

see her perform at her winter concert at school. When everybody is out with their friends getting ice cream afterward, my daughter will be ignored and taunted. It breaks my heart. If only she had one good friend. I am so thrilled that you are a happy adult. It gives me hope.

Educators' Voices

I am a fifth grade teacher. Recently, two students in my class said they only needed one bullet to take care of a particular student in the classroom. The principal gave them a "talking to" and sent them back to class. I was outraged. Even in elementary school, these threats should be taken seriously and warrant serious consequences. What can I do about the bullying that begins in elementary school and continues through middle and high school? I want to do something with these fifth graders that will stay with them, make an impact on them. I am researching on the internet and preparing lesson plans about bullying. I would like my school to get involved. What else can I do?

I'm a teacher constantly trying to help children who are being bullied. It is hard to see my students have to deal with these issues. I'm scared for their future, because I know that as they continue with their schooling, the supervision is decreased and the bullying will get worse. There are faults within our education system that need to be mended. And most importantly, we have to help the children and students who are dealing with this pain. I will never forget your story...or your strength.

I just got home after hearing you speak at my school. I was a victim of bullying during my middle school years. I am now a teacher...and see many students becoming the kind of people I feared when I entered middle school. I thank you for standing up and talking out and helping these children. If there is anything I can do for you to help you spread the word, let me know.

Thank you for taking the time to speak to my students. They were obviously moved and awakened by your story. Thank you also for having the courage to forgive those who tortured you. It was one of the most important points that you made. I was picked on and an outcast all my life, including today. I was never physically abused by my peers, but the psychological damage that was done is still there. The recovery process is very slow...

I am twenty-five years old and a special education teacher. My students struggle every day with bullying. You have made me more aware of what I can do to stop this. I was once the target of bullies, too. I thankfully overcame the torment in high school, but middle school was the toughest time of my life. Knowing that someone else experienced similar situations and overcame them was a relief. Thank you for sharing your story.

Adult Survivors' of Peer Abuse Voices

I was tormented and humiliated every day from Kindergarten on. I lived in hell the moment I stepped in school. I never knew why I had to face intense teasing and bullying and humiliation from my peers, believe it or not, from my teachers and even from my principal. The worst part was that I had no help. I had to face it alone. My parents just told me to fight my own battles. I was afraid to go to school. Afraid to stand up for myself. I would become so angry that I wanted to lash out but I held it in because I feared getting into trouble. I am forty one now and still hate myself even though my loving husband tells me I am intelligent, articulate and beautiful. Why can't I make these memories go away?

I was a geek, and probably still am, obese and gay. Since the beginning of second grade I started being called a fag. I was beaten almost to death once. I had rocks thrown at me on my way home from school. What hurt the most is that no one ever stood up for me, not even my own brother and sister. Once, after the showers in gym, someone stole all my clothes, underwear too. I just had my hands to cover myself up. I cried myself to sleep every night, dreading the sight of day. Your story helped me so much.

In my life, I played both the part of the bully and the bullied. I was picked on so much without mercy, that I brutalized other kids just as viciously. I feel terrible about that to this day. However, getting picked on has made me be perceived now a days as heartless. I wish I could change all this. Can you help me?

I am stationed in Iraq and recently came across your book which was donated to us troops by the dear people back in the states. As I was reading your book, I couldn't help but think about my own childhood and feelings of loneliness. I can't say that I had it as bad as you did, but in a way I did. I was never part of any group, always in the middle. I can't say people liked me, and I can't say that anyone really remembers me to this day. Your book made me feel better about myself and I will hold onto it for years to come and continue to reread it.

I have been ridiculed and bullied and abused since I was in third grade. In ninth grade it became too much and I attempted suicide. After that I dropped out of public school and began home schooling. I am eighteen now. It gives me so much strength to know that if I stick with it and don't give up that I too can overcome this obstacle. I think one of the most influential parts of your book for me was when you said that you had love to give that nobody wanted. I had that problem for countless years and all it did was turn into a depressing rage, until about six months ago when a member of my church asked me to volunteer some time working with children with disabilities. I love it more than words can express. I only hope that ten years from now I can forgive my tormentors also. I'm still at the horrible rage stage, but I know that eventually I too will heal. Thank you for giving me inspiration and hope.

For more information about Jodee Blanco or to book her as a speaker, please contact the Blanco Group at info@jodeeblanco.com or visit jodeeblanco.com.